HODGES UNIVERSITY
LIBRARY NAPLES

P9-DZA-251

PRIVATE PROPERTY, COMMUNITY DEVELOPMENT, AND EMINENT DOMAIN

Law, Property and Society

Series Editor:
Robin Paul Malloy

The Law, Property and Society series examines property in terms of its ability to foster democratic forms of governance, and to advance social justice. The series explores the legal infrastructure of property in broad terms, encompassing concerns for real, personal, intangible, intellectual and cultural property, as well as looking at property related financial markets. The series is edited by Robin Paul Malloy and addresses issues related to the work of the Center on Property, Citizenship, and Social Entrepreneurism sponsored by the Syracuse University College of Law. Contributions are requested from authors without regard to affiliation with the Center. Submissions are encouraged on all property-related topics.

Robin Paul Malloy is E.I. White Chair and Distinguished Professor of Law at Syracuse University College of Law, USA. He is Vice Dean of the College, and Director of the Center on Property, Citizenship, and Social Entrepreneurism. He is also Professor of Economics (by courtesy appointment) in Maxwell School of Citizenship and Public Affairs, College of Law, Syracuse University. Professor Malloy writes extensively on law and market theory and on real estate transactions and development. He has published 12 books, more than 25 articles, and contributed to 12 other books.

Private Property, Community Development, and Eminent Domain

Edited by

ROBIN PAUL MALLOY
Syracuse University College of Law, USA

ASHGATE

© Robin Paul Malloy 2008

All rights reserved. No part of this publication may be reproduced, stored in a retrieval system or transmitted in any form or by any means, electronic, mechanical, photocopying, recording or otherwise without the prior permission of the publisher.

Robin Paul Malloy has asserted his right under the Copyright, Designs and Patents Act, 1988, to be identified as the editor of this work.

Published by
Ashgate Publishing Limited
Gower House
Croft Road
Aldershot
Hampshire GU11 3HR
England

Ashgate Publishing Company
Suite 420
101 Cherry Street
Burlington, VT 05401-4405
USA

Ashgate website: http://www.ashgate.com

British Library Cataloguing in Publication Data
Private property, community development, and eminent
    domain. - (Law, property and society)
    1. Kelo, Susette - Trials, litigation, etc. 2. Eminent
    domain 3. Eminent domain - Connecticut - Cases 4. Economic
    development - Moral and ethical aspects 5. Law and economic
    development
    I. Malloy, Robin Paul, 1956-
    343' .0252

Library of Congress Cataloging-in-Publication Data
Private property, community development, and eminent domain / edited by Robin Paul Malloy.
        p. cm. -- (Law, property, and society)
    Includes bibliographical references and index.
    ISBN 978-0-7546-7211-1
    1. Eminent domain. 2. Right of property. 3. Land use--Law and legislation. I. Malloy, Robin Paul, 1956-

    K3511.P75 2007
    343'.0252--dc22

                                                            2007023737

ISBN: 978 0 7546 7211 1

Printed and bound in Great Britain by TJ International Ltd, Padstow, Cornwall.

Contents

Dedicated to
Robert E. Peters, Esq.

List of Contributors

Tom Allen Professor, Faculty of Law, University of Durham

D. Benjamin Barros Associate Professor, School of Law, Widener University

Carol Necole Brown Associate Professor, School of Law, University of North Carolina

Eric R. Claeys Associate Professor, School of Law, George Mason University

Rachel D. Godsil Professor, School of Law, Seton Hall University

Robin Paul Malloy E.I. White Chair and Distinguished Professor of Law, and Vice Dean, College of Law, Syracuse University

Marc R. Poirier Professor, School of Law, Seton Hall University

David Simunovich, Esq. (co-author with Rachel D. Godsil) School of Law, Seton Hall University

James Charles Smith John Byrd Martin Professor, School of Law, University of Georgia

Michael Allan Wolf Professor, and Richard Nelson Chair in Local Government Law, Levin College of Law, University of Florida

Series Editor's Preface

The book series on *Law, Property and Society* brings together experts from a variety of fields and institutions to discuss and explore issues related to modern Real Estate Transactions and Finance; Community Development and Housing; Global Property Law Systems; and Access to Ownership for Inclusion of the Elderly, the Poor, and Persons with Disabilities.

A core principle of the Series is that a just and accessible property law system is the basis for both good citizenship and successful economic development. Therefore, the books in this series address all areas of property law and theory; including real, personal, intangible, intellectual, and cultural property. In doing this it is understood that property, in all its forms, addresses the fundamental relationships between the state and its citizens, and among the people themselves. For this reason the books in this series examine property in terms of its ability to foster democratic forms of governance, advance social justice, promote citizenship, build sustainable and supportive communities, and enhance the stewardship of our global environment and its natural resources.

In this book on *Private Property, Community Development, and Eminent Domain* we address the relationships among private property, community development, and the exercise of the power of eminent domain. The discussion centers on a recent decision by the United States Supreme Court in the case of *Kelo v. City of New London*, 545 U.S. 469 (2005). The full opinion in this case is included in the Appendix. The contributions to this book reflect both broad and comparative perspectives on the relationships addressed in the *Kelo* case as well as specific analysis of the underlying law and rationale of the Court's opinion. The purpose of the book is to initiate an important conversation about the nature of property, and the way in which people and communities organize to address, through property law, the inherent tensions between private and public interests.

In editing this book I thank Jason Mintz and Sheila Welch for their invaluable assistance.

All notes and sources used in this book are prepared in accordance with the Uniform System of Legal Citation ('The Bluebook'), 17th Edition.

Robin Paul Malloy
E.I. White Chair and Distinguished Professor of Law
Vice Dean, College of Law
Syracuse University

Director, Center on Property, Citizenship, and Social Entrepreneurism (PCSE)
www.law.syr.edu/pcse

Chapter 1

Private Property, Community Development, and Eminent Domain

Robin Paul Malloy and James Charles Smith

Introduction

On March 16, 2007 the Chinese government, by way of the National People's Congress, announced passage of a new national property law designed to protect private property.[1] The new Property Law becomes effective October 1, 2007.[2] It defines different categories of property,[3] defines the meaning of a property right,[4] and protects private property from illegal State seizure.[5] This has been hailed as a great step forward for the market economy in China. While China has made great economic progress in recent years and has facilitated a great amount of real estate activity, private property rights have been the subject of ongoing debate. The new Property Law helps to clarify rights as between private parties, collectives, the State, and creditors. While the law provides a new reference point for negotiating the complexity of interests within a market economy, it remains to be seen how effectively the law will be enforced.

The passage of the new Property Law in China is noteworthy not only for its potential benefit to the Chinese people and the Chinese economy but also because it represents an important indicator in the ongoing recognition of the global importance of private property law for economic development and the building of institutions of citizenship.

A concern for private property has been at the core of many debates regarding the reduction of poverty in developing countries,[6] and in terms of the political and economic reorganization of states after such events as the collapse of the Soviet Union. Likewise, property law has been critical in the negotiating of regime change

---

1   Story from BBC News: http//news.bbc.co.uk/go/pr/fr/-/2/hi/asia-pacific/6429317. stm (published March 8, 2007 at 07:07:53 GMT). See also Li & Fung Research Centre, *The Promulgation of Property Law – A New Era for Private Property* 1–8, 38 CHINA DISTRIBUTION & TRADING (MARCH 2007).

2   Li & Fung, *supra* note 1.

3   *Id.* See generally CAO PEI, REAL ESTATE LAW IN CHINA (1998); PATRICK RANDOLPH, CHINESE REAL ESTATE LAW (2000).

4   Li & Fung, *supra* note 1.

5   *Id.*

6   See generally HERNANDO DE SOTO, THE MYSTERY OF CAPITAL: WHY CAPITALISM TRIUMPHS IN THE WEST AND FAILS EVERYWHERE ELSE (2000).

as witnessed in such situations as those involving the turn over by the British of Hong Kong to China, and with the transformation of political and economic order with regime change in such places as Zimbabwe (Rhodesia) and South Africa.

From a market perspective, property is fundamental legal infrastructure for trade and exchange. Property defines the interests that people own and control so that we, as market actors, know what is available for trade and whom to pay.[7] The rules of property address more than issues of ownership and control. The rules of property also clarify the quality and the quantity of the interest held and capable of exchange.[8] For instance, the quantity of a parcel of real property might be measured at 1.5 acres and described by a standardized survey process using metes and bounds. The quality of the property might also be identifiable in terms of a recognized estate interest (a life estate vs. a fee simple), and in terms of its environmental characteristics and condition. The ability to describe, qualify, quantify, and fix ownership is crucial to a market economy, and particularly so when a market extends beyond a very local reach to include potential participants who lack personal familiarity with each other.

Property rules also reduce transaction costs (reducing waste and making transactions more efficient),[9] and they can correct for problems associated with the tragedy of the commons,[10] wherein a lack of private property rights results in over-use and misuse of valuable resources.

Property law connects people to civil society.[11] Formal ownership of property connects individuals to the broader community by putting them and their property on public records, it requires them to have a known and knowable address, makes them visible to government officials by placing them on the property tax roles, and provides them with collateral for credit, thus making them visible and valuable to all manner of creditors, sales people, and merchandisers.[12] To have formal legal property is to take on an identity and a place within a given community, for property is a system of organizing social hierarchy within and across communities. Property structures relationships such as landlord-tenant, owner-trespasser, debtor-creditor, and arranges a hierarchy of interests in terms of legal position and in terms of market relationships.[13] In both legal and economic terms it is frequently better to be an owner rather than a renter. Owners, for instance, generally have higher priority legal rights and also enjoy better credit terms than renters in the marketplace.

Without a coherent and reasonably well developed system of property, market exchange, beyond a very local community, would be costly, difficult, and perhaps

---

7   See ROBIN PAUL MALLOY and JAMES CHARLES SMITH, REAL ESTATE TRANSACTIONS 3ʀᴅ (2007). See also ROBIN PAUL MALLOY, LAW IN A MARKET CONTEXT: AN INTRODUCTION TO MARKET CONCEPTS IN LEGAL REASONING (2004).

8   See *id.*

9   See MALLOY, MARKET CONTEXT, *supra* note 7, at 184–5, 177; ROBIN PAUL MALLOY, LAW AND MARKET ECONOMY: REINTERPRETING THE VALUES OF LAW AND ECONOMICS 91–4, 96, 98–100, 102–4, 108, 118, 121, 155–6 (Cambridge, 2000).

10   See MALLOY, MARKET CONTEXT, *supra* note 7, at 21, 106.

11   DE SOTO, *supra* note 6.

12   *Id.*

13   See MALLOY, MARKET CONTEXT, *supra* note 7, at 82–9. See generally MALLOY, MARKET ECONOMY, *supra* note 9 (on the idea of relational exchange and meaning).

barely existent. In saying this, we do not ignore the idea of informal property systems and exchange networks that emerge privately through custom, kinship groups, and by personal arrangement and enforcement. There is a literature addressing these kinds of market functions. But pragmatically, extensive, global, and positive market networks require a degree of transparency, stability, predictability, and access which cannot be efficiently and effectively attained by purely informal means. Property law systems establish rules and standards that favor stability of interests, predictability of outcome, and transparency of information. All of this advances economic exchange and civic institution building.

Issues arise, however, when circumstances change. In all cases of property there is tension between competing claimants to property, and with respect to the appropriate balance between public and private authority over property. When circumstances change legal systems need to be responsive and dynamic. This may be difficult however, when property rules are generally fostered to enhance stability, predictability, and a sense of permanence in the hierarchy of social organization. With the advent of new technology, changes in demographics, shifts in preferences, reorganization of political power, and the obsolescence of prior land uses, adjustments need to be made. Private reordering can be accomplished by private contract. Public reordering may be done by consent or by coercive force.

In this book we look at the issues that arise when private property rights come into conflict with public (community) interest. Whether stated as such, or not, such tensions involve changed circumstances. Technology, demographics, political structure, or preferences change, and tensions arise with respect to the perceived needs of change and the established organization of society through property. New uses are sought for properties, and questions arise with respect to the public's ability to change prior established uses and rights through the exercise of state power. This exercise of state power is typically referred to as a "takings power" or as a right of eminent domain.

In this chapter we address this tension between private property and the community. We proceed in several steps. First, we briefly address some concerns regarding the regulation of property that expresses itself in the law of various countries.[14] This includes an explanation of some of the key concepts used in land regulation generally, and relevant to eminent domain.[15] Second we put this general information into context with reference to the recent *Kelo* decision by the U.S. Supreme Court.[16] The *Kelo* case has attracted global attention by triggering reconsiderations of fundamental questions of private property and the proper exercise of the power of eminent domain.

---

14 Tom Allen, The Right to Property In Commonwealth Constitutions (2000).

15 See Daniel R. Mandelker, Land Use Law 5th (2006).

16 Kelo v. City of New London, 545 U.S. 469 (2005). (See Full Court opinion in Appendix of this book.)

General Concepts in Land Use Control and Development Law

In general there are two primary background principles involved in land use and its regulation. The first relates to traditional common law concepts of nuisance, and the second to the political and constitutional balance struck between the rights of the community and the rights of individuals to own and control private property.[17] We will explore these ideas with reference to the tension between private interest (self-interest) and public interest.[18]

In many ways land use law embodies the classic market tension between private and public interest. To understand this we need to think in terms of Adam Smith's classic metaphor of the invisible hand. Smith argued that, in general, people pursuing their own self interest will end up promoting the public interest even though the advancing of the public interest is no part of their original plan.[19] It is as if they are lead by an invisible hand that simultaneously promotes both private and public benefit. This has been referred to as the equivalence or invariance theory to understanding law in a market context and it suggests that laws promoting the pursuit of self-interest likewise advance the public interest because the market mechanism calibrates an equivalence between the two. In such an environment, private ordering of property rights is all that is needed since by definition successful private ordering would be equivalent to successful public planning. In fact, private ordering under the equivalence theory makes public gain available without having to incur administrative costs and without needing to identify a complex calculus for adjusting individual preferences across a broad exchange network. Problems arise, however, the instant that we recognize situations of variance between private (self) interest and the public interest.[20] Such variance occurs in a number of situations. Common and well explained instances of this occur in settings where decision making is governed by the dynamics of the so called prisoner's dilemma,[21] when property rights are not clearly identified as in the Tragedy of the Commons, and when there are transactions costs that hinder the ability of individuals to make rational, efficient, and optimal choices. In many cases, certain land uses and individual preferences are suboptimal because of externalities that are not internalized into the individual's decision-making process. Likewise, problems arise when individuals experience difficulty in processing complex information related to such things as long-term risk to the environment and public health due to certain types of land use.[22] For all of these reasons it is frequently the case that one can observe variance between self-interested land use preferences and the interests and preferences of the community. An important goal of public regulation of land, therefore, is to mediate these tensions between public and private interests and to

---

17 See generally MANDELKER, *supra* note 15.

18 MALLOY, MARKET CONTEXT, *supra* note 7, at 26–30.

19 *Id.* (Malloy has identified this relationship as one of equivalence or invariance. *Id.*)

20 *Id.*

21 *Id.* at 130–32, 174, 203.

22 See generally BEHAVIORAL LAW & ECONOMICS (Cass R. Sunstein, ed., 2000) (addressing a variety of behavioral and cognitive issues that make purely rational calculus difficult for individual decision makers).

navigate the delicate process of correcting for variances that might otherwise lead to negative impacts on the public health, welfare, and safety.

In seeking to achieve this balance between public and private interest a number of factors come into play concerning the basic characteristics of ownership, and the limiting principles governing the exercise of state power through the process of eminent domain.

Characteristics of Property Ownership

To best understand a discussion of state limitations on individual property rights one needs to appreciate the basic characteristics of property ownership. There are philosophical debates on the meaning and purpose of property that can be read in summary form elsewhere.[23] In this chapter we simply set out to identify the basic characteristics of property to establish a foundation for the more focused discussion of eminent domain.

Property may be categorized in various ways. Recognized legal categories include real property (land and related fixtures attached to and connected to the land), personal property (movables such as equipment, inventory, and personal goods), intangible property (contract rights and insurance), intellectual property (copyrights, patents, trademarks), and cultural property (traditional medicines and goods or products identified to a specific cultural community and context). To a large extent the legal concept of property is a conclusion. It is a conclusion in law based on an evaluation of the presence or absence of certain characteristics which permit one to identify a given interest as fitting within one of the legally recognized categories set out above. Having an interest so categorized is important because the legal designation of an interest as property generates important consequences. Property is generally given strong protection under the law. There is typically a heightened review of state action to regulate or invade a private property right relative to other types of non property interest, often involving a fundamental constitutional set of principles with respect to the terms and conditions upon which the state may intrude upon private property rights of citizens. There are also special private law remedies for intrusions on property rights. This might include, for example, the ability to demand specific performance, ejectment, or to seek an injunction rather than having to accept money damages.

The idea of a property right can vary from one legal system to the next. In general, Common Law countries (Britain and many of its former colonies; U.S.A., Australia, and Canada for instance) conceive of property in terms of a metaphor of a bundle of sticks.[24] This metaphor presents the idea of property as being a multiplicity of interests that can be divided and legally recognizable in numerous discrete ways. Thus, one might own a piece of land and reserve a life estate in it while giving a future interest to one person and an easement to a third person. All can have constitutionally protected property rights as all hold sticks in the bundle

---

23 See Laura S. Underkuffler, The Idea Of property: Its Meaning And Power (2003); Joseph William Singer, Introduction to Property 1–18 (2001); Malloy, Market Context, *supra* note 7, at 1–21.

24 Allen, Property, *supra* note 14.

of property rights associated with the land. In contrast, countries with a Civil Law legal system (France, Spain, Germany, and their former colonies, along with most of continental Europe and South America) have a different conception of property.[25] Rather than using a bundle of sticks metaphor Civil Law systems might best be understood by Common Law lawyers as having a "one big log" approach to property rights. In a Civil Law system property rights are not able to be so easily split and typically one person has a "property right" while others may enjoy "an interest in property," as opposed to a property right.[26] Again, from a Common Law perspective, the Civil Law idea would be akin to the person with the property right having an interest that would rise to the level of Constitutional protection from an unlawful government taking under a provision such as the Fifth Amendment to the United States Constitution, whereas the people with "rights in property" would have a lower status. In the common law system many people may hold a property rights stick in the bundle of property rights, and each such stick would give rise to the constitutional level of scrutiny of an interest protected by the Fifth Amendment to the United States Constitution.

Given these differences there are still similarities recognizable across countries with respect to some basic characteristics of what it means to have property, and some basic standards for limiting state interference and regulation of property. In this regard, however, our discussion will focus on the basic outline of Common Law jurisprudence (as opposed to that of the Civil Law).

There are four primary characteristics of property although various authors may identify more or different ones in given jurisdictions. Generally, when the legal conclusion is made that an individual owns property it means that the person enjoys the following four characteristics of ownership:

1) the right to use and possession;
2) the right to exclude others (private parties and the public, with the public having certain rights via the state police power and its power of eminent domain);
3) the right to transfer (by sale, gift, credit arrangement, death, etc.); and
4) the right to enjoy the profits of ownership (such as enjoying the fruits of the land, the offspring of animals, and the equity appreciation of the interest).

Basically, when these characteristics are present one can legally conclude that an interest that can otherwise fit into one of the established categories of property is going to be treated as property.

Standards for Exercising the Power of Eminent Domain

In general, the sovereign (the state) has the power and authority to define, regulate, and protect property within the reach of its jurisdiction. In most developed market economies power over property is divided between the state and private individuals.

---

25 *Id.*
26 *Id.*

Individuals are given private property rights as part of democratic political structures, as a means of promoting citizenship, and as a vehicle for advancing economic development. In both Civil Law and Common Law traditions the legislative power includes the authority to exercise control over private property.[27] The exercise of this power is, however, constrained by legal rules and standards. Professor Tom Allen has done significant work in detailing many of these rules and standards in his book *The Right to Property in Commonwealth Constitutions*,[28] and has put many of these standards into the current context of European Union human rights law in his book, *Human Rights Law in Perspective: Property and the Human Rights Act of 1998.*[29]

In this book we are primarily concerned with the exercise of the power of eminent domain which involves a physical taking of private property by the state. We are not focused on issues of "regulatory takings" which are more ambiguous as to standards applied in different jurisdictional contexts, and in fact rather unclear even in one jurisdiction such as the United States. Suffice it to say that regulatory takings involve state action that so diminishes the use and value of the property by regulation that it is argued to be the equivalent of a physical taking. The variables to be considered in all of this are many and complex. In the United States we know only that regulation which results in completely eliminating *all* economic value of ownership is considered a taking for which compensation is due under the Fifth Amendment to the United States Constitution.

Having said this we now turn our attention to outlining some of the basic standards that govern the exercise of eminent domain. These standards describe the basic considerations used in exercising the power of eminent domain, with respect to a physical taking of private property, across numerous Common Law jurisdictions.

There are three generally applicable standards used to govern the lawful exercise of the power of eminent domain. These can be identified as standards of:

1) proportionality,
2) public purpose, and
3) compensation.

A brief consideration of each is provided.

Proportionality

While exact wording and standards may vary as between jurisdictions the general requirements are that the government action be rationally connected to the stated objective; that the government action seeks reasonably to minimize the intrusion onto private property; and that the intrusion is proportional to the objective. Other ways of stating this include the idea of striking a fair balance between the need to achieve an appropriate public objective and the infringement on the rights of a

---

27 *Id.*

28 *Id.*

29 Tom Allen, Human Rights Law In Perspective: Property And The Human Rights Act of 1998 (2005).

private property owner. Generally, the attempt is to avoid placing a disproportionate burden on a discrete individual or group of individuals when seeking to advance a legitimate public interest.

Public Purpose/Use

Various jurisdictions speak to the need for the power of eminent domain to be exercised for a public purpose or a public use. The exact meaning of this standard varies but the idea is that the government is using this power to achieve a public goal, and to advance the production of public goods. There are some disputes about the nature of the government action in terms of the meaning of "use" and "purpose." Some interpretations hold that public use requires actual access and use by the public as in taking private property to build an airport, a highway, or a public school. The more difficult question concerns taking private property for a public purpose which may or may not result in a so-called public use. A public purpose may involve the taking of private property in the context of clearing out a blighted slum area for purposes of urban redevelopment. The redevelopment may or may not include public uses, as there may be construction of new private buildings and housing in the area. Similarly, in an age of privatization the state may seek to acquire private property rights for a right of way to be granted to a privately owned utility company agreeing to supply needed power to a community.

Compensation

When the state exercises its power of eminent domain to take title to property or to acquire another recognized ownership interest, such as a leasehold or an easement, the state generally must compensate the private property owner.[30] Compensation is a key restraint on the exercise of this power by the state as it requires government to think about the costs and benefits of a project and to allocate resources to the undertaking. It is also a critical component of proportionality and fair balance as it takes funds from general revenues and pays for the project, thereby more fairly equalizing the impact and burden on the discrete individuals whose property is taken for the benefit of the public at large. Requiring compensation is of course further complicated by the question of what compensation is due. The compensation standard can vary in several ways. Some tests speak in terms of market value, others in terms of fair value. Questions arise with respect to the best way to calculate these values. In addition, some jurisdictions require additional compensation based on such factors as the time period over which the individual held private ownership of the property or the costs of relocating or acquiring substitute property.

---

30 One exception is taking pursuant to a forfeiture statute, when an owner's criminal misconduct justifies the expropriation. See Bennis v. Michigan, 516 U.S. 442 (1996) (state declared forfeiture of automobile in which husband had sex with a prostitute; innocent wife, who held one-half interest, had no right to compensation under takings clause).

In general, one will observe these basic standards in many Common Law jurisdictions and in current and former Commonwealth countries.[31] Some of these basic standards prevail across the European Union and the fair balance test is being developed in this area as a result of the application to all member states of the European Convention on Human Rights.[32]

Forced Transfers to Private Owners

With this as background we turn now to one of the more interesting questions concerning the exercise of the power of eminent domain. This question concerns the appropriate limits to the use of eminent domain in situations in which the state intends to take private property from one private property owner and turn it over to another. The issue here involves consideration of the public use and purpose distinction noted above. The public purpose standard seems to offer a broader basis than that of public use for the exercise of eminent domain, and opens the door to increased tension with respect to the balance between private and public interests in the use of state power to achieve certain goals.

The United States Supreme Court's decision in 2005 of *Kelo v. City of New London* has spotlighted the tension with respect to the balancing of private and public interests. Public reaction in the United States was intense and immediate, and soon the case attracted global attention. Within the United States, a large majority of commentators both inside and outside the legal community were highly critical of *Kelo*. By the narrowest of margins, the Court held that the City could take single-family homes to develop an office park and to provide parking and retail services for visitors to an existing state park and marina. Many observers thought the Court would take this opportunity to display its "conservative" activism by reining in the power of eminent domain. After all, the Court has grown increasingly protective of property rights during the past two decades.[33] The Court, however, passed on the chance to redefine the "public use" requirement to protect property owners from many forms of government takings. However, the Court refused to turn the ship around. Instead, the majority followed its long-standing rule that the government takes for a "public use" under the Fifth Amendment whenever its purpose is to provide a public benefit. And for a public benefit to exist, members of the general public need not have a right to enter the property, and title to the property need not remain in a public entity.

The facts of *Kelo* merit close attention. In 1990, a Connecticut state agency designated the City of New London as a "distressed municipality." Six years later the United States closed a naval base in the Fort Trumbull neighborhood, and by

---

31 See ALLEN, PROPERTY, *supra* note 14; RICHARD A. EPSTEIN, TAKINGS: PRIVATE PROPERTY AND THE POWER OF EMINENT DOMAIN (1995); DAVID A. DANA and THOMAS W. MERRILL, PROPERTY: TAKINGS (2002); MANDELKER, *supra* note 15, SINGER, *supra* note 23, at 595–700.

32 ALLEN, HUMAN RIGHTS, *supra* note 29.

33 See Lucas v. South Carolina Coastal Council, 505 U.S. 1003 (1992) (right to build house notwithstanding beach protection legislation); City of Cleburne v. Cleburne Living Center, 473 U.S. 432 (1985) (right to operate group home notwithstanding zoning).

1998 the City had an unemployment rate that was roughly double the state average. A redevelopment authority began plans for the economic revitalization of Fort Trumbull. Shortly after the authority disclosed its plans, which included bond financing for the creation of a Fort Trumbull State Park, the pharmaceutical giant Pfizer Inc. announced plans to build a $300 million research facility next to Fort Trumbull. In 2000, the City approved a development plan for a 90-acre site in Fort Trumbull, which included 115 privately owned properties in addition to the former naval base. Many of the private parcels contained homes. The authority negotiated the purchase of a vast majority of these properties. Nine owners (including Susette Kelo) who owned a total of 15 lots refused to sell. They then became defendants in the City's eminent domain action.

Many but not all "economic development" takings involve land assembly plans, as in *Kelo*. Such "neighborhood buyouts" raise a fundamental issue of property ownership: Who owns the right to determine the future of a neighborhood? Changed circumstances, within the neighborhood and exterior to the neighborhood, make the question more acute and more important. When someone wants a drastic change to a neighborhood – a redevelopment or reinventing of the neighborhood – may this happen? If so, how? In other words, who owns the "redevelopment right" for the neighborhood?

The opposing sides in *Kelo* have radically different answers to this basic question of ownership. The government claims that the community as a whole may assert ownership of the right to redevelop a neighborhood by invoking the power of eminent domain. In other words, the concept of "economic development" allows the political processes to operate to determine when, if, and how a neighborhood will change. On the other hand, the *Kelo* homeowners asserted that their properties were "non blighted," that economic development was not a proper public use or purpose, and that therefore each of them individually had the right to refuse to sell to the redevelopment authority. This would mean that each neighbor owned a "veto power" over the plan to redevelop the neighborhood. Such "blockage rights," identified by Michael Heller as an anti-commons regime, often result in the inefficient use of resources.[34]

The intense public criticism of the *Kelo* Court's decision is largely undeserved. The outcome stands solidly on the shoulders of the Court's existing precedents. To understand how *Kelo* fits within the Court's eminent domain jurisprudence, we should start by considering the prototypical taking for a publicly owned facility. When a governmental entity condemns land to build a government facility, such as a school or library, its power is unquestioned. Takings for public transportation – highways and airports, for example – also raise no legal controversy about the government's right to condemn. Citizens may complain that the government's plan is not sound. They may say that there is a better site for the new school than the one selected by the school board, or it may be wiser to rebuild an existing school rather than acquire a new site. Similarly, opponents of a proposed new highway that will pass through

---

34 Michael Heller, *The Tragedy of the Anticommons: Property in Transition from Marx to Markets*, 111 Harv. L. Rev. 621 (1998).

a city may assert that its construction will destroy a valuable urban neighborhood.[35] For a new highway that will pass through sparsely populated rural land, critics may be skeptical of the government's justification that the project will spur economic development. The new airport's value may be speculative. All these objections are political in nature. If substantial, the objections may cause the government to modify or abandon its plan. But if the landowner goes to court to question the legal need to take her land for the public project, the government wins hands down. The Court applies a deferential rational basis standard of review, deferring to the decision made by the legislative branch. In such "public ownership" condemnations, issues of proportionality and the measurement of compensation may arise, necessitating judicial resolution, but under modern law the need for public ownership of the asset in question is never subjected to meaningful judicial scrutiny.

Not all exercises of eminent domain result in government ownership of the condemned property. As the Supreme Court recognized early on, the government sometimes employs eminent domain to transfer property from its present owner and transfer it to another private person. This practice became popular more than a century ago to promote the private development of transportation[36] and utility infrastructures.[37] Today, condemnations for the benefit of privately owned railroads are rare because long ago the Nation developed an extensive rail right-of-way system; and rail transportation, confronted with competition from other forms of transport, has waned. Condemnations to support power companies and other utilities, however, still happen frequently. Although few owners want an easement taken from their property for power lines, no one questions the legality of the practice. The power grid is important.

In principle, decades ago the Court could have drawn the line at privately owned transportation and utility infrastructure uses, prohibiting all other eminent domain exercises that transfer ownership to the private sector. Although such a demarcation was conceivable and justifiable, the Court, however, chose not to confine the concept of "public use" in this way. Instead, it broadly interpreted that concept to include any use that benefits the public, whether or not the land will be publicly owned, and whether or not members of the public have the right to enter the property. Of particular importance were two modern rulings. In *Berman v. Parker*,[38] the Court upheld slum clearance for urban renewal. Then in *Hawaii Housing Authority v. Midkiff*,[39] the Court permitted Hawaii to compel landlords to sell their properties to their residential tenants, thus breaking up large Hawaiian estates, the size of which had prevented the development of a normal market for the purchase of owner-occupied housing.

---

35 JOHN MOLLENKOPF, THE CONTESTED CITY (1983); Yan Zhang & Ke Fang, *Is History Repeating Itself? From Urban Renewal in the United States to Inner-City Redevelopment in China*, 23 JOURNAL OF PLANNING EDUCATION AND RESEARCH 286–98 (2004).

36 See Cherokee Nation v. Southern Kansas Railway Co., 135 U.S. 641, 657–8 (1890) (Congress may authorize railroad corporation to condemn land through Indian territory).

37 See Mt. Vernon-Woodberry Cotton Duck Co. v. Alabama Interstate Power Co., 240 U.S. 30 (1916) (Holmes, J.) (state may allow private corporation to condemn land for hydroelectric purposes).

38 348 U.S. 26 (1954).

39 467 U.S. 229 (1984).

In *Kelo*, the question was whether the public benefit theory properly extended to government efforts at economic development, designed to revitalize the community with new jobs and a higher tax base. Relying on its earlier rulings, a five-Justice majority concluded that it did.

In their dissenting opinions, Justices O'Connor and Thomas argued that the majority had stretched "public use" beyond recognition, in effect reading that limit out of the Constitution. The dissenters' opinions, however, are laced with flaws, thus suggesting that the majority reached the right result in refusing to strike down "economic development" takings. Justice O'Connor advanced a twofold argument for overturning the City of New London's development plan, without overruling *Berman* or *Midkiff*. As to *Berman*, she reasoned that economic development is different from, and less important than, rectifying urban blight.[40] The assertion (1) is not self-evident, (2) does not fit the underlying facts of *Kelo* because the state identified the entire community as a "distressed municipality," and (3) if generalized, would invite a nightmarish sprawl of litigation over whether particular takings qualify as "important." Second, Justice O'Connor claimed that *Berman* and *Midkiff* are best understood as cases in which the landowners were inflicting "affirmative harm on society" by their present use of the properties,[41] while the New London homeowners were blameless in this respect. This interpretation of the cases is especially unconvincing. There was nothing wrong with Mr. Berman's department store; indeed, the government conceded it was not blighted and did not contribute at all to the slum characteristics of the surrounding neighborhood. Whether the Hawaiian landlords in *Midkiff* were "harming" their tenants and society is debatable, to say the least. If they were, the harm they were causing by refusing to sell their properties to tenants does not look much different than a charge one could level against the New London homeowners – that they were harming their community by refusing to recognize that the office park would help the entire community. In each case, the challengers of the government's program were simply putting their own self-interest above that of their neighbors.

Justice Thomas's opinion was more radical and more forthright than Justice O'Connor's. Invoking what he perceived to be the original intent of the framers of the Constitution, Justice Thomas argued that "public use" must be narrower than "public purpose," and therefore *Berman* and *Midkiff* are wrongly decided, meriting overruling. Justice Thomas would permit forced transfers to a private owner only if "the public has a legal right to use" the property after the taking occurs.[42] It is not clear, however, why the "legal right to use" rule did not apply on the facts of *Kelo*. Members of the public, after all, could rent space in the developed project just as surely as members of the public can use a railroad if (but only if) they buy a ticket. New London's plan for the parcel that supports the state park seems especially unassailable under Justice Thomas's test because parking and retail services would presumably be open to one and all. Justice Thomas's assertion that we should look to the intent of the drafters of the Bill of Rights would also support the city's position because the Fifth Amendment

---

40 545 U.S. at 500-01.

41 Id. at 500.

42 Id. at 508.

as written limits only the federal government. The Court did not invent the "selective incorporation" doctrine until late in the 19th century.

The dispute among the *Kelo* justices can be seen in terms of the tension between private and public ordering of market relationships. The equivalence theory posits that the self interest of private landowners, guided by Smith's invisible hand, will produce the optimum public benefit. Faith in that proposition counsels for the imposition of limits on the power of eminent domain, which in the *Kelo* context would mean the invigoration of "public use" as a meaningful brake on government power. Conversely, the perspective of the City of New London, which the *Kelo* majority sanctioned, rests upon the perception that there is variance between the public interest and private (self) interest. Thus, the City's "economic development" taking was designed to overcome a problem with externalities: the *Kelo* homeowners ignored community benefits when making the decision to accept or reject the development authority's offers to purchase their homes, which preceded the judicial filing of the eminent domain action.

Kelo is a major victory for state and local governments, but it does not mean that "economic development takings" will now take place routinely in all states. The Court interpreted the Federal Constitution, and state courts may choose to interpret the takings clauses of their state constitutions more narrowly. Indeed, the Michigan Supreme Court did so just one year before the *Kelo* decision, ruling that a county could not condemn land adjacent to an airport to develop a privately owned industrial park.[43] In the future, other state courts will face the issue of whether to follow *Kelo*'s public benefit theory or to grant greater protection to property owners under principles of state law. A number of state legislatures also have entered the fray. Several of them acted to restrict the use of eminent domain even before *Kelo*, and since *Kelo*, lawmakers in Alabama, Delaware, and Texas have followed their lead. Other states are likely to adopt similar measures soon, spurred by the much-publicized ruling in *Kelo* itself.[44] Such state-law development, rejecting the broad public benefit theory, does not prove that the *Kelo* majority got it wrong. Rather, in the balance between national and local land regulation, it proves that federalism is working. The Court properly decided not to have the federal judiciary decide, for every community in every state, how broad or narrow the power of eminent domain ought to be. Within a Federal Constitutional framework, these choices – like most land-use law choices – should be informed at the state and local levels, taking into account local norms and circumstances.

Conclusion

The *Kelo* decision and the public debate arising in its aftermath provide an important opportunity for us to step back and assess the legal landscape related to the ability

---

43 County of Wayne v. Hathcock, 684 N.W.2d 765 (Mich. 2004).

44 See, e.g., Sonji Jacobs, *Legislators Give Property Seizure Laws High Priority*, ATLANTA JOURNAL – CONSTITUTION, Aug. 25, 2005, at 1C ("Grandma's house is at risk if she isn't in the best part of town and a corporate entity wants to build a plant there") (quoting Shannon Goessling of the Southeastern Legal Foundation).

of government fairly to balance the tension between private property and the public interest. This tension and the need successfully to strike a balance are not unique to any one country or any one political system. In this light, the *Kelo* decision provides an opportunity for us to explore a rich set of legal principles with broad applicability. From the United States to the United Kingdom, to the People's Republic of China, property and its legal regulation are of prime importance to matters of economic development and civic institution building.

Chapter 2

Hysteria versus History: Public Use in the Public Eye

Michael Allan Wolf

The negative public reaction to the United States Supreme Court's decision in *Kelo v. New London*,[1] in which a five-Member majority refused to second-guess the motives and methods of a redevelopment project for an economically distressed New England city, over the protests of landowners who refused buy-outs and fought the assertion that their property was then targeted for a "public use" taking, was as unexpected as it was widespread. After all, this was the third time in a half-century that the Justices had deferred to officials in the other branches of government who, in their supposed wisdom, had decided to employ the sovereign power of eminent domain in order to achieve highly defensible public policy goals. In 1954, a unanimous Court joined in Justice William O. Douglas's opinion in *Berman v. Parker*,[2] allowing the District of Columbia to use eminent domain as an urban renewal tool, over the objections of a department store owner who wanted to stay in business instead of receiving payment for the condemned property's fair market value. Three decades later, in *Hawaii Housing Authority v. Midkiff*,[3] Justice Sandra Day O'Connor, writing for another unanimous Court, refused to overturn the Hawaii Legislature's decision to attack "land oligopoly"[4] by arranging for the "taking" of landlords' property interests, which were in turn transferred to tenants upon payment of compensation. Neither of those earlier decisions, involving situations that were arguably as egregious and as far from the text of the Fifth Amendment's Takings Clause ("nor shall private property be taken for public use, without just compensation"[5]) as was the factual context in *Kelo*, resulted in public and political reactions that were in any way comparable in breadth and intensity to the furor spawned by the decision in New London's favor that the Court announced on June 23, 2005.

What was the nature of the reaction in the popular media in the hours, days, and weeks following the revelation that the Justices had refused to invalidate the use of eminent domain to take Susette Kelo's and the other plaintiffs' homes to make way for a redevelopment project? How did media coverage in the summer of 2005 compare with that in the fall of 1954 and the spring of 1984, when the pro-taking decisions

---

1   545 U.S. 469 (2005).
2   348 U.S. 26 (1954).
3   467 U.S. 229 (1984).
4   *Id*. at 242.
5   U.S. Const. amend V.

in *Berman* and *Midkiff* were announced? What factors can we identify that offer the best hope of explaining why the response to *Kelo* was so much more intense and unfavorable? This chapter will address these three important questions as a vehicle for exploring (1) the importance of context in appraising judicial decisions, (2) the implications of an important shift in the American political milieu that occurred during the closing decades of the twentieth century, and (3) the emergence of the "Public Use Clause" as the soft underbelly of government regulation of land.

Kelo and the Fourth Estate: A Chronology

First Encounters: The Story is Caught in the Web

In the Internet Age, Supreme Court observers no longer have to camp out on the courthouse steps or hang out at the clerk's office to find out how the Justices voted and what they said in the latest case. By the noon hour on June 23, 2005, those browsing the MSNBC web site, for example, could scan a report with the following headline: "Homes May be 'Taken' for Private Projects."[6] Underneath a photograph of Suzette Kelo's pink house (with multi-story structures and a construction crane in the background), the Associated Press story included some disturbing "facts" (highlighted by italics below):

> The Supreme Court on Thursday ruled that local governments may *seize people's homes and businesses* – even against their will – for private economic development.

> It was a decision fraught with huge implications for a country with many areas, particularly the rapidly growing urban and suburban areas, facing countervailing pressures of development and property ownership rights.

> As a result, cities now have wide power to bulldoze residences for projects such as shopping malls and hotel complexes in order to generate tax revenue.[7]

Only those readers who took the time to read beyond the alarming headline and opening passages would find an account of the case that included quotations from majority and dissenting opinions, from disappointed residents, and from the city's legal brief. The web story also included a link to a video news story by NBC correspondent Pete Williams that similarly conveyed a mixed message. While the "Flash News" imposed on the bottom of the screen read, "Supreme Court: Cities Can Seize Property for Economic Development,"[8] Williams, like the AP story, related information from both sides of the issue.

---

6   http://www.msnbc.msn.com/id/8331097/.

7   *Id.* (emphasis added).

8   *Id.* Apparently, NBC was prepared for the announcement of another controversial case, as the first version of "Flash News" read, "U.S. Supreme Court Rules on Ten Commandment Displays." As it turns out, the Court's two rulings on that subject appeared a few days later, on June 27, 2005.

Foxnews.com carried the same basic AP story with its own "fair and balanced" twist. Under a headline reading "High Court Expands Reach of Eminent Domain,"[9] the first two paragraphs painted a dire picture indeed:

Cities may bulldoze people's homes to make way for shopping malls or other private development, a divided Supreme Court ruled Thursday, giving local governments broad power to seize private property to generate tax revenue.

In a scathing dissent, Justice Sandra Day O'Connor said the decision bowed to the rich and powerful at the expense of middle-class Americans.[10]

During or soon after lunchtime, many Americans would already have discussed what appeared to be the latest example of judicial overreaching by the nation's highest tribunal.

Shock and Awe on Cable and Network News

All three leading cable news networks complemented their web site coverage with *Kelo* stories on the day the decision was announced. On "CNN Live Today" (10am on the East Coast), correspondent Kimberly Osiris informed the anchor, Daryn Kagan, that "the Supreme Court has issued a decision on eminent domain, siding basically with big business,"[11] noting twice that the Justices were split 5-4. When CNN Legal Analyst Jeffrey Toobin was asked about whether anything could be "read into" the 5-4 split, he tied the *Kelo* story to speculation about the possible retirement of the Chief Justice:

Well, you know, I think it's an example of Chief Justice Rehnquist, who may be leaving the court shortly, not having had his way on several important issues. And this is an issue he has believed in for a long time, limiting the power of government, limiting eminent domain. But he's in the minority. He never persuaded his colleagues.

And 5-4 is the same as unanimous. It's the law of the land. So this gives local politicians, local government authorities, more or less carte blanche to condemn property and give it to other private people if they believe it's in larger term interests of the community.[12]

By the early afternoon, CNN's coverage featured a video clip of Institute of Justice attorney Scott Bullock, who represented Kelo and the other landowners. Bullock issued this troublesome (and bellicose) warning, "The people who will be most affected by today's decision are the poor and working, and middle class homeowners,

---

9   http://www.foxnews.com/story/0,2933,160479,00.html.

10 *Id.* In similar fashion, the following afternoon CNN.com's version of the decision cried, "Supreme Court Backs Municipal Land Grabs." http://www.cnn.com/2005/LAW/06/24/scotus.property/.

11 *CNN Live Today: Supreme Court Allows Seizures of Private Property; Senate Armed Services Committee Hearing On Iraq Military Operations; Killen Sentenced to 20 Years on Each Count* (June 23, 2005) (transcript available on LEXIS).

12 *Id.*

who may now see their neighborhoods and their homes and small businesses targeted by governments and their corporate allies. This battle will continue.'[13] Soon, George Washington University law professor Jonathan Turley offered this sobering, if somewhat confused, assessment of the Court's decision:

> You know, many Supreme Court cases have only limited effect on citizens across the country. This one is going to have an enormous effect. And what the court is saying here is that local officials can simply decide that someone else could do better with your property. And there are many cities that want to expand their tax base, bring in some more jobs. And so they literally can bulldoze your house and give you the market value.

> And the thing to remember is, a lot of these people turned down the market value. You could have a family home where someone's offered you twice the market value then you turned down previously. The city can give you half of what you were offered and bulldoze your home whether you like it or not.[14]

Luckily, Professor Turley identified a cure for the Court's dramatic and disturbing ruling (a strategy suggested by Justice John Paul Stevens in his opinion for the Court[15]): "Now, if citizens are upset, they can go to their state governments and seek state laws that bar this type of use of eminent domain. It can be eliminated through state legislation."[16] As the afternoon turned into night, and as the CNN baton passed from Wolf Blitzer to Lou Dobbs to Anderson Cooper to Paula Zahn and to Aaron Cooper ("In America, your home, they say, is your castle. But if it lies in the path of a riverfront shopping mall, the government can take it away and knock it down. That's, in effect, what the U.S. Supreme Court ruled today."),[17] Cable news watchers were treated to additional accounts of the *Kelo* decision. Viewers of the Fox News Network and MSNBC were also informed about the Court's already controversial eminent domain decision.[18]

By the dinner hour on the East Coast, broadcast network news writers and producers had put their own spin on the *Kelo* tale. Elizabeth Vargas, sitting in for Peter Jennings on ABC, opened the broadcast with this attention-grabber: "On 'World News Tonight,' a major defeat for homeowners. A huge win for big business. The supreme court says your home can be taken away if your city thinks it's a good

---

13 *Live From ... : Iraq War: What Next?; Eminent Domain; Mississippi Murder Trial; Aruba Disappearance Update* (June 23, 2005) (CNN transcript available on LEXIS).

14 *Live From ... : 5-4 Supreme Court Decision Asserts Preeminence of Eminent Domain; Senate Sparks Over War in Iraq* [hereinafter *5-4 Supreme Court Decision*] (June 23, 2005) (CNN transcript available on LEXIS). Professor Turley did not explain how the offer that the landowner turned down would not be considered in a determination of "market value."

15 See *Kelo*, 545 U.S. at 489 ("We emphasize that nothing in our opinion precludes any State from placing further restrictions on its exercise of the takings power.").

16 *5-4 Supreme Court Decision, supra* note 14.

17 *CNN Newsnight: Paul Van Der Sloot Arrested; China Bids for U.S. Oil Company* (June 23, 2005) (transcript available on LEXIS).

18 MSNBC viewers of "The Abrams Report" (6pm on the East Coast) could hear Joseph Sax, University of California law professor plus Fox News. See *Fox Special Report with Brit Hume: Rove Remarks on 9/11; Senate Hearing on Iraq; Supreme Court Eminent Domain Case* (June 23, 2005) (transcript available on LEXIS).

idea." She continued by noting that the "ruling that will have major implications for every person who owns a home," before turning to Manuel Medrano's report, which, like the body of the internet stories released earlier in the day, was a balanced account featuring the pros and cons of the Court's ruling.[19] Brian Williams opened his NBC "Nightly News" broadcast in a similar, alarmist fashion: "House rules. The US Supreme Court makes it much easier for the government to take your private property. Tonight, critics are calling the decision a violation of the Founding Fathers."[20] Williams then brought the decision down to the personal level of every American homeowner: "The US Supreme Court today made it a whole lot easier for someone to come in and take your house, take your private property, against your will, as long as the state can prove there's a better public use for it."[21] Once again, the actual report contained information supporting and attacking the decision.

On CBS's "Evening News," an American general's Senate testimony on the strength of the insurgency in Iraq took top billing. Later in the broadcast, the anchor, Bob Schieffer, introduced reporter Wyatt Andrews's well-balanced *Kelo* story in a comparatively tepid manner: "The US Supreme Court today affirmed the power of local governments to seize private property. In a 5-to-4 ruling, the court said governments may take private property even for private development as long as the project is for the public good."[22] While somehow *Kelo* did not rate coverage later in the evening on Fox's "The O'Reilly Factor," MSNBC talking head Tucker Carlson did his part to chum the political waters by dropping the "L word." The lead story on "The Situation" was, in host Carlson's colorful phrase, "A high court low blow for homeowners."[23] Who was to blame for delivering the "low blow"? The answer was "the liberals":

> The majority, dominated by the court's liberal wing, ruled that the confiscations will benefit the city, and so they're constitutional.
>
> I mean, to say this is setting a bad precedent is probably the understatement of the week. The idea that your house can be taken away by someone who thinks he can make more money on the same property is terrifying ...
>
> I'm struck more than anything by the fact it was the liberal wing of the Supreme Court that did this.[24]

Later in the show, Carlson bantered with the winning attorney in the case, Wesley Horton, who tried to explain to the unconvinced host that what the Court allowed

---

19 *World News Tonight with Peter Jennings* (June 23, 2005) (transcript available on LEXIS). Another *Kelo* story ran on ABC's "Good Morning America" the next day. See *News Headlines: Good Morning America* (June 24, 2005) (transcript available on LEXIS).

20 *NBC Nightly News* (June 23, 2005) (transcript available on LEXIS).

21 *Id.*

22 *CBS Evening News: Supreme Court Affirms the Power of Local Governments to Seize Private Property* (June 23, 2005) (transcript available on LEXIS). Andrews's story also ran the next morning on CBS. See, e.g., *CBS Morning News: Supreme Court Rules That Government May Take Property for Public Use* (June 24, 2005) (transcript available on LEXIS).

23 *The Situation with Tucker Carlson* (June 23, 2005) (transcript available on LEXIS).

24 *Id.*

was the use of eminent domain when there "was a well-planned, comprehensive economic development plan for a whole area and wasn't just targeting one piece of property."[25] Many Americans would go to bed with visions of government-controlled bulldozers dancing in their heads.

The Poison of the Pen

On the morning of June 24, 2005, many of the nation's newspapers featured headlines on the news and editorial pages designed to inform and, it cannot be denied, distress the American people about the latest offering from the High Court. The words of woe and warning issued forth from sea to shining sea included:

U.S. Supreme Court Trashes People's Right to Their Homes (*Detroit News*, editorial, at 10A);

High Court Bolsters Municipal Land Grabs (*Boston Herald*, at 6);

Supreme Court Ruling on Private Property Seizures a Clunker That Invites Great Abuse (*Asheville Citizen-Times*, editorial, at 8A);

Court Curbs Property Rights (*Orlando Sentinel*, at A1);

The Little People Get Hit (*Providence Journal*, editorial, at B-04);

Dangerous Property Rights Ruling (*Post and Courier* (Charleston, South Carolina), editorial, at 12A);

Liberalism Bulldozes Over Society's Little Platoons (*Houston Chronicle*, op-ed by George F. Will, at B11);

Dark Days Ahead for Property Owners (*Rocky Mountain News* (Denver), editorial, at 48A);

Is Your Home Safe? (*Chicago Tribune*, editorial, at 24);

Your Home Could Be Up for Grabs (St. Petersburg Times (Florida), column, at 1D);

So the City Says It Has a Plan for Your Property – A New Shopping Center to Benefit Everyone. Start Packing. (Virginian-Pilot (Norfolk, Virginia), at A1);

Ruling Leaves Door Open to Abuse (*USA Today*, at 14A);

Preeminent Domain; Court Eviscerates the Takings Clause (*Union Leader* (Manchester, New Hampshire, editorial, at A10).

Court Shows Homeowners Door; Development Trumps Property Rights (*Chicago Sun-Times*, at 65);

Ruling Sanctions Property Seizures (Lincoln Journal Star (Nebraska), at A1);

Land's Not Your Land (Newsday (New York), at A03);

High Court Sticks it to the Little Guy (Orange County Register (Santa Ana, California), editorial);

Tear Down the Castle (St. Louis Post-Dispatch, editorial, at B8);

Cities Get More Power to Seize Homes (Star Tribune (Minneapolis), at 1A).[26]

While, as with the cable and network news reports, the news stories were, typically, balanced presentations that offered comments from the winning and losing sides

---

25 *Id.*

26 The editorial attacks did not end on June 24, as evidenced by June 25 editorials in the *Richmond Times-Dispatch* ("Court-Endorsed Theft," at A-10), the *Chattanooga Times Free Press*

and quotations or summaries of majority and dissenting opinions, the editorials and guest commentaries whose titles are included above were predominantly negative. Although in most cases the content of the text matched the message conveyed by the title, there were exceptions. For example, those *St. Louis Post-Dispatch* readers who read beyond the title and all the way to the end of "Tear Down the Castle" would find this balanced summary of the import of the decision: "The court's decision may fuel the trend for big box stores to displace little businesses and homes ... But it also will help cities improve their economic health or aesthetics. In essence, the decision is a bow to modernity. There aren't castles anymore."[27]

Two major exceptions to the editorial trashing of the majority opinion in *Kelo* could be found in the nation's most prominent left-leaning, East-Coast dailies. A *Washington Post* editorial titled "Eminent Latitude" opened, "It's hard to take satisfaction in the Supreme Court's decision yesterday in the case of Kelo v. City of New London – the result of which is quite unjust. Yet the court's decision was correct."[28] The editorial writer then provided this assessment of the difficult question of judicial deference that the case posed:

> This is not to say that a "public use" is anything government says it is. But the Fifth Amendment's takings clause was never meant to ensure good judgment or wise policy. Indeed, it was intended less as a restraint on the substance of what government does than as a guarantee that it will pay reasonably. However unfortunate New London's plans may prove, stopping the city based on a standardless judicial inquiry into how "public" its purpose really is would be far worse.[29]

Similarly, the *New York Times* editorial – "The Limits of Property Rights" – perceived the risks of uncontrolled use of the sovereign power of eminent domain, noting that "the dissenters provided a useful reminder that eminent domain must not be used for purely private gain."[30] Nevertheless, the newspaper applauded the fact that the decision was "a setback to the 'property rights' movement, which is trying to block government from imposing reasonable zoning and environmental regulations."[31]

Editorial cartoonists had a field day with *Kelo*, portraying the Court or individual Justices as court jesters smiling at the proposition that "DEVELOPERS CAN SEIZE YOUR HOMES,"[32] as a group named the "Supremes" singing "THIS LAND IS NOT YOUR LAND," as a corrupt judge who rules that property will be "SOLD TO THE POLITICALLY WIRED DEVELOPER," as a wrecking ball in the shape of a

---

("Your Home, Freedom Attacked," at B7), and in the *ARIZONA REPUBLIC* (Phoenix) ("Supreme Court Ruling Shreds 5th Amendment," at 6B).

27 Editorial, *Tear Down the Castle*, ST. LOUIS POST-DISPATCH, June 24, 2005, at B8.

28 Editorial, *Eminent Latitude*, WASHINGTON POST, June 24, 2005, at A30.

29 *Id.*

30 Editorial, *The Limits of Property Rights*, N.Y. TIMES, June 24, 2005, at A22.

31 *Id.* The fact that these two prominent newspapers were outliers was not lost on observers from the ideological right. See, *e.g.*, Matt Welch, *Why The New York Times's Eminent Domain*, REASON, Oct. 2005, at 18, *available at* http://www.reason.com/0510/co.mw. why.shtml.

32 All of the editorial cartoons discussed in this paragraph are available on-line at http://www.politicalcartoons.com.

gavel about to raze a home, as a modern-day version of the Ku Klux Klan ("ROBED GROUP THAT THREATENED HOMEOWNERS"), and as a butcher with a cleaver in one hand and a still-bleeding heart torn from the Constitution in the other hand. The post-*Kelo* alarmism, though predominant, was not universal, as illustrated by one cartoonist who paired an hysterical chicken crying "EMINENT DOMAIN! THEY'RE TAKING OUR FARM!", with a cow who calmly observed, "THE SKY IS ALWAYS FALLING FOR CERTAIN CREATURES ... "

Rushing to Judgment

In the days, weeks, and months that followed, radio talk-show hosts and politicians, among others active on the national scene, fanned the anti-*Kelo* flames, and private property rights activists were on hand to provide kindling in the form of provocative quotations. On his June 27, 2005, radio broadcast, Rush Limbaugh reduced *Kelo* to its (supposed) partisan essentials for the benefit of a caller who saw the majority's opinion as "revert[ing] power back to the states" and asserted, "This really isn't a question of liberal or conservative." Limbaugh responded:

> It most definitely is liberal versus conservative because there's no conservative court in the land that would decide to kick you off your property for some other private citizen to build something else. This is not the same thing as the State of Wisconsin saying, "Joe, we need to put a boat dock there. The state is going to run it. We need to put a road through your property to improve living conditions here, and here's the price we're going to give you. It's the fair market value. You can go move somewhere else." This is the state saying to another group of private citizens, who are wealthier than you, Joe, they want your property.[33]

Similarly, three days later, the second hour of Bill O'Reilly's "Radio Factor" was set aside for "Debating eminent domain":

> Armed with an activist Supreme Court decision, local governments have nearly tripled the rate at which they seize private property. Is your home no longer your castle? The Factor will let you know if your home is vulnerable, and what you can do to protect yourself.[34]

Right-wing radio resonated with this rhetoric even as *Kelo* became weeks and months old.

Making Political Hay While the *Kelo* Sun Shines

It would not be long before the media attacks bore political fruit. In the October, 2005 issue of *Reason*, Matt Welch, reported on the progress of the multi-front battle to date:

---

33 *Limbaugh Legal Division: Liberals Stick it to the Little Guy*, http://www.rushlimbaugh. com/home/stacks/liberals_stick_it_to_the_little_guy_in_eminent_domain__06_27_05_ .guest.html.

34 Screen capture of www.billoreilly.com June 30, 2005, in possession of the author.

"The vast majority of newspapers have editorialized against it," says Scott Bullock, senior attorney at the Institute for Justice, who unsuccessfully litigated Kelo in front of the Supreme Court. "The only real exceptions were the elite-opinion papers."

As the [Washington] *Post* and the [New York] *Times* cheered on the government's ability to break a few individual eggs in order to make a more perfect public-interest omelette, Kelo was prompting an ideologically diverse backlash against eminent domain abuse. The week after the decision, far-left California Democrat Rep. Maxine Waters joined far-right Texas Republican Rep. Tom DeLay in supporting an amendment to an appropriations bill barring federal Community Block Grant funds for any locale that doesn't prohibit eminent domain seizures for private development. It passed 231 to 189, and a similar bipartisan bill has been introduced in the Senate.[35]

Alabama successfully prohibited such transfers in nonblighted areas on July 27 (joining eight other states with similar laws); Texas is trying to get a ban on the November ballot, and several other state legislatures are contemplating quick action in the wake of Kelo. Supporting these efforts is a politically broad variety of groups, from the National Association for the Advancement of Colored People to RightMarch.com. Outrage at Kelo united columnists Molly Ivins and George Will, fire breathers Rush Limbaugh and Ralph Nader. "The only people who supported the decision," Bullock says, "were cities who want the tax dollars, their projects approved, and then a couple of random academics."[36]

With such an impressive array of *Kelo* protesters, we should not be surprised at the legislative deluge that ensued. Shortly after the first-year anniversary of the

---

35 The vote was on an amendment to H.R. 3058, offered by Representative Scott Garrett (a New Jersey Republican), reading, "None of the funds made available in this Act may be used to enforce the judgment of the United States Supreme Court in the case of Kelo v. New London, decided June 23, 2005." The final version of the legislation, Pub. L. 109–115, 119 Stat. 2396, which was passed by both chambers and signed by the President in late November, 2005, contains the following much more moderate restriction:

SEC. 726. No funds in this Act may be used to support any Federal, State, or local projects that seek to use the power of eminent domain, unless eminent domain is employed only for a public use: Provided, That for purposes of this section, public use shall not be construed to include economic development that primarily benefits private entities: Provided further, That any use of funds for mass transit, railroad, airport, seaport or highway projects as well as utility projects which benefit or serve the general public (including energy-related, communication-related, water-related and wastewater-related infrastructure), other structures designated for use by the general public or which have other common-carrier or public-utility functions that serve the general public and are subject to regulation and oversight by the government, and projects for the removal of an immediate threat to public health and safety or brownsfield as defined in the Small Business Liability Relief and Brownsfield Revitalization Act (Public Law 107-118) shall be considered a public use for purposes of eminent domain: Provided further, That the Government Accountability Office, in consultation with the National Academy of Public Administration, organizations representing State and local governments, and property rights organizations, shall conduct a study to be submitted to the Congress within 12 months of the enactment of this Act on the nationwide use of eminent domain, including the procedures used and the results accomplished on a state-by-state basis as well as the impact on individual property owners and on the affected communities.

36 Welch, *supra* note 31.

controversial decision, lawmakers in more than half of the states could tell their constituents that they had responded to *Kelo* by passing an eminent domain reform law.[37] On September 30, 2006, Louisiana voters jumped on the anti-*Kelo* bandwagon by passing two ballot initiatives that provided a detailed definition of "public purpose"[38] and placed restrictions on the resale of property that the state had previously expropriated.[39] In November, 2006, voters in several other states would be given the opportunity to register their dissatisfaction with the *Kelo* Court by considering ballot questions proposing legislative or constitutional changes to eminent domain law.[40] It seemed as if politicians and activists throughout the nation felt the need to respond to the anti-*Kelo* sentiment, to take advantage of that sentiment to achieve their preexisting goal of placing restraints on government acquisition and regulation of real property, or both.

Pages from the Past: The Media Response to *Berman* and *Midkiff*

When the Court decided *Berman v. Parker* in the early 1950s, coast-to-coast network television news was in its infancy, so Americans relied chiefly on daily newspapers to keep informed about important national developments. In fact, during this period,

---

37 See, e.g., POWELL ON REAL PROPERTY, §79F.03[3][b][iv] (Michael Allan Wolf, gen. ed., 2006):

> Public reaction against the majority opinion in *Kelo* was swift, intense, and unprecedented. State lawmakers in every region of the nation took up the cause of making clear that "'public use'" was not elastic enough to include private economic development projects. Within a little more than one year after the date on which the Court announced its holding, more than half of the states enacted eminent domain reform legislation. The states that have made it to the finish line are, in order, Delaware, Alabama, Texas, Ohio, South Dakota, Utah, Idaho, Indiana, Kentucky, Wisconsin, Georgia, West Virginia, Maine, Nebraska, Vermont, Pennsylvania, Florida, Kansas, Minnesota, Tennessee, Colorado, New Hampshire, Alaska, Missouri, Iowa, and Illinois. In several states, voters will be given the opportunity to change constitutional takings provisions.

> A review of the chief elements of the new statutes reveals that, not surprisingly, when given the opportunity to revisit often outdated eminent domain provisions, many state legislators used this opportunity to tweak existing law in areas beyond public use. Some of the more common changes involve enhanced public notice requirements, provisions for enhanced attorney's fees, and additional compensation for targeted landowners, and stiffer requirements for the taking of property in blighted areas.

North Carolina joined the list when the governor signed House Bill 1965 on August 10, 2006.

38 Ballot Number 5, based on La. House Bill No. 1 (2006).

39 Ballot Number 6, based on La. House Bill No. 707 (2006).

40 The states include Arizona (Proposition 207), California (Proposition 90), Florida (Amendment 8), Georgia (Amendment 1), Idaho (Proposition 2), Michigan (Proposal D), Nevada (Ballot Question 2), New Hampshire (Question 1), North Dakota (Measure Number 2), Oregon (Measure 39), and South Carolina (Amendment 5), and Washington (Initiative 933).

more than one newspaper was sold for each American household.[41] In stark contrast with the shrieking headlines and the widespread news and editorial attention focused on *Kelo*, newspaper coverage of *Berman* was downright noncontroversial – even mellow. Forty-eight pages after its front page on November 23, 1954, the *New York Times* included an article titled, "Congress Upheld in Slum Clearing: Supreme Court Says Federal and State Legislatures Have Wide Redevelopment Power."[42] The descriptive article quoted generously from Justice Douglas's unanimous opinion for the Court, which turned back a department store owner's challenge to the use of eminent domain under the District of Columbia Redevelopment Act of 1945.[43] Similar reportage appeared in newspapers such as the *Atlanta Constitution*[44] and the *Chicago Daily Tribune*,[45] while in other dailies the *Berman* opinion was quickly summarized along with other Court developments from the previous day.[46] Not surprisingly, given the fact that the case had important local implications, the *Washington Post* complemented its front-page news coverage of *Berman*[47] with a positive editorial two days after the decision was announced. The author of "City's Right to Beauty" declared:

> The effect [of *Berman*] is to give the RLA [Redevelopment Land Agency] a bright and prolonged green light for its redevelopment projects. That is good news for the whole city. With all the obstacles to major redevelopment removed, the public will now expect the RLA to move ahead with dispatch as well as determination. It is time for extraordinary efforts to get these great undertakings into the construction stage.[48]

Similar praise appeared on the pages of a leading West coast newspaper, the *Los Angeles Times*, in which the author of "A Wide Decision on Blighted Areas" was intrigued by the fact "that a governing body, in considering the need for redevelopment, may take into account the fact that the changes will contribute to the beauty of a neighborhood as well as to its sanitation."[49] Even in the conservative political milieu of the first Eisenhower term, the editorial singled out approvingly

---

41 *The State of the News Media 2004: An Annual Report of American Journalism*, http://www.stateofthenewsmedia.org/narrative_newspapers_audience.asp?cat'3&media'2. By 2000, the percentage dropped to 53 percent. *Id.*

42 *Congress Upheld in Slum Clearing: Supreme Court Says Federal and State Legislatures Have Wide Redevelopment Power*, N.Y. TIMES, Nov. 23, 1954, at 49.

43 60 Stat. 790 (cited in Berman v. Parker, 348 U.S. 26, 28 (1954)).

44 *High Court Upholds Slum Re-Reprojecting: Ruling Okays Broad Powers of Federal, State Legislatures*, ATLANTA CONSTITUTION, Nov. 23, 1954, at 2 (from New York Times News Service).

45 *Supreme Court Delays Segregation Action*, CHICAGO DAILY TRIBUNE, at 7.

46 See, e.g., *Immigration Debate Put Off*, CHRISTIAN SCIENCE MONITOR, Nov. 22, 1954, at 7 (from AP); *What's News: World Wide*, WALL ST. JOURNAL, at 1; *Integration Hearings Postponed: Supreme Court to Wait for Full Membership Before Acting*, MORNING TRIBUNE (Tampa, Florida), Nov. 23, 1954, at 1 (from UP).

47 See Frank R. Kent, Jr., *Development Act of D.C. Upheld: U.S. Supreme Court Opinion Removes Major Obstacle to Rebuilding Here*, WASH. POST AND TIMES HERALD, Nov. 23, 1954, at 1.

48 Editorial, *City's Right to Beauty*, WASH. POST & TIMES HERALD, Nov. 24, 1954, at 12.

49 Editorial, *A Wide Decision on Blighted Areas*, L.A. TIMES, Nov. 26, 1954, at II-4.

one departure that Justice Douglas and his colleagues had made from traditional doctrines: "The law has, in general, been held to be strictly utilitarian; and the idea that esthetics may also be considered would not, we think, have appealed to courts in the 19th century." In this column, as in the news reports and the other editorial responses to *Berman*, there seemed to be little if any concern about the private property rights of the disgruntled owners of going concerns who were being forced out of their locations by the government bulldozer.

When, on May 30, 1984, Justice O'Connor presented the Court's *Midkiff* opinion for the eight participating Justices, the response in the national media attention was, as was the case nearly thirty years before, generally neutral or supportive. For example, the two network news stories on the case that appeared on the evening of the 30th were anything but sensational or alarmist. Jim Lehrer's text on PBS's MacNeil/Lehrer NewsHour updated a story that appeared on the show two months previously:

> [T]oday the Court ruled in the state's favor in an eight-to-zero unanimous decision. It means the state can force the sale of the land under a plan Justice Sandra Day O'Connor, writing for the Court, said attacked the perceived evils of concentrated property ownership.[50]

With a picture of the Supreme Court in the background (upon which was superimposed the title, "LAND REFORM"), CBS news anchor Dan Rather also reported on the decision, quoting from the opinion and noting that the Court "upheld the principle of a land reform program designed to end the concentration of real estate in the hands of the few, not in some third-world country, but in the fiftieth state – Hawaii."[51]

Several newspaper headlines that appeared the day after the decision also highlighted the land reform and breakup of large landholding aspects of the case:

> Justices Uphold Hawaii Land Reform (*Miami Herald*, May 31, 1984, at 13A);
> Supreme Court Upholds Program to Reform Hawaii Land Ownership (*Atlanta Constitution*, May 31, 1984, at A2 (UPI));
> Court Oks Break-up of Big Land Holdings (*Chicago Tribune*, May 31, 1984, at 13);
> Justices Uphold Hawaii's Statute on Land Reform: Estates May Be Split Up; Court Decides State May Use Power of Eminent Domain to Transfer Ownership (*New York Times*, May 31, 1984, at A1);
> Court Sustains Hawaiian Law Dividing Large Land Holding (*Washington Post*, May 31, 1984, at A2).[52]

The longer articles included quotations from the Court's opinion and detailed the high concentration of property in the hands of a small number of Hawaiian landowners.

---

50 *MacNeil/Lehrer NewsHour, Immigration: Political Hot Potato; India: Religious Unrest; Healing an Old Wound; Book Review: Jacob's Well*, May 30, 1984 (Transcript #2263 available on LEXIS).

51 *CBS Evening News*, May 30, 1984 (recording in possession of author).

52 This same themes were also part of the *Midkiff* coverage in the nation's two leading weekly news magazines. See *State's Right; Hawaii Land Reform is Upheld*, TIME, June 11, 1984, at 27; *The High Court: This Property Is Condemned*, NEWSWEEK, June 11, 1984, at 69.

While *Wall Street Journal* readers would learn that "the decision *reaffirms* the broad power of states to regulate resources, like land, to serve public needs,"[53] the headline in the *Los Angeles Times* article was somewhat unusual in noting that the Court had "Expand[ed] Government's Power of Eminent Domain."[54] The latter article not only quoted the winning counsel, Harvard law professor Lawrence H. Tribe, but also "John Findley, deputy director of the Pacific Legal Foundation in Sacramento and one of the attorneys who opposed the law, [who] expressed dismay with the sweeping nature of the court's ruling."[55] The *Washington Post* noted that, while the "immediate impact" of the decision was limited to Hawaii and its special situation, attorneys on both sides of the dispute could foresee an expansion of the notion of "public use," "strengthening the hand of cities attempting to keep sports teams in town by condemning them, for example, or of governments wishing to restrict condominium conversion or enact laws rearranging land rights in the West."[56]

The editorial pages of three important national newspapers indicated some emerging concerns about the potential abuse of the sovereign power of eminent domain. In the *New York Times*, the editorial opened by observing that the Court's validation of the "dramatic land reform has a radical ring to it," which "sounds startling at first blush."[57] "In truth," we learn, however, "the decision is neither radical nor unprecedented and demonstrates, if anything, judicial restraint."[58] In its editorial, "Paradise Divvied," the *Christian Science Monitor* praised *Midkiff* as "a welcome advance toward an otherwise unobtainable equity for Hawaii's middle class" and compared the state program favorably with land-reform efforts that the United States government supported in El Salvador.[59] Still, the editorial had one "cautionary note" for its readers: "It should be used only with great care as a precedent. Any state efforts to legislate redistribution of other scarce resources – recreational land, or services – should be viewed with the greatest caution."[60] More in line with the emerging property-rights rhetoric that grew louder as the Reagan years rolled on was the *Wall Street Journal*'s editorial offering, "Lords of the Manor."[61] *Midkiff* changed the law, according to this column, as the Justices "vastly broadened the government power of eminent domain – with national consequences that the court itself refused to contemplate."[62] Indeed, "Justice Rehnquist, Justice O'Connor and

---

53 *Powers in* Stephen Wermiel, *Justices, in a Hawaii Land Case, Reaffirm States' Regulation of Resources*, WALL ST. JOURNAL, May 31, 1954, at 60 (emphasis added).

54 Philip Hager, *Hawaiian Law on Breakup of Estates Upheld; High Court Expands Government's Power of Eminent Domain*, L.A. TIMES, May 31, 1984, at 1.

55 *Id*. "'If the state is going to take away private property, it should be for some public use as a highway, courthouse or something else everyone can use,' Findley said. 'What the court has sanctioned is taking property from one individual to give to another.'"

56 Fred Barbash, *Court Sustains Hawaiian Law Dividing Large Land Holdings*, WASH. POST, May 31, 1984, at A2.

57 Editorial, *Eminent Sense on Eminent Domain*, N.Y. TIMES, June 1, 1984, at A30.

58 *Id*.

59 Editorial, *Paradise Divvied*, CHRISTIAN SCIENCE MONITOR, June 1, 1984, at 15.

60 *Id*.

61 Editorial, *Lords of the Manor*, WALL ST. JOURNAL, June 1, 1984, at 1.

62 *Id*.

their colleagues have engineered a vast expansion of governmental powers," in turn abandoning essential, historical American values:

> Eminent domain may be the most devastating of government powers, especially in a country based on John Locke's theory of a social contract designed to protect property. Very few things hit as close to a person's identity as the threat to take away his home ...
>
> A well-intentioned court has just opened this sphere to a host of unforeseeable harassments. We may all live to regret the day we heard about Hawaiian land reform.[63]

This editorial is notable not only for its dead-on prediction (at least according to Susette Kelo and her supporters) and for its invocation of John Locke one year before the publication of Richard Epstein's landmark *Takings*,[64] but also for the author's respectful acknowledgment that the *Midkiff* Court, unlike the *Kelo* majority in the eyes of many editorialists, was "well-intentioned."

Why the Difference?

It would be presumptuous (and dismissive of the multi-layered nature of history) for any commentator to identify the *one, sure reason* for the dramatic difference between the media and political outcry after *Kelo* and the much more temperate responses to *Berman* and *Midkiff*, the two key precedents upon which the *Kelo* Court relied. This is particularly true given the fact that the Justices in 1954 and 1984 were considering unprecedented fact patterns that pushed the "public use" envelope farther than ever before, even farther, I would assert, than New London's redevelopment plans. We will have to be satisfied with identifying a set of factors that, considered collectively, help us to understand why we moved from history to hysteria in 2005.

The first factor considers the newsworthiness of the Court's decision at the time it was announced. *Berman* was not necessarily the most important story on the Supreme Court to appear in newspapers on November 23, 1954. The headline (and opening paragraphs) of the *Chicago Daily Tribune* article discussing the *Berman* holding read, "Supreme Court Delays Segregation Action: Arguments Await 9th Justice."[65] The story lead ran as follows: "Arguments on when and how to end racial segregation in public schools were postponed by the United States Supreme court [*sic*] today because of the vacancy on the bench.[66] While President Eisenhower had nominated John Marshall Harlan for the seat formerly held by the late Justice Robert Jackson, members of the Senate had announced the week before that they would hold up the confirmation process. As reported in the *Washington Post* article the same day, Senator James O. Eastland, a Mississippi Democrat, "explained that he had an 'open mind' on the nomination, but said 'several Democrats' wanted additional time to find

---

63 *Id.*

64 RICHARD A. EPSTEIN, TAKINGS: PRIVATE PROPERTY AND THE POWER OF EMINENT DOMAIN (1985).

65 Philip Dodd, *Supreme Court Delays Segregation Action: Arguments Await 9th Justice*, CHICAGO DAILY TRIBUNE, Nov. 23, 1954, at 7.

66 *Id.*

out more about Harlan. Many Southern Senators have been upset about the makeup of the court since it banned dual court systems."[67] In other words, still smarting over *Brown v. Board of Education* (*Brown I*),[68] which the Court announced the previous May 17, southern Democrats put the brakes on the Court's efforts to follow up their highly controversial decision with its enforcement plan.[69] The unanimous opinion in *Brown II*, with the Court at full strength after Harlan's confirmation, would not appear until May 31, 1955.[70]

The second factor is the existence of two stinging dissents in *Kelo*, in contrast with the unanimity of *Berman* and *Midkiff*. When reporters, writers, producers, radio hosts, and talking heads sought colorful and stirring rhetoric in opposition to Justice Stephens's opinion for the Court in *Kelo*, they did not have to look beyond Justice O'Connor's ringing dissent, in which she warned, "Nothing is to prevent the State from replacing any Motel 6 with a Ritz-Carlton, any home with a shopping mall, or any farm with a factory."[71] Indeed, her hotel hypothetical along with other

---

67 Jeanne Rogers, *High Court Delays School Arguments*, WASH. POST AND TIMES HERALD, Nov. 23, 1954, at 29.

68 347 U.S. 483 (1954).

69 For examples of similar coverage in other newspapers, see Luther A. Huston, *School Bias Case to Await Harlan: Implementation Arguments Delayed by Supreme Court Till There is a Full Bench*, N.Y. TIMES, at 49; *Segregation Arguments Postponed: U.S. High Court Acts After Senate Delays Action on Harlan Nomination*, MIAMI HERALD, Nov. 23, 1954, at 1 (UP).

70 *Brown v. Bd. of Education*, 349 U.S. 294 (1955). As it turns out, the thirtieth anniversary of *Brown I* fell two weeks before the Court announced its decision in *Midkiff*. The anniversary was noted in numerous news articles, editorials, and network broadcasts that considered *Brown*'s mixed legacy. See, e.g., Ted Gest et al., *School Desegregation Grinds to a Halt in the South*, U.S. NEWS & WORLD REPORT, May 21, 1984, at 49; Lawrence Feinberg, *30 Years After Brown Decision, Its Impact Debated*, WASH. POST, May 18, 1984, at C1; Opinion, Derrick Bell, *Brown and Pocketbook Segregation*, CHRISTIAN SCIENCE MONITOR, May 17, 1984, at 18; *Persian Gulf Violence – Oil Crisis Near?; Mondale's Record; School Desegregation – Thirty Years Later*, MacNeil/Lehrer NewsHour, May 17, 1984 (Transcript #2254 available on LEXIS); Walter Goodman, *Brown v. Board of Education: Uneven Results 30 Years Later*, N.Y. TIMES, May 17, 1984, at B18.

71 Kelo v. City of New London, 545 U.S. 469; 125 S. Ct. 2655, 2676 (2005) (O'Connor, J., dissenting). Justice O'Connor had this specific fact pattern in mind when she questioned the city's counsel during oral argument. See Transcript of Oral Argument at 26, Kelo v. City of New London, 545 U.S. 469; 125 S. Ct. 2655 (2005) (No. 04–108), 2005 U.S. TRANS LEXIS 11:

JUSTICE O'CONNOR: For example, Motel 6 and the city thinks, well, if we had a Ritz-Carlton, we would have higher taxes. Now, is that okay?

MR. HORTON: Yes, Your Honor. That would be okay – because otherwise you're in the position of drawing the line. I mean, there is, there is a limit. I mean –

JUSTICE KENNEDY: Well, if that, if that's so then the occasional statements that we see in the writing that you can't take from A to give to B is just wrong?

MR. HORTON: No. I don't agree with that.

Later in the oral argument, Horton explained why the hotel hypothetical was not likely to occur in reality:

MR. HORTON: I think there is [*sic*] two good reasons for it, and that it's a theoretical more than a practical problem. First of all, you've got all sorts of transaction costs when you, when you go through eminent domain, as opposed to doing things voluntarily.

quotations from her dissent and that of Justice Clarence Thomas's can be found in dozens of news articles and transcripts of radio, television, and cable programs.[72] While those writing news articles on *Midkiff* could turn to the Ninth Circuit's opinion in the landowners' favor,[73] such was not the case in *Berman*, in which the three-judge district court panel agreed with the Justices that the Redevelopment Act was not unconstitutional.[74]

The third factor is the Reagan Revolution. In his first presidential inaugural address, Ronald Reagan conveyed the essence of his long-held conservatism in two memorable phrases: "government is not the solution to our problem; government is the problem."[75] In the minds of many Americans, this day marked the beginning of the end of the identification of the state with the promotion of the overall general welfare even at the expense of the needs of one or a few. After nearly a quarter-decade of watching politicians at all levels taking credit for shrinking government, freeing Americans from burdensome regulations, and fostering individual freedom, *Kelo* appeared to be a return to the uncaring, power-hungry government behemoth of the pre-Reagan past. It was too easy for the media to take advantage of the fact that the overwhelming majority of Americans – comfortable with the rhetoric of individualism and uneasy with the power of the state – had never considered the expansive legal understanding of the term "public use" or the true nature of eminent domain.

The fourth factor is the explosive growth of national, right-leaning radio, television, and cable. Rush Limbaugh, Sean Hannity, and Bill O'Reilly were years away from national syndication and network exposure in 1984. CNN was only four years old in 1980, while the Fox News Channel, the current home of many conservative taking heads, was still more than a decade away when the Court issued

---

So you are not going to do things – yes, as a practical matter, to take Justice Scalia's earlier example, for one piece of property because of the transaction costs involved. I mean, you're never going to make up – unless it's to, you know, to favor the governor's friend or something like that, as you say.
Id. at 42.

72 See, e.g., David Harsanyi, *Court Gives Land Robbery a Thumbs Up*, DENVER POST, June 27, 2005, at B-01 (column); Gail Gibson, *High Court Upholds Eminent Domain; Private Homes, Businesses Can Be Seized as Part of Economic Revitalization; Cities Are Handed Broad Powers*, BALTIMORE SUN, June 24, 2005, at 1A; Michael McGough, *Court Upholds Eminent Domain; Property Rights Movement Suffers Narrow Defeat*, PITTSBURGH POST-GAZETTE, June 24, 2005, at A-1; *CBS News Transcripts, CBS Evening News: Supreme Court Affirms the Power of Local Governments to Seize Private Property*, June 23, 2005 (available on LEXIS); *National Public Radio, Talk of the Nation: David Savage Discusses the Issue of Eminent Domain and the Constitution*, June 23, 2005 (transcript available on LEXIS).

73 Midkiff v. Tom, 702 F.2d 788 (9th Cir. 1983), *rev'd*, Haw. Hous. Auth. v. Midkiff, 467 U.S. 229 (1984). See e.g., Barbash, *supra* note 56, at A2 ("Lawyers for the large landowners, and a panel of the 9th U.S. Circuit Court of Appeals, said the Hawaii scheme was different because it resulted in the transfer of property into private hands without changing its use.").

74 See Schneider v. District of Columbia, 117 F. Supp. 705 (D.C.D.C. 1953), *aff'd*, Berman v. Parker, 348 U.S. 26 (1954).

75 Ronald Reagan, *Inaugural Address (Jan. 20, 1981)*, *in* PUBLIC PAPERS OF THE PRESIDENTS OF THE UNITED STATES: RONALD REAGAN, 1981: JANUARY 20 TO DECEMBER 31, 1981, at 1 (1981).

its *Midkiff* opinion. Today, the competition in talk radio and round-the-clock cable news and talk is much more fierce than it was twenty years ago, and a Supreme Court decision on an otherwise dry and largely settled jurisprudential point that could be spun as a struggle between a greedy and uncaring government and a few middle-class homeowners would prove hard to resist (and easy to exploit).

The fifth factor is the growth of effective public interest law firms dedicated to the protection of property rights. The homeowners in *Kelo* were represented by the Institute of Justice (IJ), which describes itself and its mission in this way:

> As our nation's only libertarian public interest law firm, we pursue cutting-edge litigation in the courts of law and in the court of public opinion on behalf of individuals whose most basic rights are denied by the government – like the right to earn an honest living, private property rights, and the right to free speech, especially in the areas of commercial and Internet speech.[76]

Since 1991, the IJ has filed amicus briefs in opposition to a wide range of land-use and environmental regulation in several important Supreme Court cases,[77] many of which were crafted at least in part by Richard Epstein, whose important and controversial ideas have inspired the modern private property rights movement.[78] This has by no means been a lonely struggle for the IJ, as, for example, the following groups were among the many that filed *amicus curiae* briefs in support of the petitioners in *Kelo*: Mountain States Legal Foundation, Defenders of Property Rights, Cato Institute, Property Rights Foundation of America, Reason Foundation, James Madison Institute, John Locke Foundation, and Rutherford Institute. Other effective legal organizations in support of property rights include the Pacific Legal Foundation and the Washington Legal Foundation, early warriors in this struggle who today have a lot more company than they did in the *Midkiff* period.

The five factors above, when considered together, created a potent, unprecedented, and largely unexpected atmosphere for the explosive reaction to *Kelo*. The Supreme Court's careful, though disputed, holding exposed the "soft underbelly" of government regulation of land regulation. There are fervent opponents of traditional and innovative planning, zoning, and environmental regulations who are taking advantage of the dramatic reaction to the use of eminent domain to take private homes in furtherance of private economic development. One tactic, on the ballot on November 7, 2006, in four western states (successfully in Arizona, but failing to win voter approval in California, Idaho, and Washington), is for citizens to propose

---

76 *Institute Profile: Who We Are*, http://ij.org/profile/index.html.

77 See, e.g., http://ij.org/cases/index.html.

78 See, e.g., Douglas T. Kendall & Charles P. Lord, *The Takings Project: A Critical Analysis and Assessment of the Progress So Far*, 25 B.C. Envtl. Aff. L. Rev. 509, 510 (1998) ("many of the changes in takings law that have taken place over the last 11 years correspond quite closely to a blueprint for takings doctrine proposed by Professor Richard Epstein in his now-famous book called *Takings* … ").

and gather signatures for initiatives designed to merge anti-anti-regulatory taking
provisions with a public use "fix" for state laws.[79]

Those who believe that these and other anti-*Kelo* reverberations in the media,
courthouses,[80] state and federal legislatures, and statewide ballot measures would, on
balance, do more harm than good to the nation should consider how the five factors
can help yield effective strategies for containing the current excessive anti-eminent
domain hype and for anticipating similar overreactions in the future. Defenders
of enlightened land-use regulation can no longer assume that court decisions that
even peripherally involve property rights are not worthy of news coverage. Even
if a court majority sides with government regulators, legal commentators who are
asked for reactions from the press should be prepared to address the points made
by the dissenters. Regulators and their defenders need to be aware that, to many
Americans who have sipped generously from the cup of Reaganism, assertions that
government officials are acting on behalf of the general welfare, in the absence of
strong demonstrations of *concrete public* benefits, will be utterly unconvincing. The
proliferation of conservative media voices and public interest lawyering cannot be
neutralized overnight, nor without considerable time, energy, and expense. The first
step is realizing the extent of the lay and legal opposition to government and public-
private initiatives to regulate and redevelop land. The opponents of zoning and
environmental regulations have conjoined regulatory takings measures with more
popular efforts to narrow the definition of "public use." The supporters of those
regulations should educate the public that the constitutionality and legality of their

---

79 According to one news report, "The spate of ballot proposals is being bankrolled
largely by libertarian organizations controlled by New York City real estate investor Howie
Rich. The groups, Americans for Limited Government and the Fund for Democracy, have
donated $4 million to ballot drives in eight states." Martin Kasindorf, *Voters Get a Say on
Land Rights; State Laws Limit High Court Ruling*, USA TODAY, Sept. 25, 2006, at 1A. See
also Patrick Hoge, *Mogul's Network Bankrolls Prop. 90; Web of Advocacy Groups Funnels
Millions to Pass Property Rights Initiative*, SAN FRANCISCO CHRONICLE, Oct. 5, 2006, at A1;
NPR: Morning Edition: Western Voters Consider Property Rights Changes, Sept. 19, 2006
(transcript available on LEXIS).

In September, 2006, Louisiana became the first of several states to amend their state
constitution's takings provisions when voters passed a ballot measure based on Act No. 851.
The new provision limits the definition of "public purpose" and makes clear that "[n]either
economic development, enhancement of tax revenue, or any incidental benefit to the public
shall be considered in determining whether the taking or damaging of property is for a public
purpose." In November, 2006, voters in Florida, Georgia, Michigan, New Hampshire, and
South Carolina approved similar constitutional changes to eminent domain law that were
placed on the ballot by state lawmakers, while eminent domain ballot measures originating in
citizen petitions were successful in Arizona, North Dakota, Oregon, and Nevada. According
to state law, the Nevada measure requires a second positive statewide vote before it becomes
law. The Arizona statutory change not only narrows the definition of "public use," but it also
includes a "regulatory takings" provision that puts at risk land-use regulations that reduce
property values. Voters in California, Idaho, and Washington struck down ballot measures that
would have added this anti-regulatory measure.

80 See, e.g., City of Norwood v. Horney, 853 N.E. 2d 1115 (Ohio 2006) (invalidating
city's use eminent domain for a redevelopment project in a "deteriorating area").

favorite "green" program, such as the protection of wetlands or sand dunes, is only as strong as the weakest link in the land-use control chain, for all of these measures have the potential of reducing the real estate values or the property rights of at least one disgruntled potential litigant. And who knows, that litigant might be the next Susette Kelo.

Chapter 3

Kelo, the Castle, and Natural Property Rights

Eric R. Claeys[1]

The United States Supreme Court galvanized an important and high-profile political debate about eminent domain when it handed down its 2005 decision in *Kelo v. City of New London*.[2] In *Kelo*, the Supreme Court held that states and state agencies may condemn and redistribute private property if the redistribution promises to promote general economic growth and revenue in the context of a comprehensive redevelopment plan. *Kelo* unleashed strong political protests, and it has prompted many state legislatures to reconsider their states' policies toward eminent domain and urban redevelopment.

Somewhat surprisingly, this political debate has prompted an academic debate about the old proverb "A man's house is his castle." This maxim, which is associated with Lord Coke and Sir William Blackstone,[3] is used in different contexts to suggest a few different themes: that the home is a place of privacy; that the home is dignified; and that the common man deserves treatment by the law and state equal to any castle baron. *Kelo*'s opponents have used the "castle" maxim as a metaphor to advance the latter two themes: Developers are modern-day castle barons who get preferential treatment over home owners.

Yet the "castle" metaphor is ambiguous. If one puts the emphasis on "castle," the proverb suggests that property is and ought to be sacrosanct, even beyond regulation. That emphasis construes the proverb in a manner that is hard to square with our government practice, which *does* allow for the regulation and taking of property in many situations. If, in the proverb, one emphasizes "house," the proverb suggests that home ownership deserves priority over other forms of property ownership. While that suggestion sounds appealing, it also seems to justify cynical special-interest politics by home owners against everyone else. If these are the best available interpretations of the "castle" metaphor, perhaps the "castle" metaphor misguidedly encourages *Kelo*'s opponents to mobilize in favor of a reform program that is privately interested but publicly anarchistic.

---

1   I thank Christopher Stagg for his research assistance.
2   545 U.S. 649 (2005).
3   See Sir Edward Coke, Third Institute of the Laws of England 162 (1644); 4 William Blackstone, Commentaries on English Law 223 (1765–69); see also Semayne's Case, 77 Eng. Rep. 194 (K.B. 1603).

This chapter proposes an alternative interpretation. It interprets the proverb "A man's house is his castle" consistently with the principles of takings and regulation that follow from American natural-rights theory. In previous scholarship, I have articulated and defended an approach to public use law grounded in American natural-rights theory.[4] In simplified form, this is the theory, expressed in the United States Declaration of Independence and other public documents of the American Founding, holding that the primary object of government is to secure to individuals a zone of negative freedom, consistent with the like rights of others, in which to care for themselves and to pursue their own chosen callings.

If the "castle" metaphor is interpreted in light of American natural-rights theory, it is a call for a specific kind of equality and liberty. The liberty claim is that no property – castles, homes, or land uses in between – should be condemned without a convincing justification. The natural right to property, I hasten to add, is not an absolute and unbounded right. The natural-law principles that justify the individual right to property lay down corresponding duties to reflect the equal health, safety, moral, and property rights of neighbors. This interplay between duty and rights generates specific justifications for the regulation of property under the police power, and the taking of property under the eminent domain power. The equality claim is that the state should not condemn the property of the not-very-rich (proverbial "home" owners) using any grounds it would not use against the rich ("castle" owners). The state should not take or condemn by regulation homes on any grounds different from the narrow grounds it would probably cite to take or condemn castles.

To make sense of the "castle" metaphor, this chapter updates my previous natural-rights scholarship to account for several new and important criticisms associated with the "castle" metaphor. This analysis provides a less extreme and more sensible interpretation of the "castle" metaphor. No doubt, academics have studied the "castle" metaphor precisely because it is politically potent. Understood the natural-rights way, the "castle" metaphor provides a justification for government condemnation policy less susceptible of straw-man criticisms than other interpretations provided to date. If one goes by current scholarship about the castle metaphor, the post-*Kelo* debate is a debate between anarchistic libertarianism and home owners-first special-interest politics on one side, and pragmatic urban redevelopment policy on the other. This Essay does not settle the debate, but it does make it seem less lopsided. The more interesting and serious debate is between two rivaling forms of liberalism – the classical liberalism reflected in American natural-rights theory, and the modern, expertise-driven liberalism that informs contemporary redevelopment policy.

---

4   See Eric R. Claeys, *That '70s Show: Eminent Domain Reform and the Administrative Law Revolution*, 46 Santa Clara L. Rev. 867 (2006) [hereinafter "Claeys, *Administrative Law Revolution*"] ; Eric R. Claeys, *Don't Waste a Teaching Moment:* Kelo*, Urban Renewal, and Blight*, 15 J. Affordable Hous. 14 (2006) [hereinafter "Claeys, *Teaching Moment*"]; Eric R. Claeys, *Public-Use Limitations and Natural Property Rights*, 2004 Mich. St. L. Rev. 877 [hereinafter "Claeys, *Public-Use Limitations*"].

The Castle Metaphor after *Kelo*

In *Kelo v. City of New London*, the U.S. extended its public-use case law to hold that a state does not violate the Public Use Clause of the Fifth Amendment to the United States Constitution when it transfers condemned property to a private developer if the condemnation is part of a redevelopment project guided by a comprehensive plan, and if the plan documents that the condemnation will generate general economic benefits like increased jobs, taxes, and sales revenue. Suzette Kelo and eight other petitioners owned 15 properties in a New London, Connecticut neighborhood called Fort Trumbull. New London undertook to redevelop Fort Trumbull to generate more business opportunities and more economic growth next to a drug-manufacturing plant that the Pfizer Corporation had committed to build next door.[5] As part of that redevelopment project, New London condemned the lots of Kelo and the other plaintiffs and leased them to a private developer for a dollar per year. New London did not make any findings suggesting that the condemned properties were blighted; it proceeded instead solely under the chapter of Connecticut law authorizing "economic development" condemnations. As a result, the question before the Court was "whether a city's decision to take property for the purpose of economic development satisfies the 'public use' requirement of the Fifth Amendment."[6]

The Court held that economic development does satisfy the Public Use Clause. Broadly speaking, there are two basic ways to interpret "public use" as a constitutional term of art. The "use by the public" test is narrow and favors property owners; it requires the government or a regulated common carrier to own and control the property after eminent domain. The "public purpose" test, by contrast, is broad and favors governments; it allows the government to redistribute property between private parties whenever doing so promotes general public policies, benefits, or purposes. The Court rejected the use-by-the-public test on the ground that the test had "proved to be impractical given the diverse and always evolving needs of society."[7] The Court therefore examined "whether the City's development plan serves a 'public purpose.'" The Court construed the concept of "public purpose" "broadly," meaning in a spirit inclined to give government strong benefit of the doubt, "reflecting our longstanding policy of deference to legislative judgments in the field."[8] The Court drew the following deferential rule from the precedent: "'When the legislature's purpose is legitimate and its means are not irrational, our cases make clear that empirical debates over the wisdom of takings ... are not to be carried out in the federal courts.'"[9]

The Court then concluded that the condemnations in question were constitutional because the Fort Trumbull redevelopment project passed the public-purpose test. The Court praised Fort Trumbull for having "carefully formulated an economic development plan that it believes will provide appreciable benefits to the community,

---

5   See *Kelo*, 549 U.S. at 473–5.

6   *Id.* at 477.

7   *Id.* at 479.

8   *Id.* at 480.

9   *Id.* at 488 (quoting Hawaii Hous. Auth. v. Midkiff, 467 U.S. 229, 242 (1984)).

including – but by no means limited to – new jobs and increased tax revenue," and it praised this plan for its "comprehensive character" and "thorough deliberation." The Court stated that "Promoting economic development is a traditional and long accepted function of government." The Court therefore upheld New London's "determination that the area [taken] was sufficiently distressed to justify a program of economic rejuvenation."[10]

The *Kelo* decision has provoked considerable protest. While the decision can be read narrowly, its critics have chosen to read it broadly – to stand for the proposition that a state agency may reassign property from one private owner to another whenever the transfer will increase local jobs, taxes, or other general economic benefits. That reading explains why, for example, the Texas and Alabama state legislatures among others, have enacted laws barring state and local agencies from condemning property solely to generate general economic benefits.[11]

Some states, however, have gone even farther in reaction against *Kelo*. For example, the Georgia legislature has has not only barred economic-redevelopment takings but also sharply limited blight condemnations. In Georgia, state agencies may no longer use blight as a ground for condemning and redistributing property unless they can prove that the property meets objective standards like uninhabitability, imminent harm to life, repeat illegal activity, and conduciveness to ill health, disease, infant mortality, or crime. A separate provision specifically denies governments authorization to blight property on purely aesthetic grounds.[12] This last provision repudiates case law, going back to the 1954 U.S. Supreme Court decision in *Berman v. Parker*, suggesting that blight programs can promote values "spiritual as well as physical, aesthetic as well as monetary."[13]

In debates over eminent domain in these states and elsewhere, the "castle" metaphor has become a rallying cry against *Kelo*. Most notably, the Institute for Justice, a non-profit libertarian public-interest organization, created its anti-*Kelo* education and reform project with the name the "Castle Coalition."[14] Scholars have picked up on this metaphor to describe and rationalize the strong outrage many homeowners have expressed against *Kelo*. As Professor Joseph Singer recognizes, *Kelo* is unusually threatening for a judicial decision because it offends an intuition, "deeply embedded in our consciousness," that "a man's house is his castle."[15]

Yet as powerful and appealing as the "castle" seems, it also seems incoherent. Proverbs are dangerous and unreliable guides to decision making because they can be interpreted in different and conflicting ways. Coke and Blackstone's proverb suffers from this problem. To begin with, the "castle" metaphor has not been used as much in the context of eminent domain as it has in other contexts: for instance

---

10 *Id.* at 483–4.

11 See ALA. CODE § 11-47-170(b) (2005); TEX. GOV'T CODE ANN. § 2206.001 (Vernon 2005).

12 GA. CODE ANN. § 22-1-1 (West 2006).

13 348 U.S. 26, 33 (1954).

14 See Castle Coalition: Citizens Fighting Eminent Domain Abuse, available at http://www.castlecoalition.com/.

15 Joseph William Singer, *The Ownership Society and Taking Of Property: Castles, Investments, and Just Obligations*, 30 HARV. ENVTL. L. REV. 309, 314 (2006).

searches and seizures of the home,[16] and defense of the home against intruders.[17] And as applied to eminent domain, the "castle" metaphor can be read in different ways, each of which is subject to different criticisms.

The metaphor could be used to give owners a strong claim to veto any unconsented uses of their property. In this respect, it would operate much like Sir William Blackstone's description of property as "that sole and despotic dominion which one man claims and exercises over the external things of the world, in total exclusion of the right of any other individual in the universe." This position, however, seems unjustifiable if not totally incoherent. In Professor Singer's words, it is an "extreme libertarian position" rejected by all state and federal constitutions in the United States, and it begs serious questions why property should be off-limits.[18]

The "castle" metaphor could also be read to suggest that homes are especially sacrosanct. In Professor Eduardo Peñalver's words, the metaphor speaks statement "not so much about the power of the property owner to do as he pleases, but about the inherent dignity of homeownership" and "a statement about the subjective importance and status that society attaches to homeownership."[19] If so, however, the proverb begs serious questions about why homes are so special.

These doubts raise several fundamental questions: Is the "castle" metaphor useful in public-policy debates about eminent domain? Or does it encourage home owners to be obstinate in defense of their financial and emotional attachments to their homes, to the point of convincing them that they need not respect any principled limitations on their property rights?

Public-Use Limitations in Natural-Rights Theory

It depends. The more sympathetically the "castle" metaphor is interpreted, the more it fits the special demands of home owners within a coherent, public-interested theory of regulation. In this section, I offer such an interpretation and theory. My interpretation of the castle metaphor sounds in American natural-rights theory. To focus on the castle metaphor, I pass over other important criticisms of American natural-rights property theory; interested readers will need to consider those criticisms and my responses in previous scholarship.[20] Because I focus here on how natural-rights theory applies to eminent domain and the problems associated with contemporary redevelopment policy, I abstract away from how the theory applies in many other contexts for property regulation. Here, my main focus is to make

---

16 See, e.g., THOMAS M. COOLEY, A TREATISE ON THE CONSTITUTIONAL LIMITATIONS WHICH REST UPON THE LEGISLATIVE POWER OF THE STATES OF THE AMERICAN UNION 299 and n. 3 (1st ed. 1868).

17 See, e.g., 4 SIR WILLIAM BLACKSTONE, COMMENTARIES ON THE LAWS OF ENGLAND 223 (1765–69) (Stanley Katz ed., 1979).

18 2 *id.* at 2; *see* Singer, *supra* note 15, at 315.

19 Eduardo M. Penalver, *Property Metaphors and Kelo v. New London; Two Views of the Castle* 74 FORDHAM L. REV. 2971, 2973 (2006).

20 See, e.g., Claeys, *Administrative Law Revolution, supra* note 3, at 869–75; Claeys, *Public-Use Limitations, supra* note 3, at 884–6, 905–28.

sense of the "castle" metaphor and use it to illustrate an approach to eminent domain that rationalizes most of the public opposition to *Kelo* within a rigorous theory of government. This section sketches the theory of government; the next section interprets the "castle" metaphor to fit the theory of government sketched here.

Read in the context of the natural-rights tradition, the "castle" metaphor applies to property an understanding of human equality grounded in negative human freedom. One of the primary objects of natural-rights government theory is to secure to individuals a zone of non-interference, qualified properly for the like rights of others, in which all can apply their own talents and personalities to take care of their own needs. "Property" consists of the legal rights necessary to extend that zone over land, chattels, intangibles, and other ownable and usable things. Ownership is dignifying because it frees owners from being destitute or from being dependent on the will and generosity of others. In this sense, the home owner receives as much dignity and opportunity for self-advancement from his home as the manor lord does from his castle.

Understood in this sense, however, the metaphor does not exempt property from regulation, condemnation, or other government action. The moral principles that entitle owners to the dignity and benefits of ownership require owners to respect the like dignity and rights of others and the genuine needs of the public. That general proviso converts into three general legal duties on property ownership: to sacrifice property on just compensation for *bona fide* public uses; not to use property to trench on the public's rights to health, safety, morals, and property; and to submit to regulatory schemes that secure affected owners an average reciprocity of advantage. Home owners and castle owners are equal, not in being equally free from public responsibilities, but in enjoying the same liberty subject to the same responsibilities.

In American natural-rights theory, the regulation and protection of property rights are just two elements of a broader project to secure natural liberty. Natural liberty describes the state in which man acts simultaneously freely and morally. Men are self-motivated to pursue the goods that make them happy, and their inherent faculties for reasoning and judging enable them to regulate their motivating passions. They are therefore entitled to pursue the goods of human life within a range of moral freedom. Natural liberty is the state in which each person freely uses his natural talents, his reason, and his morality, to obtain for himself the full range of human goods he is capable of obtaining, each as far as it contributes to the completely happy life. James Wilson, drafter of the Constitution, member of Congress, and U.S. Supreme Court Justice defined it as "the right to exert intellectual and active powers for his own happiness, in such a manner, and upon such objects, as his inclination and judgment shall direct; provided he does no injury to others; and provided more public interests do not demand his labours." Natural liberty encompasses the "inalienable rights" mentioned in the Declaration, "Life, Liberty, and the pursuit of Happiness."[21] As Wilson explains, it encompasses both the low but necessary goods, like "preservation" and "security," and the goods that aspire to human excellence,

---

21 THE DECLARATION OF INDEPENDENCE para. 2 (U.S. 1776).

like "improvement" and "happiness."[22] This understanding was appreciated even 180 years later, by the district court in *Schneider v. District of Columbia*, the precursor case to the blight case *Berman v. Parker*.[23] The *Schneider* court defined property rights with reference to "the right of the individual to own property and to use it as he pleases [, a]bsent impingement upon the rights of others, and absent public use or compelling public necessity."[24]

Because natural liberty is the freedom to pursue genuine goods and human excellence, natural liberty does not mean freedom from any restraint on one's will. To act in violation of natural law is to choose to act no better than an animal, to be a slave to one's passions. Natural rights are thus bounded by the duties and limitations imposed by principles of natural law, which spell out when and how different objects of human life are good. The inalienable rights of the Declaration are thus bounded by "laws of Nature and Nature's God."[25] In James Wilson's words, "the laws of nature are the measure and the rule; they ascertain the limits and the extent of natural liberty."[26] Elsewhere, he asked rhetorically, "What would be the fate of man and of society, was every one at full liberty to do as he listed, without any fixed rule or principle of conduct, without a helm to steer him – a sport of the fierce gusts of passion, and the fluctuating billows of caprice?"[27]

Civil society is dedicated to ordering social life so that every member may enjoy this state of natural liberty. In Wilson's definition, civil society means "a complete body of free persons, united together for their common benefit, to enjoy peaceably what is their own, and to do justice to others."[28] Because such a society exists to secure and promote the common benefit of its members, the individual rights of its members are coterminous with the common good of the society. As Wilson explains:

> The wisest and the most benign constitution of a rational and moral system is that, in which the degree of private affection, most useful to the individual, is, at the same time, consistent with the greatest interest of the system; and in which the degree of social affection, most useful to the system, is, at the same time, productive of the greatest happiness to the individual.[29]

Specifically, when civil society tries to promote the individual interests of its members, it does so by securing and enlarging the natural liberty of its members – on equal terms for all. Because, as the Declaration holds, "all men are created equal," civil society is obligated to secure individual rights on equal terms for all.

---

22 1 JAMES WILSON, *Lectures on Law*, THE WORKS OF JAMES WILSON 69, 239, 242 (Robert McCloskey ed., 1967).

23 117 F. Supp. 705 (D.D.C. 1953), *rev'd sub nom.* Berman v. Parker, 348 U.S. 26 (1954).

24 *Id.* at 724.

25 THE DECLARATION OF INDEPENDENCE para. 1 (U.S. 1776).

26 1 WILSON, *supra* note 21, at 242.

27 See *id.* at 129–30.

28 1 *id.* at 239.

29 1 *id.* at 238.

This obligation follows from the fact that all men are equally rational and moral animals. By equality, James Wilson warns, the Founders do not mean that all men are equal in "their virtues, their talents, their dispositions, nor their acquirements." In fact, it is fit that men be unequal in these respects, because the differences render men mutually dependent upon one another. These dependencies encourage the formation of society. But men are equal in that they have freedom of moral action, they have talents and moral faculties they can use to pursue happiness, and they deserve the opportunity to exercise those talents. As Wilson explains, "there is an equality in rights and obligations ... . The natural rights and duties of man belong equally to all." Specifically, every person "has a right to exert those powers for the accomplishment of those purposes, in such a manner, and upon such objects, as his inclination and judgment shall direct; provided he does no injury to others; and provided more public interests do not demand his labours. This right is natural liberty."[30]

The natural right to property applies this broad understanding of natural liberty to the specific case of property.[31] Natural property rights take the shape they take because of two important insights. First, "property" recognizes that people share in common connections between passions, reason, and moral sense that tie work to reward. As U.S. Supreme Court Justice William Patterson explained in the 1795 case *Van Horne's Lessee v. Dorrance*: "Men have a sense of property: Property is necessary to their subsistence, and correspondent to their natural wants and desires; its security was one of the objects, that induced them to unite in society. No man would become a member of a community, in which he could not enjoy the fruits of his honest labor and industry."[32] Second, different individuals apply these common productive passions to extremely different uses and purposes. As James Wilson explained, "[m]any are the degrees, many are the varieties of human genius, human dispositions, and human characters. One man has a turn for mechanics; another, for architecture; one paints; a second makes poems; this man excels in the arts of a military; the other, in those of civil life. To account for these varieties of taste and character, is not easy; it is, perhaps, impossible."[33] That insight explains why, for instance, in *Federalist 10*, James Madison assumed that "the rights of property originate" in "[t]he diversity of the faculties of men."[34]

These two insights, particularly the latter, have powerful implications for the condemnation and regulation of natural property rights. Let us begin with condemnation.[35] Assume for a minute that the law clearly delineates the bundle of control, use, and disposition rights that attach to different species of property. In natural-rights theory, the state should use eminent domain to reassign any of those rights only when the rights condemned goes to a state agency, or to a private entity

---

30 1 *id.* at 240–41.

31 The discussion in the following paragraph is adapted and derived from Claeys, *Public-Use Limitations, supra* note 3, at 892–905.

32 2 U.S. (2 Dall.) 302, 310 (C.C.D. Pa. 1794).

33 1 WILSON, *supra* note 21, at 240–41 (anachronistic spellings modified).

34 THE FEDERALIST PAPERS, No. 10, at 45, 47 (Charles R. Kesler intro. & Clinton Rossiter ed. 1999) (Madison).

35 The following five paragraphs are adapted and derived from Claeys, *Public-Use Limitations, supra* note 3, at 887–91.

with standard common-carrier duties of non-discrimination and reasonable rates. In a republic dedicated to securing individual natural rights, government may force an owner to sacrifice his property for public objects, but only if the sacrifice is for the "public" in the narrow sense of the word. The social compact can be likened to a partnership. A partnership violates its organizing principles when it requires one partner to contribute property for the benefit of other partners without compensation guaranteeing that the partner recoups not only his contribution but also a proportionate profit. Usually, in eminent domain, the just-compensation requirement returns the owner's "property" sacrifice in cash; in a few cases, the owner is compensated implicitly by in-kind benefits in some other form. In social-compact theory, once the owner is held harmless by just compensation, she then profits in the sense that, as a member of the public, she enjoys whatever benefits or public services the government or common carrier is providing with the taken property. But when the state condemns property and redistributes it to a private party without common-carrier duties, such a condemnation eliminates the owner's independent right to dispose of the property on an open market at her own price and provides no corresponding corporate public access to her. Such a forcible private transfer counts as a case in which "the lands of A shall be taken and given to B" and violates the natural law.[36]

While these natural-law principles of eminent domain are fairly straightforward, the natural-law approach to contemporary "public use" law is more complex because these principles are qualified by natural-law principles of "regulation." Natural-law "regulatory" principles are important in two respects. In general, because they help define the specific content of owners' bundles of rights, they define the rights that are properly takeable in eminent domain. More specifically, in "public use" law as it is understood in contemporary practice, natural-law principles lay down two important justifications to which the state may appeal to condemn an owner's property without recourse to eminent domain. When the state condemns an owner's property by regulation, eminent-domain public-use limitations do not apply. At the same time, the principles that justify the exercise of such regulatory power lay down important regulatory-takings limitations on private-to-private property transfers. These limitations establish standards by which contemporary public-use law and practice may be judged.

In general, the object of natural-rights property regulation is "to make property rights regular." The public-use proviso limits acts of eminent domain, but not acts of police regulation. Since the institution of property recognizes that people put possessions to different uses, neither the laws of nature nor positive-law regulations can favor any legitimate uses of property over any others. The laws of nature merely prescribe that positive laws ought to protect in each owner a zone of freedom to decide what mix of uses will best suit her own individual tastes, talents, and goals. Kent confirmed the same when he concluded that "every individual has as much freedom in the acquisition, use, and disposition of his property, as is consistent with good order, and the reciprocal rights of others."[37]

---

36 Robinson v. Barfield, 6 N.C. (2 Mur.) 390, 421 (N.C. 1818).

37 2 KENT, *supra* note 36, at 264–5.

"Regulations" may protect public order and the reciprocal rights of others in one of two ways. One type of "regulation" will be called here "harm-prevention" regulations. Such regulations serve two purposes: They define the substantive rights of use, control, and disposition that attach to various species of property, and then they protect owners against unconsented takings of those rights. Basic trespass and anti-pollution nuisance laws define and then protect the possessory interests of control and use that attach to land; the possessory interests that run with patents are defined in different respects and then protected by patents; and so forth for chattels, water, and other species of property. The other kind of regulation reorders owners' use rights for their mutual advantage; they are called here "reciprocity of advantage" regulations.[38] Traffic laws and conveyancing laws count as reciprocity of advantage regulations. These two conceptions of "regulation" explain, for instance, why James Kent spoke of the concept of "general regulations" as the power "to prescribe the mode and manner of using" property "so far as may be necessary to prevent the abuse of the right."[39]

While modern public-use law does not speak explicitly in terms of "regulations" or "regulatory-taking" principles, the problems it confronts implicate both types of natural-rights property regulation.[40] First, the state may justifiably condemn property under the harm-prevention rationale. To do so, the state must show that the property is generating substantial and concrete threats of crime, disease, or other hazards to neighbors and the general public, and if it can show that no remedy short of condemnation will abate the hazard created by the property.[41] Because owners are by nature entitled to the widest zone of active use compatible with the like rights of others, the state bears the burden to prove that an owner's land use is dangerous to the rights of others, and the state is obligated not to take more property than necessary to abate the danger. Thus, "blight" programs can count as harm-prevention regulations, but only if the blight is concrete, physical, and documented, and only if the state has run out of other regulatory options. The most prominent case advocating this position is the opinion in *Schneider v. District of Columbia*,[42] the district court opinion reversed by the Supreme Court in *Berman*. Contrary to the Supreme Court, the three-judge district court that decided *Schneider* barred slum clearance except when a condemnation was "reasonably necessary to the accomplishment of the asserted public purpose," and specifically when "the clearance of the slum is impracticable without taking the title to the land or that proposed restrictions which

---

38 This phrase comes from Supreme Court substantive due process cases including Jackman v. Rosenbaum Co., 260 U.S. 22 (1922); and Penn. Coal Co. v. Mahon, 260 U.S. 393 (1922).

39 2 Kent, *supra* note 36, at 276.

40 To track contemporary public-use law, the following discussion will focus primarily on regulatory-takings principles as they apply to land.

41 The following discussion is adapted and derived from Claeys, *Public-Use Limitations*, *supra* note 3, at 914–19.

42 117 F. Supp. 705 (1953), *rev'd*, Berman v. Parker, 348 U.S. 26 (1954).

can be imposed only through the medium of a resale are fairly calculated to prevent recurrence of slum conditions."[43]

The "reciprocity of advantage" ground for regulation comes into play less frequently.[44] However, it can arise in cases in which neighboring owners are in a genuine bilateral monopoly, the deadlock cannot be attributed to the fault of either party, and there is no way practicably to break the deadlock without assigning one parties' land to the other. In such cases, the state may intervene to transfer ownership of both land lots to one party and equitable compensation to the other. To be sure, these standards are vague and imprecise – how much compensation is properly "equitable" and (especially) whether a bilateral monopoly is "genuine" and "not the fault" of either party. Even so, these standards sketch a justification by which the law justifiably "regulates" by condemning one party's property rights *in toto* and transferring them to a second party. Ordinarily, natural-rights "regulation" does not allocate property rights by evaluating competing uses of property. However, there may be cases in which two land uses conflict so severely that the practice of one makes impossible the practice of the other – hence the requirement that there be a genuine bilateral monopoly. Ordinarily, natural-rights regulation encourages parties to resolve such disputes by encouraging one party to acquire the rights of the other by private transaction – hence the requirement that the monopoly not be the fault of either party. In such cases where neither party can be blamed, however, natural-law and -rights principles cannot provide any more guidance to resolve the dispute. In such pure cases of necessity, the state may pick one or the other use interests depending on which contributes the most to public interests. Before doing so, however, the state must make a genuine effort to protect *all* of the ousted owner's property interests and to guarantee that the ousted owner shares especially in the public benefit generated. Equitable compensation thus sets a standard of compensation which is higher than just compensation or fair market value and which guarantees the ousted owner some profit.

During the nineteenth century, this rationale justified certain mill-dam statutes, including a New Hampshire statute upheld by the U.S. Supreme Court in *Head v. Amoskeag Manufacturing Co.*[45] The New Hampshire mill-dam statute challenged in *Head* created legal rights in mill and dam builders to overflow riparian land needed for their mills and dams. The statute gave the owners of the land flooded a right to seek a judicial determination, by a committee of disinterested parties, whether the dam was necessary for a public use or benefit. If the committee concluded that the dam was so necessary, the statute required the dam builder to pay the owners of the land flooded their damages plus a 50 percent mark-up.[46] The U.S. Supreme Court upheld this scheme on the ground that the water rights were "property, in which several persons have a common interest," and which therefore "cannot be fully and beneficially

---

43 *Schneider*, 117 F. Supp. at 717, 719. For a longer list of cases illustrating similar principles, consider J.E. Macy, *Constitutional Rights of Owner As Against Destruction of Building by Public Authorities*, 14 A.L.R.2d 73 (1950).

44 The discussion in the next two paragraphs is adapted and derived from Claeys, *Public-Use Limitations, supra* note 3, at 919–28.

45 113 U.S. 9 (1885).

46 See *id.* at 10–11 n.*.

enjoyed in its existing condition." Here, the Court satisfied the requirements that there be a genuine bilateral monopoly, and that the monopoly not be attributable to the fault of either party. The Court also noted that laws for dissolving co-tenancies often used remedies like owelty and set-offs to make "equitable compensation to any whose control of or interest in the property is thereby modified."[47] Of course, legislatures could try to specify in greater detail than New Hampshire did when a condemnation is "necessary," and there is nothing magical about the New Hampshire act's 50 percent damage mark-up. Even so, the act confirms that states may regulate property by condemning and transferring it – when the competing land uses are incompatible in a fairly strict sense of the term, and when the ousted owner shares in the public benefits created by the transfer.

This libertarian understanding of property is commonly criticized on the ground that it cannot give a convincing account where rights end and duties begin. In Professor Singer's words, such an understanding cannot explain "*what it means to stay within one's borders*," or how to distinguish between "self-regarding" and "other-regarding" acts.[48] In principle, however, borders provide a useful starting point for distinguishing between rights and duties, and self- and other-regarding consequences. The natural-rights approach does not protect physical borders for their own sake. These borders are means to natural ends – particularly labor, in the service of one's own talents and desires. Many actions within one's own borders have ripple effects elsewhere. When one land owner builds a new gas station on the cater-corner from an existing gas station, the later station to some extent diverts the earlier station's customers and diminishes its sales. This ripple effect is not noxious, however, because the physical-invasion test rewards both owners' labor. A first-in-time rule would privilege the labor of one to the exclusion of the labor of everyone else, much like the "race to the patent" phenomenon in intellectual property. A rule that requires owners to seek community pre-approval for all new gas stations ties each owner's labor to the wishes of outsiders who are probably disinterested, selfish, and lack the wrong incentives.

To appreciate the problem from another light, consider how the natural-rights tradition considered aesthetic zoning. Modern land-use lawyers often eschew natural-rights influenced law in favor of modern because the latter encourages aesthetic, historic, and preservation regulation where the former does not. Aesthetic, historic, and preservation ideals are "other-regarding," it is said, and not adequately considered by the crude boundaries of the physical-invasion test. But the advocates of such ideals are not always entirely other-regarding. Aesthetic, historic, and preservation goals force a choice between the useful and the beautiful, and their advocates regard the beautiful without sufficiently regarding the impact on those who dearly need the useful. Aesthetic, historic, and preservation ideals are the sorts of goods that a community seeks once a control group in it has acquired plenty of life's useful necessities and is now striving for noble and refined luxuries. Aesthetic and other "community character" goals usually cannot be accomplished unless many owners conform their properties to a common intention. Such other-regarding

---

47 *Id.* at 21.
48 See Singer, *supra* note 14, at 317, 319, 320.

goals therefore often require a tremendous amount of co-ordination. To promote such common goals, they suppress the energetic and disorderly desires of many individual land owners. They have a pronounced tendency to freeze certain land uses in place. They often also have the side tendency to lock in expensive land uses at the expense of cheaper land uses more affordable and useful to poorer community entrants. By contrast, because the physical-invasion test assigns to individual owners a share of free action and policy control, it empowers them to use land for the many boring and humble purposes for which it is used before it can be a source of beauty.

Under natural-rights theory, while aesthetic, historic, and preservation goals ought to be recognized as genuine goods, local officials ought to consider the bitter with the sweet. Before 1930, many jurists did so by deeming such commons to be "public uses," creatable only after localities used eminent domain to take from land owners use servitudes marked off by the physical-invasion test. As several courts insisted in passing on aesthetic restrictions of billboards: "Æsthetic considerations arc a matter of luxury and indulgence rather than of necessity, and it is necessity alone which justifies the exercise of the police power to take private property without compensation."[49]

The Natural Right to Have One's Home be Treated as a Castle

When such principles guide eminent domain, they flesh out the proverb "A man's house is his castle" in a distinct manner. "A man's house is his castle" stands for two propositions. One is a claim about liberty: No property – castles, homes, or land uses in between – should be condemned without a convincing justification as sketched in the last section. The other claim is about equality: The state should not condemn the property of the not-very-rich (proverbial "home" owners) using any grounds it would not use against the rich ("castle" owners).

This interpretation follows because, in natural-rights theory, property consists of a zone of negative liberty allotted to each individual, to empower her to use her own distinct talents, on her own assets, to fulfill her own goals. In a leading case invalidating a mill law – in which the mills were neither common carriers nor governed by the necessity and mark-up rules noted in the *Head* decision – Michigan Chief Justice Thomas Cooley defined liberty as follows: "A person may be very unreasonable in insisting on retaining his lands; but half the value of free institutions consists in the fact that they protect every man in doing what he shall choose, without the liability to be called to account for his reasons or motives, so long as he is doing only that which he has a right to do."[50]

In all but the most extreme cases, then, the natural law refrains from picking and choosing among owners or land uses. As long as owners are respecting their neighbors' like zones of liberty and the public does not need their property for public uses, all should be left alone so that all may pursue happiness in their own ways.

---

49 Varney & Green v. Williams, 100 P. 867 (Cal. 1909), *overruled by* Metromedia, Inc. v. City of San Diego, 592 P.2d 728 (Cal. 1979) (quoting Passaic v. Paterson Bill Posting, Adver. & Sign Pointing Co., 62 A. 267, 268 (N.J. 1905)).

50 Ryerson v. Brown, 35 Mich. 333, 342 (1877).

Castle and home owners are alike metaphorically in the specific substantive sense that both have a general right to be left alone within their legitimate rights. This theme was explained especially well by the three-judge court that invalidated the portions of the District of Columbia slum-clearance law later upheld in *Berman*. For the panel, Judge Prettiman criticized D.C.'s slum-clearance law because it promoted the policies favored by expert planners and developers over those favored by the modest: "Choice of antiques is a right of property … The poor are entitled to own what they can afford. The slow, the old, the small in ambition, the devotee of the outmoded have no less right to property than have the quick, the young, the aggressive, and the modernistic or futuristic."[51]

One can see this theme in the few eminent domain opinions that appealed to the castle proverb between the Civil War and the rise of modern urban planning. To be clear, not all courts used the "castle" metaphor as an argument for natural-rights theories of regulation and eminent domain. In particular, enthusiasts for Euclidean zoning occasionally used this metaphor as Peñalver suggests that it be used now – to protect the home as "the one sacred spot where his liberty, his rights, and his comfort shall not be interfered with or impaired by the action of another."[52] Yet in a significant number of cases, jurists who subscribed to natural-rights principles used the metaphor to reinforce the vision just described.

For example, in the 1927 case *City of Winston-Salem v. Ashby*,[53] the North Carolina Supreme Court was called on to interpret a condemnation statute to determine whether the statute required the city to negotiate with owners before condemning their property. The court held that the statute did require such negotiations. Citing the maxim "every man's house is his castle," the court argued, "[i]t is not reasonable and right, no matter how important the undertaking, that a landowner or homeowner be brought into court without first negotiations looking to an amicable sale."[54] The court did not mean to suggest that property ownership required the state to keep eminent domain entirely off limits. Nevertheless, eminent domain necessarily deprives owners of valuable disposition rights and peculiarly personal attachments they may hold to their land. Before depriving those rights, the court concluded, the better policy was to protect owners' dignity and disposition rights where possible.

Separately, in the 1942 case *Metropolitan Housing Authority v. Thatcher*,[55] the Ohio Supreme Court considered whether subsidized housing counted as a public or private use of property for the purposes of state constitutional limitations on the taxing power. "It seems to us clear," the court concluded, "that where dwellings are leased to family units for the purposes of private homes, the use of such dwellings is private and not public … That every man's house is his castle has not yet been erased from our laws."[56] While the public-private distinction in tax was technically

---

51 *Schneider*, 117 F. Supp. at 719.

52 Blakemore v. Cincinnati Metropolitan Housing Authority, 57 N.E. 2d 397, 401 (Ohio Appt. 1943) (en banc) (White, J., dissenting).

53 139 S.E. 764 (N.C. 1927).

54 *Id.* at 767.

55 42 N.E.2d 437 (Ohio 1942).

56 Metropolitan Hous. Auth. v. Thatcher, 42 N.E. 2d. 437, 442 (Ohio 1942).

distinct from the same distinction in eminent domain, the court's discussion regarded the substantive issue as the same in both cases; if subsidized houses were public for taxation purposes, they would also be public for eminent domain and many other purposes. To be sure, the *Thatcher* court's understanding was distinguished and rendered irrelevant in subsequent cases about newly written blight laws. Even so, when later courts upheld Ohio blight laws, they treated the *Thatcher* court's use of the proverb "A man's house is his castle" as a serious substantive objection, which needed to be considered and rejected in favor of new policy arguments about public policy and public purpose.[57]

Equally interesting, in the same case law, the "castle" metaphor was cited surprisingly often as a *justification* for condemnations about as often as it was cited as a *limitation* on condemnations. Historically, the "castle" metaphor therefore has not always been understood as the "extreme libertarian" rights claim represented by Singer. Normatively, these cases help refute the typical impression that a libertarian "castle" model of property "marginalizes" citizens' sense of obligation, or "suppress[es] consciousness of the obligations inherent in ownership, to draw attention away from them."[58]

In general, natural-rights theory does not create rights independent from duties. Even though the natural right to property is a negative right, it is still a freedom *for*, not a freedom *from*. The right takes the character it has because a general analysis of human nature reveals that property reconciles an active and productive faculty of labor (which all men share) with many specific talents, interests, and goals (which they do not). By claiming rights, owners automatically become bound by correlative duties to respect the equal labor and diversity of others.[59] For instance, when the *Schneider* court criticized the District of Columbia's slum-clearance law, it appealed to the conception of natural rights embodied in the Declaration of Independence. Curiously, however, the court did so to highlight that citizens need government mainly to enforce the duties that come with their rights: "To secure those rights governments were instituted, says the Declaration, and to secure them governments may impose limitations upon them."[60]

---

57 57 N.E. 2d. 397, 401 (Ohio App. 1943).

58 Singer, *supra* note 14, at 330.

59 This general claim probably needs to be qualified slightly to fit the prescriptions of different theorists the text classifies loosely as being in "the natural-rights tradition." Different theorists understood the obligatory character of rights and duties differently depending on their foundational commitments. Some theorists, most prominently Locke, were "hedonistic" or "eudaimonistic" – meaning that they were consequentialists who justified moral rules by their tendency to refine and enlarge individuals' happiness, understood in a classical and philosophical sense. For such theorists, rights and duties were hypothetical as a strict matter of philosophy even if they were obligatory in practical politics and ethics. By contrast, other theorists, including prominent Scottish Enlightenment philosophers and many theologians, held that men's sense of obligation issued from a faculty of conscience independent from and prior to men's faculty for practical reasoning. Such theorists tended to portray rights and duties as categorical both in theory and in practice. This chapter passes over such theoretical differences to focus on the practical effects of natural-rights theory generally.

60 *Schneider*, 117 F. Supp. at 716.

Men therefore need government both to give real-life content to their rights and to give teeth to the duties that attach to rights. As condition for getting protection for their own property, owners owe duties to respect the equal rights of labor and active use in their neighbors. Property owners are also obligated to respect other natural rights civil society protects – the rights to personal health and safety, the public's corporate interest in a moral order that is minimally peaceful and not scandalized by opinions that corrupt the family, and so forth. More extreme, because citizens need a vigorous government, they also owe a duty to sacrifice their own for eminent domain when doing so contributes to genuine public uses. The end result is a broad private sphere, but a government that is lean and mean within its narrow public sphere.

Consider for example the claim made by an owner for compensation in *Dawson v. Kuttner*.[61] To stop an on-coming fire, Dawson authorities destroyed Kuttner's store-house and all the goods in it. The applicable condemnation statute followed general principles regulating the privilege of necessity; it compensated owners only for damages that were caused by the public authorities' destruction and would not have been caused by the fire. (This statute's drafters appreciated the distinction between regulation and eminent domain sketched in the last part, for the statute's preamble justified its power "from necessity," as a power only "[a]nalogous to the right of eminent domain.") Dawson's authorities paid Kuttner for the damage to his store house, but contested whether he was also entitled to statutory "damages" for the goods in it. The court held that Kuttner was entitled to both, reasoning that a rule was:

> not only unjust to the citizen whose property is destroyed, but would be a limitation on the power of a town, city or county, often seriously hurtful. Suppose a fire is about to reach a board-yard, or a lot of loosely packed cotton, or a quantity of any other combustible material, classed as personal property, must the flames be permitted to go on because the public dare not treat this trumpery stuff as it might a man's house – his castle – the home of his family?[62]

For the *Dawson* court, the castle metaphor acted as the foundation for an *a fortiori* argument. If the statutory term "damages" did not cover personal property, the city of Dawson would not have had the utmost power to contain fires. If the statute clearly authorized the city to condemn homes and castles, it surely authorized the city to condemn personalty. But for our purposes, the important point is that the *Dawson* court took for granted that the city needed the power to condemn homes. As majestic as castles are, they are still limited by natural-law duties to submit to necessity-based regulations when emergencies threaten the public safety.[63]

---

61 48 Ga. 133 (1873).

62 *Id.*

63 See also Brocket v. Ohio & P. R.R. Co., 14 Pa. 241 (1850) (holding that the term "land" as used in a state eminent domain statute "includes every thing fixed to the ground, and every thing above or below the surface of it; that it comprehends castles, houses, and other buildings; and that, not only the soil, but every thing in it or on it, passes by it. It, therefore, distinctly includes a mansion, when its generality is not restrained by the context").

The Castle Metaphor after *Kelo*

Let us finish where we started, by teasing out of the "castle" metaphor a road map for contemporary political and legislative debates about eminent domain. The castle model of eminent-domain policy prescribes both a theory of rights and a theory of urban development policy. Both can be used to justify laws like the act recently passed by Georgia, to bar economic-redevelopment takings and to curtail blight takings sharply.

Let us start with the theory of rights. Ultimately, natural-rights theory judges government by the extent to which it secures the freedom of its citizens. In the case of property rights, that freedom usually is best understood as a negative liberty, a right to be let alone to use one's own possessions for one's own ends. Strict public uses and blight restrictions do ordinarily limit owners' property rights, and in cases as extreme as mill floodings the state may also intervene to dislodge innocently-caused bilateral monopolies. But overly-aggressive blight laws and standard economic-redevelopment policies go beyond these limits. In doing so, they take use and disposition rights from some land owners and transfer them to developers who promise to use land for private purposes in line with local government's interests. Such policies promote the general social welfare by disproportionately taking the rights of a few citizens. By treating ordinary owners' properties as less than castles, such policies violate the grounds of the social compact.

Separately, these schemes are part of a larger project to cultivate republican character, the habits and political opinions necessary to sustain the people's commitment to natural rights over the long term. In natural-rights theory, the majority is entitled to legislate and regulate, but only on condition that it do so to protect and enlarge the equal rights of all. The majority must accept constitutional limitations, including limitations on the regulation of property, to restrain its worse impulses and habituate and teach it to follow its better impulses. When the law protects natural property rights, it calms society, orders it, and makes it harmonious. In recent years, we have seen how regular and swift law enforcement can turn cities that seemed ungovernable and crime-ridden hospitable and vibrant. Similarly, in *Van Horne's Lessee v. Dorrance*, in a circuit opinion handed down by United States Supreme Court Justice William Patterson, if government regulates property regularly, under general laws and established tribunals, the law promotes "security and safety, tranquillity and peace. One man is not afraid of another, and no man is afraid of the legislature."[64] By treating ordinary property as less than castles, the law encourages all owners but especially developers to take on the most overbearing tendencies of castle barons.

Separately, nineteenth-century jurists assumed that to protect equal and natural rights, common opinions needed to prefer the useful over the beautiful. If land-use law focuses on securing and ordering individual freedom, it leaves individual owners with most of the choices on how to use their own land. That commitment requires tradeoffs. Because people have different talents, tastes, and needs, they will use their property for different purposes. Regulations promote the well-being

---

64 2 U.S. (2 Dall.) 302, 312 (C.C.D. Pa.1794).

of society when they secure natural rights, because they put individual owners in the best position possible to use their own talents to satisfy their own needs and desires. But by the same token, those regulations make it more difficult to obtain goals such as coordinated economic growth, or state of the art development and design. Such goals cannot be obtained without forcing owners to subordinate their own tastes and projects to community goals. But if human tastes differ as widely as natural-rights theory holds, that subordination forces a bad tradeoff. Everyone can agree that property serves basic useful ends, but goods like coordinated growth and design are more controversial and divisive. Better that the law foster security and diversity, which in turn generate a dynamic market. In such a market, even if the entire community will not respond to a problem, most owners will be able to respond to it in part with their own property to their own level of interest. According to James Kent, the protection of property encourages not only "the cultivation of the earth," but also "the institution of government, the acquisition of the comforts of life, the growth of the useful arts, the spirit of commerce, the productions of taste, the erections of charity, and the display of the benevolent affections."[65] In a free society, the law will never attain the order and beauty one expects from a well-designed castle; but the rewards from having many individual owners take care of their own are far more satisfying.

This vision is subject to several serious responses. One general criticism of natural-rights theory holds that it does not leave the law with enough leeway to redistribute property. If the existing allocation of entitlements is skewed against the poor, the law ought to intervene on their behalf. This criticism deserves attention in other contexts, such as debates about welfare and other entitlements, but it does not deserve attention here in the context of eminent domain policy. Contemporary eminent domain policy tends to redistribute from relatively powerless poor and low/middle homeowners to relatively powerful developers, to attract relatively powerful upper and upper/middle class homeowners.

Some respond to this critique by suggesting that there is something unjust or ignoble about (in Professor Singer's words) a "user fee model of government."[66] Singer criticizes the natural-rights view because it "suggests ... that any sacrifice that is disproportionate to the benefit is not one that can be fairly asked of an owner in the absence of compensation"; he prefers "a citizenship model [which] contains a more expansive understanding of 'what we owe each other.'"[67]

Yet the natural-rights approach makes its own claim about citizenship. From its perspective, if citizens already owe each other equal duties correlative to their equal rights, why should they make further sacrifices for a broad but fuzzy vision of community? The Founders were not acquainted with modern-day communitarian calls, but such calls have more than a whiff about them of the longing for the beautiful that used to attract some to pre-Enlightenment aristocratic government. Consider the warning Judge Robert Earl issued when he struck down New York's cigar-making restriction in the 1887 New York decision *In re Jacobs*. Since Earl did not have any

---

65 2 KENT, *supra* note 36, at 257.
66 Singer, *supra* note 14, at 330.
67 *Id.* at 331.

experience with modern land-use administrators to rely on, he hearkened back to examples of feudal and guild-based regulation:

> Such legislation may invade one class of rights to-day and another to-morrow, and if it can be sanctioned under the Constitution, while far removed in time we will not be far away in practical statesmanship from those ages when governmental prefects supervised the building of houses, the rearing of cattle, the sowing of seed and the reaping of grain, and governmental ordinances regulated the movements and labor of artisans, the rate of wages, the price of food, the diet and clothing of the people, and a large range of other affairs long since in all civilized lands regarded as outside of governmental functions. Such governmental interferences disturb the normal adjustments of the social fabric, and usually derange the delicate and complicated machinery of industry and cause a score of ills while attempting the removal of one.[68]

Of course, modern redevelopment policy does not interfere with property rights nearly as much as these feudal and guild restrictions used to. Even so, both the European feudal-guild system and modern redevelopment policy presume that a select few (priests and guilds then, planners now) can coordinate land uses and predict how the community will respond to such coordination in a regular way. As Dennis Coyle has observed, "[a]rguments for feudallike encumbrance of private property have been heard throughout this century," particularly by the property-law scholars from the early- and mid-twentieth century who legitimized Euclidean zoning and urban redevelopment. As Coyle explains, "Francis S. Philbrick waxed nostalgic for feudalism in 1938, writing that 'in the case of feudalism it is regrettable that there could not have been preserved the idea that all property was held subject to the performance of duties – not a few of them public.' These sentiments were echoed nearly thirty years later by John Cribbet, who asserted that 'the concept behind [feudal duties] was sound ... [T]he use of land is of more than private concern.'"[69] The "user fee" vision of government limits coordinated government action, but it does force government to justify the actions it takes by the effects they have on owners. In the context of eminent domain, that justification requirement protects individual owners from appeals to community that empower majorities, developers, or planners.

Another criticism holds that economic redevelopment is necessary because cities need concentrated political power to break depression cycles and energize their local economies. As Singer explains, "Low property values mean low taxes, and low taxes mean bad public services, and bad public services are what make the middle class flee – it is a vicious cycle."[70] This argument, however, raises the same questions about expertise as the argument just considered. Singer presumes that cities can predict more likely than not which redevelopment projects will be cost-justified and successful and jump-starting a local economy. If a local land economy is static and expertise is effective, this presumption may not be unreasonable. But in the American

---

68 *In re Jacobs*, 98 N.Y. 98, 114–15 (1885).

69 DENNIS J. COYLE, PROPERTY RIGHTS AND THE CONSTITUTION 217 (1993) (quoting Francis S. Philbrick, *Changing Conceptions of Property in Law*, 86 U. PENN. L. REV. 691, 710 (1938), and John Cribbet, *Changing Concepts in the Law of Land Use*, 50 IOWA L. REV. 245, 247 (1965).

70 Singer, *supra* note 14, at 337.

natural-rights tradition, "property" is a cluster of legal rights organized around different presumptions: that individuals are more ignorant than knowledgeable about competing land uses; that owners' self-love makes them better judges of their own uses and policy choices than of their neighbors; and that in conditions of ignorance and productivity it is institutionally safer to push land-use policy decisions as close to owners as possible.[71]

If this critique is accurate, cities may go farther by setting their sights lower.[72] John Norquist, former mayor of Milwaukee and now president of the Congress for New Urbanism, gave a sense of the alternatives in an *amicus* brief in *Kelo*.[73] Private real-estate markets have room for land banks, which amass real estate for years. Developers know how to use purchase options to pit homeowners against each other and steer around hold-outs. Norquist cited the example of the Focus Property Group, which managed to assemble 2,400 acres to build a master-planned community near Las Vegas.[74] While it took five years to assemble the land for this project, publicly-sponsored redevelopment routinely takes longer because the political process is slow and gets tied up more often in court. Cities ought to focus on doing what they do well: rezoning, laying down infrastructure, making sure that basic public services are met, and providing basic police and fire protection. As Norquist has argued, if cities establish basic conditions in which people feel safe and private markets can operate, the people will develop a vibrant community and land markets will blossom. If cities disregard the basics, redevelopment will probably not succeed anyway.[75]

Before concluding, it should be noted that eminent-domain reforms like Georgia's fall short of the natural-rights approach in at least one and perhaps two respects. First, Georgia's scheme does not make any provisions for situations like riparian mill-dam disputes – in which competing owners are truly deadlocked and the deadlock stems from the nature of the land uses and not the conduct of either party. However, this shortcoming may not be fatal, for these disputes are fairly rare and it is vexing to establish legislative rules to determine whether it is truly necessary to condemn by regulation as happened in *Head*. Such cases may properly be dealt with by more case-specific legislation.

Separately, however, the natural-rights portrait of eminent-domain policy sketched here has important repercussions for zoning. The natural-rights interpretation of the "castle" metaphor offers a public-interested justification why homes deserve to be treated as castles in the face of local redevelopment programs. But to get the political benefit of that theory, middle-class home owners would be obligated, at least in

---

71   This argument has been developed at greater length in Claeys, *Administrative Law Reform, supra* note 3, at 870–75.

72   The following paragraph is adapted and derived from Claeys, *Teaching Moment, supra* note 3, at 17.

73   See Brief Amicus Curiae of John Norquist, President, Congress for New Urbanism, in Support of Petitioners, Kelo v. City of New London, No. 04-108 (filed 3 December 2004) (available at 2004 WL 2811055).

74   See Hali Bernstein Taylor, "Focus Provides Service to Builders, LAS VEGAS NEWSPAPERS, 17 January 2004 (available at http://www.lvnewspapers.com/realestate/REJan-17-Sat-2004/Front/22950800.html).

75   See Norquist, *supra* note 72, at 10–15.

principle, to subscribe to a castle theory of zoning. Contemporary zoning laws and policies, especially as administered in suburbs, have some institutional tendencies to lock in and encourage single-family residential home-ownership patterns.[76] As I have explained elsewhere, the natural-rights approach to zoning limits zoning's functions dramatically.[77] According to natural-rights principles of property regulation, zoning should concentrate on controlling pollution and separating residential uses from commercial and industrial uses – but it ought otherwise to leave developers generally free to develop land uses, and it ought not to discriminate generally between different gradations of residential use.

In short, the castle metaphor challenges home owners whether *they* are prepared to take the bitter with the sweet. As interpreted here, the metaphor gives home owners a public-interested justification why their homes should treated as castles in the face of entreaties by developers and urban planners, but in return it challenges them to give castle status to developers, businesses, and low-income tenants and home buyers in zoning disputes. Practically, that choice tests more effectively than anything else whether American home owners understand the "castle" only to extend to themselves, as Professor Peñalver suggests, or are willing to extend the "castle" to other property owners in their communities.

---

76 See, e.g., WILLIAM A. FISCHEL, THE HOMEVOTER HYPOTHESIS: HOW HOME VALUES INFLUENCE LOCAL GOVERNMENT TAXATION, SCHOOL FINANCE, AND LAND-USE POLICIES (2001).

77 The following is adapted and derived from Eric R. Claeys, Euclid *Lives? The Uneasy Legacy of Progressivism in Zoning*, 73 FORDHAM L. REV. 731, 737–9 (2004).

Chapter 4

Nothing "Errant" About It: The *Berman* and *Midkiff* Conference Notes and How the Supreme Court Got to *Kelo* with Its Eyes Wide Open

D. Benjamin Barros[1]

Introduction

Few judicial opinions have received as much immediate and strong public disapproval as the Supreme Court's decision in *Kelo v. City of New London*.[2] The Court's holding in *Kelo* that a municipality can use eminent domain to take private homes and transfer the property to a private developer to promote economic development came as a rude shock to most laypeople and many lawyers. How, people asked, could taking property and giving it to a private party for private development possibly be a "public use" within the meaning of the Fifth Amendment's Just Compensation Clause?

For people familiar with the Court's public-use precedents, however, *Kelo* was nothing of a surprise. In two prior cases, *Berman v. Parker*[3] and *Hawaii Housing Authority v. Midkiff*,[4] unanimous opinions of the Court had articulated broad conceptions of "public use" and narrow conceptions of the role of the judiciary in reviewing legislative exercises of eminent domain. Although the facts of *Berman* and *Midkiff* could be distinguished from those in *Kelo*, the broad principles articulated in the prior cases supported New London's argument that its proposed taking met the public use requirement. Unsurprisingly, these broad principles from *Berman* and *Midkiff* featured prominently in the Court's decision in *Kelo*.[5]

This chapter draws on archival material to gain insight into the Court's decision-making process in *Berman* and *Midkiff* and to test the accuracy of assertions made by Justice O'Connor about those cases in her *Kelo* dissent. For those unfamiliar with the Court's inner workings, the Justices meet in conference to discuss and vote on cases. Only the Justices (not clerks or anyone else) are present at the conference.

1   Thanks to Michael Dimino and Charles Cohen for their comments. Thanks also to Widener University School of Law for research support.
2   545 U.S. 649;125 S. Ct. 2655 (2005).
3   348 U.S. 26 (1954).
4   467 U.S. 229 (1984).
5   See *Kelo*, 125 S. Ct. at 2663–6.

Many Justices take notes at the conference, and some of the Justices included their notes in their personal papers given to the Library of Congress or archives at other institutions. The Justices' files also include memoranda circulated to the other members of the Court (often also called in the context "the conference") on cases.[6]

The conference notes certainly are not anything close to stenographic notes of the Court's discussions. They are handwritten, often shorthand and equally often cryptic. Because they were typically written in pencil, and because some of the Justices weren't very compulsive about pencil sharpness, they can be hard to read. They therefore must be viewed with caution. The Court's written opinions also are the only authoritative statements of its position on a particular case.

All of this said, however, it can be helpful to know what the Justices were thinking behind the scenes, and the conference notes add valuable context and richness to our knowledge of Supreme Court cases. This additional knowledge can be particularly valuable in a murky area of law like takings. Many of the arguments made in this chapter could be made based on the Court's published opinions alone, but without the conference notes and other internal documents the arguments would be less complete and comprehensive.

The focus of this chapter is to draw on the Court's conference notes and other internal documents in *Berman* and *Midkiff* to contest Justice O'Connor's assertion in her *Kelo* dissent that "there is a sense in which this troubling result [in *Kelo*] follows from errant language in *Berman* and *Midkiff*."[7] The Court's internal deliberations in those cases in fact reveal that the Court used broad language intentionally (in *Berman*) and was aware of the risk of broad language (in *Midkiff*). Further, the broad language that O'Connor found objectionable was essential to the Court's holdings in *Berman* and *Midkiff*, and the cases could not have been decided on narrower grounds. Justice O'Connor's suggestion that the broad language in *Berman* and *Midkiff* was mere dicta or the result of a judicial slip of the pen therefore is incorrect.

The Court's decisions in *Berman* and *Midkiff* consciously avoided the hard questions presented by the issue of public use and deferred those questions to the legislature. The intentional abdication of the judicial role in reviewing issues of public use reflected in the *Berman* and *Midkiff* conference notes reinforce the position that *Kelo* is entirely consistent with the Supreme Court's public use precedents, and that *Kelo* could not be distinguished on a principled basis from the prior cases. A more compelling dissent by Justice O'Connor therefore would have argued not that *Berman* and *Midkiff* contained loose language, but that with the benefit of hindsight *Berman* and *Midkiff*'s deference to the legislature was a mistake that should be corrected by overruling the prior cases.

---

6   DEL DICKSON, THE SUPREME COURT IN CONFERENCE, 1940–1985: THE PRIVATE DISCUSSIONS BEHIND NEARLY 300 SUPREME COURT DECISIONS (2001) is an outstanding source for more detailed information about the conference and conference notes generally.

7   *Kelo*, 125 S. Ct. at 2675 (O'Connor, J. dissenting).

Conscious Abdication: *Berman v. Parker* and Deference to the Legislature

Berman v. Parker involved a constitutional challenge to condemnations made under the District of Columbia Redevelopment Act of 1945. The Act created the District of Columbia Redevelopment Land Agency and gave it broad power "to acquire and assemble, by eminent domain and otherwise, real property for 'the redevelopment of blighted territory in the District of Columbia and the prevention, reduction, or elimination of blighting factors or causes of blight.'"[8]

Berman and his co-appellants owned a department store that was not itself blighted but that was slated to be taken by eminent domain as part of the clearance of a larger blighted area.[9] As summarized by the Court, Berman argued that "[i]t is commercial, not residential property; it is not slum housing; it will be put into the project under the management of a private, not public, agency and redeveloped for private, not public, use … To take for the purpose of ridding the area of slums is one thing; it is quite another … to take a man's property merely to develop a better balanced, more attractive community."[10]

Berman's reference to "a better balanced, more attractive community" raises an important contextual point about *Berman* that is not abundantly clear from the face of the Court's opinion. The District of Columbia Redevelopment Act, like many contemporaneous redevelopment acts enacted by legislatures around the country, was not concerned only with clearance of property that was blighted in the traditional sense of being decrepit and unfit for human habitation. Rather, the Redevelopment Act also was concerned with using the broader concept of blight clearance to encompass the taking of property "that owing to technological and sociological changes, obsolete lay-out, and other factors" might lead to the development of blight.[11] In other words, the broader concept of redevelopment was concerned not just with slum clearance but with modernization of the urban environment. Both the lower court and the Supreme Court had the validity of this broader idea of redevelopment squarely in mind when they considered Berman's challenge to the District of Columbia Redevelopment Act.[12]

The Court rejected Berman's arguments in an opinion that was highly deferential to the legislative branch and that articulated a broad conception of public use. The conference notes for *Berman*, discussed further below, indicate that the Court's broad language was deliberate and intended to repudiate the narrower conception of public use articulated in the opinion appealed to the Court.[13] This part therefore first examines the lower court opinion to provide context to the Court's conference notes. It then discusses the conference notes themselves and the light they shed on Justice O'Connor's dissent in *Kelo*.

---

8   *Berman*, 348 U.S. at 29.

9   *Id.* at 31.

10   *Id.*

11   District of Columbia Redevelopment Act of 1945, 60 Stat. 790, Ch. 7 § 5-701.

12   See *infra* notes, 24–5, 46–9 and accompanying text.

13   See *infra* notes 32–6 and accompanying text.

Setting the Stage: Judge Prettyman's Skeptical Analysis of the Redevelopment Act

The opinion that offended the Court was written by E. Barrett Prettyman, a respected D.C. Circuit judge sitting as part of a special three-member district court convened to hear Berman's challenge to the constitutionality of the District of Columbia Redevelopment Act.[14] In light of *Kelo*, Judge Prettyman's opinion comes as something of a revelation, much more fully engaging in the complexity of the public use issue than any of the Supreme Court's public use opinions. Prettyman's opinion therefore is worth considering, and in a few instances worth quoting, in some detail.

Judge Prettyman approached the key issue in *Berman* – the scope of government power to take property as part of a blight clearance project and transfer the taken property to private developers – in three steps. The first step involved the dilapidated physical structures that are at the core of the idea of blight:

> A slum is made up of houses (or substitutes for houses), the appurtenances thereto, and people. The houses and appurtenances are such that the people live in filth and breed disease and crime. A slum can be eliminated by tearing down the houses, destroying the appurtenances, and either building new housing on the spot for the people or moving the people away.[15]

Judge Prettyman had no difficulty with the government's ability to use eminent domain to clear blighted structures, which could be seen as the abatement of a public nuisance. "Since the Government can condemn such property without compensation under the police power [as a public nuisance], a fortiori it can condemn and pay reasonable compensation."[16]

The second step of Judge Prettyman's analysis involved the land on which blighted physical structures are located. The land itself, Judge Prettyman observed, has nothing to do with blight:

> The land itself neither contributes to nor detracts from a slum. It is the same whether a slum or a model building exists upon it. The land cannot be destroyed or moved. Only its ownership and its use can be changed. If cleared, the land upon which a slum presently exists would have no harmful effects upon the public. Neither does naked ownership of land, apart from use, have any harmful public effects. A slum and the legal title to the naked land upon which it exists are separate things.[17]

Why is it, then, that the government should have the power to take the underlying land once it has cleared the public-nuisance-causing blighted structures? If the taken "land is to be devoted to schools, roads, parks and such" then the exercise of eminent

---

14 Schneider v. District of Columbia, 117 F. Supp. 705 (D.D.C. 1953). (As a side note of trivia, the D.C. Circuit now sits in a courthouse named after Judge Prettyman.)

15 *Id.* at 714.

16 *Id.* at 715.

17 *Id.* at 714.

domain clearly would be proper.[18] But where the taken property was to be sold "to a private person for a purely private use" then the issue was more complex.[19]

Judge Prettyman recognized that the trend in caselaw was to define the permissible scope of eminent domain in terms of public purpose, rather than public use, representing a "progression in thought" based on the idea "that the taking itself, as distinguished from the subsequent use of the property, may be required in the public interest."[20] Based on this idea that an exercise of eminent domain is permissible if the taking itself, as opposed to the later use of the property, serves a public purpose, Judge Prettyman concluded that the government could take the underlying land, "provided (1) that the seizure of the title is necessary to the elimination of the slum or (2) that the proposed disposition of the title may reasonably be expected to prevent the otherwise probable development of a slum."[21] Although confused somewhat by his language about "the proposed disposition of title," Judge Prettyman's point was that the taking of title to the land was allowable if the act of taking the land from its current owner served the purpose of combating blight.

Judge Prettyman, however, was hesitant to go even this far. He observed that "[t]hese extensions of the concept of eminent domain, to encompass public purpose apart from public use, are potentially dangerous to basic principles of our system of government."[22] The government, Prettyman stated, cannot seize title to property "merely because a slum presently exists on the land," and in the ordinary circumstance the seizure of title "would seem to be neither necessary nor reasonably incidental to the clearance of a slum."[23] And for Judge Prettyman, the boundaries of the *constitutional* scope of public use were for the courts to determine:

> Whether the taking of a certain piece of property is necessary for a certain public use or purpose is initially and almost wholly a legislative question. But like every other legislative determination it is subject to the Constitution. Congress itself could not deprive a person of his property without due process of law. It is the duty of the courts, when a legislative act is challenged as violative of the Constitution, to determine that issue.[24]

The third step of Judge Prettyman's analysis moved beyond the issue of slum clearance to the broader issue of redevelopment and the use of blight as a justification to engage in what from a post-*Kelo* perspective would constitute a taking to promote economic development:

> [T]here are sections of cities which are not at the present time used to their fullest economic possibility, or are not arranged to fit current ideas of city development. An outstanding example is Trinity Church and its surrounding cemetery at the corner of Wall Street and Broadway in New York City. Old streets are not so wide as new ones would be. Apartment houses would be more economically efficient than are single dwellings. Phrases used to

---

18 *Id.* at 716.
19 *Id.*
20 *Id.*
21 *Id.*
22 *Id.*
23 *Id.* at 717.
24 *Id.* at 718.

describe this situation are "inadequate planning of the area," "excessive land coverage by the buildings thereon," "defective design and arrangement of the buildings thereon," "faulty street or lot layout," "economically or socially undesirable land uses." The statutes dealing with these areas are usually called "urban redevelopment" laws. The areas are frequently called "blighted." They are in no sense slums, or similar to slums; they are out-of-date. They do not breed disease or crime; they fail to measure up to their maximum potential use in terms of economic, social, architectural, or civic desirability.[25]

Judge Prettyman clearly stated that this type of taking would be unconstitutional, but read the Redevelopment Act narrowly as not permitting this type of taking. In light of *Kelo*, it is worth quoting from Judge Prettyman's analysis at some length:

The hypothesis in the first phase of this consideration is an urban area which does not breed disease or crime, is not a slum. Its fault is that is fails to meet what are called modern standards. Let us suppose that it is backward, stagnant, not properly laid out, economically Eighteenth Century – anything except detrimental to the health, safety or morals. Suppose its owners and occupants like it that way. Suppose they are often old-fashioned, prefer single-family dwellings, like small flower gardens, believe that a plot of ground is the place to rear children, prefer fresh to conditioned air, sun to fluorescent light. In many circles, all such views are considered "backward and stagnant." Are those who hold them "therefore blighted"? Can they not, nevertheless, own property?...

Is a modern apartment house a better breeder of men than is the detached or row-house? Is the local corner grocer a less desirable community asset than the absentee stockholder in the national chain or the wage-paid manager? Are such questions as these to be decided by the Government? And, if the decisions be adverse to the erstwhile owners and occupants, is their entire right to own the property thereby destroyed? ...

The terms "public use" and "public purpose" have never been defined with precision, and cannot be. Localities, customs and times change, and with them the needs of the public may change. But even the most liberal courts have put boundaries upon the meanings ...

We are of the opinion that Congress, in legislating for the District of Columbia, has no power to authorize the seizure by eminent domain of property for the sole purpose of redeveloping the area according to its, or its agents', judgment of what a well-developed, well-balanced neighborhood would be ... [26]

Finally, Judge Prettyman addressed the issue of whether the government could take non-blighted property such as Berman's department store that was located in an otherwise blighted area. Judge Prettyman characterized the government's argument on this point as "if slums exist the Government may seize, redevelop and sell all the property in any area it may select as appropriate, so long as the area includes the slum area."[27] This, Judge Prettyman said, "amounts to a claim on the part of the authorities for unreviewable power to seize and sell whole sections of the city," and could not withstand constitutional review because "a public purpose must be the

---

25 *Id.* at 714.

26 *Schneider*, 117 F. Supp at 719–20.

27 *Id.* at 721.

reason for the seizure of private property, not merely the excuse for the seizure."[28] Judge Prettyman allowed that non-blighted property could be taken for the same reason that the underlying title to blighted property could be taken – if taking the property could be tied to the prevention of blight.[29] But Judge Prettyman clearly stated that the government could not use eminent domain to take private property to improve the economic or aesthetic condition of a neighborhood:

> Of course the plan as pictured in the prospectus is attractive.[30] In all probability it would enhance the beauty and the livability of the area. If undertaken by private persons the project would be most laudable. It would be difficult to think of a village, town or city in the United States which a group of artists, architects and builders could not improve vastly if they could tear down the whole community and rebuild the whole of it. But as yet the courts have not come to call such pleasant accomplishments a public purpose which validates Government seizure of private property. The claim of Government power for such purposes runs squarely into the right of the individual to own property and to use it as he pleases. Absent impingement upon rights of others, and absent public use or compelling public necessity for the property, the individual's right is superior to all rights of the Government and is impregnable to the efforts of the government to seize it. That the individual is in a low-income group or in a high-income group or falls in the middle of the group is wholly immaterial. One man's land cannot be seized by the Government and sold to another man merely in order that the purchaser may build upon it a better house or a house which better meets the Government's idea of what is appropriate or well-designed.[31]

All of this said, Judge Prettyman construed the statute narrowly to avoid constitutional problems, and granted the government's motion to dismiss with leave to the plaintiffs to amend.[32] Thus, as the case came to the Supreme Court, the Redevelopment Act had been narrowly held to be constitutional in an opinion that forcefully raised serious doubts about the use of eminent domain in broad redevelopment projects.

The Berman *Conference Notes*

The conference notes for *Berman* show that the Supreme Court wanted nothing to do with Judge Prettyman's restrictive view of public use or with having the judiciary ask hard questions about legislative public-use determinations. Justice Douglas's notes have Chief Justice Warren's position as: "project is within the statute + is constitutional – what they [the District of Columbia] did was reasonable – he [the Chief Justice] would go further than the Ct. of Appeal [i.e., Judge Prettyman sitting as part of the district court panel] which unduly restricted the Act – affirm on broader

---

28 *Id.*

29 *Id.*; see *supra* note, 20 and accompanying text.

30 Prettyman's reference to the prospectus and its elegance foreshadowed the prominent, and unusual, use at oral arguments in *Kelo* of a display showing the proposed redevelopment plan for the Fort Trumbull area of New London.

31 *Schneider*, 117 F. Supp. at 724.

32 *Id.* at 724–5.

ground than the ct of appeal."[33] Justice Burton's notes also have Warren's position as "go beyond Court of Appeals."[34] Justice Reed's notes have Warren saying "In affirming, I would correct the CA. Put emphasis on parcel."[35] There are no remarks for any of the other justices beyond "agree with CJ" or "affirm and modify" in any of the Justices's notes, indicating a remarkable degree of consensus on the Court.

The opinion in *Berman* was assigned to Justice Douglas. A handwritten note dated November 12, 1954 from Justice Burton to Justice Douglas shows that Burton apparently felt that Douglas's first circulated draft did not go far enough in repudiating Judge Prettyman's position:

Dear Bill,

While I believe I agree with the statements you make in the Redevelopment case it seems to me that the specific interpretations made by Prettyman will cause much trouble and confusion unless treated more specifically. Therefore, unless you or someone else does it, I shall probably want to attempt it in a concurrence. This means some delay. H.H.B.[36]

Another memorandum dated November 17, 1954 indicates that Justice Douglas's next draft was more to Justice Burton's liking:

Dear Bill:

I appreciate the modifications in the recirculated opinion and see no adequate reason for me to write anything. Please include me in your "Court." H.H.B.[37]

And indeed, Justice Douglas's opinion for a unanimous Court clearly and specifically repudiated the views expressed by Judge Prettyman. Judge Prettyman's opinion had raised three hard questions about blight clearance takings: (1) Why does the existence of blight give the government power to take title to the underlying land? (2) Why should the government be able to take nonblighted property in a blighted area? and (3) Why should the government be able to use the blight clearance justification to take property that was used in a non-ideal but non-harmful way? The Court answered (or avoided) these questions by linking the scope of the power of eminent domain to the broad scope of the police power.[38] If the government was acting in furtherance of an end permitted by the virtually-limitless police power, the government was permitted to pursue that end through the means of an exercise of eminent domain.[39]

---

33 Justice William O. Douglas Papers, Manuscript Division, Library of Congress, Washington, D.C. (hereinafter "Douglas Papers"), Box 1156.

34 Justice Harold Burton Papers, Manuscript Division, Library of Congress, Washington, D.C., Box 251, Folder 15.

35 Justice Stanley Reed Papers, University of Kentucky Library, Lexington, Kentucky.

36 Douglas Papers, Box 1159.

37 Douglas Papers, Box 1159.

38 *Berman*, 348 U.S. at 32–3. On the virtually limitless scope of the police power, see generally D. Benjamin Barros, *The Police Power and the Takings Clause*, 58 U. Miami L. Rev. 471, 473–98 (2004).

39 *Berman*, 348 U.S. at 32.

As a result, the Court held that the relevant inquiry was not whether the taking of private property was for a public use, but whether the taking was in furtherance of the public welfare. This "broad and inclusive" concept represents values that "are spiritual as well as physical, aesthetic as well as monetary."[40] It therefore "is within the power of the legislature to determine that the community should be beautiful as well as healthy, spacious as well as clean, well-balanced as well as carefully patrolled."[41] If the government wants the community to "be beautiful as well as sanitary, there is nothing in the Fifth Amendment that stands in the way."[42]

This conception of the constitutionally permissible scope of eminent domain took the gradual shift from "public use" to "public purpose" to its logical, if extreme, conclusion, where eminent domain can be used as a means to achieve any conceivable governmental end. This view of public purpose not only permits *Kelo*-style economic development takings, but by the Court's own language would permit aesthetic takings of property deemed ugly by government officials to transfer to a private party who would erect a structure more pleasing to the eye.

With such a limitless conception of public purpose, it is unsurprising that the Court in *Berman* articulated a very narrow role for the judiciary in reviewing legislative exercises of eminent domain – what, after all, was there for a court to decide? Indeed, the Court's statement of deference to the legislature by its terms reflects the Court's view that the words "public use" in the Fifth Amendment do not act as a substantive limit on legislative power:

> Subject to specific constitutional limitations, when the legislature has spoken, the public interest has been declared in terms well-nigh conclusive. In such cases, the legislature, not the judiciary, is the main guardian of the public needs to be served by social legislation … This principle admits of no exception merely because the power of eminent domain is involved. The role of the judiciary in determining whether that power is being exercised for a public purpose is an extremely narrow one.[43]

The initial language in this passage, "Subject to specific constitutional limitations," was added by Douglas at the request of Chief Justice Warren.[44] Clearly, the Court did not view "public use" as a "specific constitutional limitation." By suggesting that the level of judicial review would be higher in other contexts involving constitutional language that the Court felt warranted additional judicial protection, this passage highlights both the limitless nature of the substantive standard set by the Court and the narrowness of the Court's conception of the judicial role in the eminent domain context.

Consistent with this general approach to the role of the judiciary and the permissible scope of public use, the Court specifically addressed (albeit in a conclusory way) two of the hard questions asked by Judge Prettyman. As to the government's power

---

40 *Id.* at 33.

41 *Id.*

42 *Id.*

43 *Berman*, 348 U.S. at 32.

44 Douglas Papers, Box 1159. Chief Justice Warren sent a memorandum dated November 18, 1954 to Justice Douglas requesting the change in language. *Id.* Douglas agreed to make the change in a memorandum to the Conference dated November 19, 1954. *Id.*

to take the property underlying a blighted structure, the Court simply observed that "[t]he District Court indicated grave doubts concerning the Agency's right to take full title to the land as distinguished from the objectionable buildings located on it. We do not share those doubts."[45] As to the government's power to take non-blighted property in an otherwise blighted area, the Court held that:

> It is not for the courts to oversee the choice of the boundary line nor to sit in review on the size of a particular project area. Once the question of the public purpose has been decided, the amount and character of land to be taken for the project and the need for a particular tract to complete the integrated plan rests in the discretion of the legislative branch.[46]

In one sense, the Court could have stopped here, because this holding allowing the taking of non-blighted property located in a blighted area effectively resolved the litigation about the taking of Berman's department store. The larger question of the constitutionality of broad redevelopment schemes, however, was expressly placed before the Court not only by Judge Prettyman's opinion but by the position taken by the government on appeal. The Solicitor General filed a Memorandum specifically asking the Court to consider the broader issues presented by the case even though the government had technically won in the court below. The Memorandum argued that the restrictions imposed by the District Court would "seriously impair, if not frustrate, the purpose" of the Redevelopment Act in part because it would reduce the government's ability to address problems "such as haphazard and mixed land uses, overcrowding of the land, outmoded street patterns, lack of light, air and living space, [and] inadequate room for necessary community facilities."[47] It also highlighted the national importance of the issue before the Court, noting that "[s]imilar redevelopment programs have been adopted in some thirty-two states" and that Congress had provided support for redevelopment plans in the Housing Act of 1949.[48] The Solicitor General further noted that the constitutionality of redevelopment acts had been at issue in courts around the country.[49]

As it was considering *Berman*, the Court therefore was well aware that it would at some point have to consider the broad constitutionality of urban redevelopment and to address the issue raised by Prettyman's third question – why should the government be able to use the blight clearance justification to take property that was used in a non-ideal but non-harmful way? The Court did not speak as directly to Prettyman's position on this issue as it had on others. The Court's lack of difficulty with this type of taking, however, is clear from its link between the permissible scope of eminent domain and the broad scope of the police power and its deference to legislatures in determining the means by which they accomplished legitimate legislative goals.[50] The Court's observation that it is "within the power of the

---

45 *Berman*, 348 U.S. at 36.

46 *Id.* at 35–6.

47 Memorandum Stating Position of Appellees, January 1954, at 7 (Berman v. Parker, 348 U.S. 26 (1954)).

48 *Id.* at 8.

49 *Id.* at 8–9.

50 *Berman*, 348 U.S. at 33.

legislature to determine that the community should be beautiful as well as healthy, spacious as well as clean, well-balanced as well as carefully patrolled,"[51] directly addresses Prettyman's question and conclusively established the constitutionality of urban redevelopment laws.

Berman *and Justice O'Connor's* Kelo *Dissent*

As the forgoing discussion demonstrates, *Berman* strongly supported the validity of economic development takings – indeed, it arguably contemplated them. It is therefore unsurprising that *Berman* was used prominently, and accurately, in the majority opinion in *Kelo*.

In her *Kelo* dissent, Justice O'Connor initially tried to discount the precedential value of *Berman* by asserting that the takings in *Berman* were justified by "the extraordinary precondemnation use of the targeted property [which] inflicted affirmative harm on society ... through blight resulting from extreme poverty."[52] Although Justice Stevens's opinion of the Court correctly noted that this view of *Berman* is severely undercut by the fact that Berman's department store itself was not blighted,[53] there is something to Justice O'Connor's position. On its surface, *Berman* can plausibly be viewed as merely deferring to the legislative judgment that the taking of non-blighted property was necessary to the broader goal of eliminating blight. Or, as Justice O'Connor put it, "[h]aving approved of Congress' decision to eliminate the harm to the public emanating from the blighted neighborhood ... we did not second-guess its decision to treat the neighborhood as a whole rather than lot-by-lot."[54]

Consistent with this view, Justice O'Connor suggested that the Court's broad language was "errant" and unnecessary to the holding in *Berman*.[55] Justice O'Connor was particularly disturbed by two assertions in *Berman*: the link established by the Court between the scope of public use to the scope of the police power and the declaration that the legislature could use any means, including eminent domain, to pursue a permissible governmental end.[56] In a technical sense, Justice O'Connor was correct that this broad language was unnecessary to the holding in *Berman*. The Court could have affirmed on the narrow grounds used by Judge Prettyman to hold the Redevelopment Act constitutional. Alternatively, the Court could have rested its holding in *Berman* on the grounds Justice O'Connor later attributed to it – deference to the legislature regarding the scope of the taking in a neighborhood that was unquestionably pervaded by blight.

As the *Berman* conference notes show, however, the Court's use of broad language in *Berman* was in no way "errant." Rather, the Court's broad language was a result of the Court's conscious decision to repudiate the ideas expressed by

---

51 *Id.*
52 *Kelo*, 125 S. Ct. at 2674 (O'Connor, J., dissenting).
53 *Id.* at 2665–6 nn. 13 and 16.
54 *Id.* at 2673 (O'Connor, J., dissenting).
55 *Id.*
56 *Id.* at 2675.

Judge Prettyman and to remove the judiciary from reviewing legislative exercises of eminent domain. In this context, looking to the narrow facts surrounding Berman's department store can be misleading. Both Judge Prettyman's opinion and the Solicitor General's memorandum placed the broader validity of redevelopment laws before the Court. The Court was well aware that the constitutionality of redevelopment laws had been the subject of controversy in courts around the country, and was therefore aware that if it ducked the issue in *Berman* it would have to address the issue in another case. These laws, aimed at problems "such as haphazard and mixed land uses, overcrowding of the land, outmoded street patterns, lack of light, air and living space, [and] inadequate room for necessary community facilities"[57] could not be held constitutional merely on blight-clearance grounds. The Supreme Court clearly and intentionally addressed this problem in *Berman* by removing any substantive limit to legislative exercises of eminent domain.

Indeed, confronted with the hard questions asked by Judge Prettyman, the Supreme Court had two choices – to admit that even in blight-clearance cases the scope of eminent domain must be limited or to remove limits on the exercise of eminent domain altogether. This stark choice highlights another weakness in Justice O'Connor's dissent in *Kelo*. It is hard to see how the Court could articulate a principled reason why the takings in *Berman* were permissible but those in *Kelo* were not unless it was willing to say that the governmental end in *Berman* (prevention of blight) was permissible while the governmental end in *Kelo* (promoting economic development) was impermissible. Justice O'Connor's statement that the Court in *Berman* had "approved of Congress' decision" to engage in blight clearance suggests that she felt that part of the Court's role was to review the substance of Congressional ends. This in turn suggests that her positions on *Berman* and *Kelo* were based not on principle but on policy preference – exactly the type of judicial second-guessing of legislative policy making in the takings context that Justice O'Connor had repudiated in an opinion of a unanimous Court just a few months before *Kelo*.[58] That Justice O'Connor's positions were based on policy preference becomes more apparent when her position in *Kelo* is compared to the Court's other leading pre-*Kelo* public use case, which ironically had been authored by Justice O'Connor herself.

Justice O'Connor, *Midkiff* and *Kelo*

Midkiff involved a challenge to a very unusual law enacted in response to a very unusual set of circumstances. For several historical reasons, land ownership in Hawaii was unusually concentrated. On Oahu, for example, 22 landowners owned 72.5 percent of the fee simple titles. Many of these landowners were hesitant to sell parcels of their property because of potentially large federal tax liabilities. The result was that most people leased, rather than owned, their homes. The Hawaii Legislature therefore enacted the Land Reform Act of 1967, which set up a process

---

57 Memorandum Stating Position of Appellees, January 1954, at 7 (Berman v. Parker, 348 U.S. 26 (1954)).

58 See Lingle v. Chevron, U.S.A. Inc. 125 S. Ct. 2074 (2005).

for using eminent domain to take the fee simple ownership of a single-family home and transfer it to the tenant living in the home.[59]

Midkiff therefore presented a very clear public use issue: the State of Hawaii was using eminent domain to transfer single-family homes from one private party (the landlord) to another private party (the tenant). In the opinion appealed to the Court, the Ninth Circuit had held that the Act did not constitute a valid public use, and instead was "a naked attempt on the part of the state of Hawaii to take the private property of A and transfer it to B solely for B's private use and benefit."[60]

One preliminary issue discussed by the Court in conference was whether to abstain and let the state courts decide the issue of public use. Justices Powell and O'Connor were the only Justices to advocate for abstention in the conference. Justice Blackmun's notes of the conference have Justice O'Connor saying that she "liked abstention and let state courts develop the public purpose."[61] Justice Brennan's notes for Justice O'Connor simply state "Favor abstention, will reverse";[62] Justice Powell's notes for Justice O'Connor state "Abstention in first vote."[63] Justices Brennan and Blackmun made explicit statements at the conference opposing abstention, and the other justices who spoke addressed the merits, implicitly rejecting abstention.[64]

---

59 Hawaii Housing Authority v. Midkiff, 467 U.S. 229, 232–4 (1984). As an aside, E. Barrett Prettyman, Jr., the son of the Judge Prettyman involved in *Berman*, was one of the lawyers who represented the landowners in *Midkiff*. See *id.* at 231. As another aside, the *Midkiff* files include one exchange that might be of more interest to scholars of abortion politics than to takings scholars. As the formal votes of the Justices were filtering in in the case, Justice Blackmun wrote a memo to Justice O'Connor, asking "if I may raise a point of personal privilege. I shall be in Honolulu May 20–22. Do you think the decision in [*Midkiff*] could be withheld until after the 22nd? I run into enough flak as it is these days, and I think it would be better if I were out of the State by the time the decision comes down." Justice Harry Blackmun Papers, Manuscript Division, Library of Congress, Washington D.C., Box 405, Folder 9. Justice O'Connor replied that "I will be more than happy to get you safely back on the Mainland before lowering the boom by announcement of this decision." *Id.* For those unfamiliar with the issue, Justice Blackmun received a tremendous amount of "flak" as the author of *Roe v. Wade*.

60 Midkiff v. Tom, 702 F.2d 788, 798 (9th Cir. 1983).

61 Justice Harry Blackmun Papers, Manuscript Division, Library of Congress, Washington D.C., Box 405, Folder 9.

62 Justice William Brennan Papers, Manuscript Division, Library of Congress, Washington D.C., Box 627, Folder 5. It is understandable that Justice O'Connor, having recently been a state appellate court judge, would lean towards deference to state courts. Twenty years later, however, Justice O'Connor had no inclination to defer to the public use determination of the Connecticut Supreme Court in *Kelo*. One explanation for this shift could be that Justice O'Connor became less deferential to state courts in her time on the Supreme Court. Alternatively, it could be that her deferential attitude in *Midkiff* was motivated by approval of the legislation at issue in that case, where her *Kelo* dissent was motivated by disapproval of the takings at issue there.

63 Justice Lewis F. Powell, Jr. Papers, Washington & Lee University, Lexington, Virginia.

64 Blackmun Papers, Box 405, Folder 9; Brennan Papers, Box 627 Folder 5; Powell Papers.

Consistent with the position of the other justices, O'Connor's opinion for a unanimous Court ultimately rejected the argument that abstention was appropriate in *Midkiff*.[65]

On the merits, the Justices seemed to be in agreement that the Act met the "public use" requirement and fell within the scope of the Court's prior precedents, especially *Berman*. Chief Justice Burger referred to the "precedent in slum clearance cases," and the "great mkt control" exercised by the property owners in *Midkiff*.[66] Justice Brennan referred to "Berman et al" and Justice Blackmun noted that "On merits, [there has been] no case yet where we've held a taking was not for public use."

Justice Rehnquist, a later dissenter in *Kelo*, observed that the opinion "can be done narrowly but this is open and shut case; at best very narrow review of what is public purpose" (Brennan notes);[67] "can be done [illegible] narrowly but case is not close; stay within Berman" (Blackmun notes).[68] The idea that this was a narrow case was also raised by Justice Powell, who said that the case "has to be treated as unique situation it is – its history etc." (Brennan notes);[69] "a special case, but to be carefully written" (Blackmun notes);[70] "This is a very special situation." (Powell notes).[71]

Despite these comments that *Midkiff* could be written narrowly, Justice O'Connor drafted an opinion that followed *Berman* and articulated a broad conception of public use and a very narrow role for the judiciary in determining the validity of exercises of eminent domain. After summarizing *Berman*, the opinion stated that "[t]he 'public use' requirement is thus coterminous with the scope of a sovereign's police powers."[72] The opinion similarly contained a lengthy exegesis on the importance of judicial deference containing statements such as "where the exercise of the eminent domain power is rationally related to a conceivable public purpose, the Court has never held a compensated taking to be proscribed by the Public Use Clause,"[73] and "Judicial deference is required because, in our system of government, legislatures are better able to assess what public purposes should be advanced by an exercise of the taking power."[74] Indeed, the opinion was so broad that Justice Blackmun's clerk noted in a memo that "I am a bit surprised at the breadth of the opinion since SOC's comments at Conference indicated that she wanted a narrow opinion."[75] This remark that Justice O'Connor wanted a narrow opinion is not reflected in the conference notes. It may be that she had made such a remark, but that the remark

---

65 *Midkiff*, 467 U.S. at 236–9.

66 Blackmun Papers, Box 405, Folder 9. Justice Brennan has the Chief Justice similarly stating "Slum clearance, waterfront is not that much unlike this." Brennan Papers, Box 627, Folder 5.

67 Brennan Papers, Box 627, Folder 5.

68 Blackmun Papers, Box 405, Folder 9. Justice Powell's notes simply have Justice Rehnquist's position as "Reverse. Narrowly." Powell Papers.

69 Brennan Papers, Box 627, Folder 5.

70 Blackmun Papers, Box 405, Folder 9.

71 Powell Papers.

72 *Midkiff*, 467 U.S. at 240.

73 *Id.* at 241.

74 *Id.* at 244.

75 Blackmun Papers, Box 405, Folder 9.

was not reflected in the notes, or that the clerk was attributing to Justice O'Connor the sentiments raised by Justices Powell and Rehnquist.

The remarkable breadth of the circulated opinion caused Justice Powell to write the following prescient and strikingly ineffective memorandum to Justice O'Connor:

Dear Sandra:

This refers to our brief conversation yesterday. I should have been in touch with you sooner. My suggested changes, set forth below, do not affect your basic analysis. I have been concerned by the sweep of language that can be read as saying that any "social" purpose may justify the taking of private property. The language to this effect is primarily on page 14.

I suggest the following as a substitute for the next to the last sentence in the paragraph on p. 14 that carries over from p. 13:

"As the unique way titles were held in Hawaii skewed the land market, exercise of the power of eminent domain was justified. The Act advances its purposes without the state taking actual possession of the land. In such cases," ...

* * *

The paragraph that begins on p. 14 also can be read broadly to the effect that "social problems" may be addressed by taking private property pursuant to "social legislation". I suggest revisions of some of the language of this paragraph, beginning with the second sentence, along the following lines:

"Judicial deference is required here because, in our system of government, legislatures are better able to assess what public purposes should be advanced by an exercise of the taking power. State legislatures are as capable as Congress of making such determinations within their respective spheres of authority. See *Berman v. Parker*, 348 U.S., at 32. Thus, if there are substantial reasons for an exercise of the taking power, courts must ... "

* * *

The first full sentence on page 13 states that "redistribution of fees simply to reduce the economic and social evils ... is a rational exercise of the power of eminent domain." Again, I am troubled by the emphasis without limits on "economic and social evils." In this case we are concerned only with a very specific and unique evil. I would suggest omission of the phrase "reduce the economic evils," replacing it with "correct deficiencies in the market."

* * *

This is a unique case, and I think we may regret language that could encourage Congress and state legislatures to justify taking private property for any perceived social evil.

I am not sending this letter to the Conference, in the hope that changes along these lines will be acceptable to you. If not, I probably will write briefly.

I do appreciate your willingness to consider these.

Sincerely,

[LFP][76]

Justice Powell's proposed language was included in Justice O'Connor's opinion of the Court,[77] but is completely overwhelmed by the broad language in the rest of the opinion. It is remarkable that Justice Powell, having seen the potential danger in the broad language in *Midkiff*, thought that the problem could be fixed with some minor wordsmithing.

Justice Powell, of course, did not live to see his prediction that "we may regret language that could encourage Congress and state legislatures to justify taking private property for any perceived social evil" come true in *Kelo*. Justice O'Connor, however, had the opportunity to eat her words, calling the broad language in *Midkiff* "errant" and "unnecessary to the specific holdings of" the case.[78] As with *Berman*, there is an element of truth to this observation. The case perhaps could have been decided in a narrow fashion, highlighting the unique facts of the case and omitting the broad language that was later used so effectively by the *Kelo* majority.[79] The Court discussed exactly that approach in conference, and Justice Powell raised the unique nature of the case in his memorandum to Justice O'Connor. The broad language in *Midkiff* therefore cannot be seen as "errant" in the sense that its presence was a mistake – the Court was aware of the risks of a broadly-written decision, but none of the Justices chose to address these risks by proposing meaningful changes to Justice O'Connor's opinion or writing a separate concurrence.

Justice O'Connor's suggestion that the broad language in *Midkiff* was unnecessary to the decision in that case – in other words, that the broad language was mere dicta – is equally problematic, and begs the question of how *Midkiff* had been decided on a principled but narrow basis.[80] Certainly, the Court's opinion could have focused on the unique facts presented by the case, but exactly why did those facts meet the requirement of the public use clause? If the permissible scope of public use is not coterminous with the scope of the police power, what could justify taking fee title to property from one private party to give it to another private party? Put another

---

76 Memorandum from Justice Powell to Justice O'Connor, May 18, 1984 (Powell Papers).

77 *Midkiff*, 467 U.S. at 243–4.

78 *Kelo*, 125 S. Ct. at 2675 (O'Connor, J., dissenting).

79 See *Kelo*, 125 S. Ct. at 2663–4.

80 My colleague Michael Dimino has noted that any time the Justices start talking about a case being very narrow it is worth looking hard for the constitutional principle they are about to break. For similar criticism of Justice O'Connor's dissent, see Ilya Somin, *Controlling The Grasping Hand: Economic Development Takings After* Kelo, 15 S. Ct. Econ. Rev. 183 (2007); Charles E. Cohen, *Eminent Domain After* Kelo v. City of New London*: An Argument For Banning Economic Development Takings*, 29 Harv. J.L. & Pub. Pol'y 491, 524–5 (2006).

way, if the Court is going to engage in review of the merits of exercises of eminent domain, is there any principled basis to distinguish between prevention of blight and elimination of oligopoly on the one hand and elimination of economic depression on the other?

In her *Kelo* dissent, Justice O'Connor tried to distinguish *Midkiff* in the same way she tried to distinguish *Berman*, arguing that the taking in *Midkiff* was permissible because "the extraordinary, precondemnation use of the targeted property inflicted affirmative harm on society ... through oligopoly resulting from extreme wealth."[81] As explained above, the harm-preventing characterization of *Berman* fails because that case concerned issues beyond the clearance of blight. With *Midkiff*, the harm-preventing argument has even less appeal, because the asserted harm to the housing market caused by oligopoly is far more attenuated from traditional conceptions of harmful land use than is blight clearance.

Even if the harm-preventing characterization of *Berman* and *Midkiff* were factually accurate, however, Justice O'Connor's argument is inherently flawed because the inquiry into whether a legislative act is intended to prevent harm is an inquiry into the substance and merits of the legislative act. Indeed, it is exactly the same inquiry that many *Lochner*-era courts used to try to limit the scope of the police power under the doctrine of substantive due process.[82]

This tie between Justice O'Connor's analysis and that of *Lochner*-era substantive due process highlights the fundamental problem with Justice O'Connor's dissent in *Kelo*, a problem that is underscored by Justice Powell's memo in *Midkiff*. Ultimately, the exercises of eminent domain in *Berman*, *Midkiff*, and *Kelo* all took property from one private party and transferred it to another private party. For Justice O'Connor, the question of whether the takings were permissible depended on the legislative end the government was trying to achieve. Justice Powell was explicit on this score, expressing concern that "any 'social' purpose may justify the taking of private property." The prevention of blight or elimination of land oligopoly, of course, can be seen as "social purposes." Why should these purposes justify the exercise of eminent domain where other legislative ends do not? The implication of Justice Powell's remark is that eminent domain should not be used to promote less important social purposes. But who gets to decide whether a social purpose is sufficiently important? In this context it is hard to imagine a justification for favoring one social purpose over another that is not based on mere policy preference for one type of government activity over another. Making this type of policy decision is supposed to be the realm of the legislature, and legislative exercises of eminent domain should not stand or fall because of the Court's views on whether the legislature's stated end is worthwhile.

This is not to say that it is impossible to take a principled position that *Kelo* is wrong. Rather, it appears to be impossible to take a position that *Berman* and *Midkiff* were correct but that *Kelo* was incorrect without making a policy choice that should belong to the legislature. As the Court's internal deliberations show, the broad language in *Berman* and *Midkiff* was in no way errant. A more compelling *Kelo* dissent by Justice O'Connor therefore would have argued that with the benefit

---

81 *Kelo*, 125 S. Ct. at 2674 (O'Connor, J., dissenting).
82 See Barros, *Police Power*, *supra* note, 37 at 488–90.

of hindsight, the core holdings of *Berman* and *Midkiff* were wrong and that the cases should have been overruled.

Conclusion

The argument that *Berman*, *Midkiff*, and *Kelo* must stand or fall together can be made based on the Court's published opinions alone. The Court's conference notes and internal memoranda, however, add useful layers to our understanding of the cases and richness to the discussion of the positions on each side of the debate. They also establish that Court's language in *Berman* and *Midkiff* was not "errant." In *Berman*, the conference notes and memoranda show the Court unanimously and strongly rejecting Judge Prettyman's nuanced approach to public use. In *Midkiff*, they show a concern by some members of the Court about the risks of a broadly-written opinion. Although some Justices suggested that the case could be decided narrowly and based on its unique facts, no one on the Court came up with a principled way to do so.

The error in Justice O'Connor's dissent in *Kelo* is highlighted more than anything by Justice Powell's memorandum in *Midkiff*, which sought to distinguish the use of eminent domain to transfer title to homes from landlords to tenants from other types of social legislation that Justice Powell thought were undesirable. The Court could take a principled position that "public use" should mean actual ownership by a public entity, or it could take a principled position based on deference to the legislature that "public use" should mean "public purpose." Having made the choice to treat "public use" as "public purpose," however, the Court could not make policy choices between legitimate public purposes without intruding on an area of decision making that should belong to the legislature. Confronted in *Kelo* with the degree to which legislatures had used the freedom created by *Berman* and *Midkiff*, the Court could have decided that its prior decisions were in error. It could not, however, have invalidated the taking in *Kelo* without rejecting the analysis in *Berman* and *Midkiff*.

Chapter 5

Controls over the Use and Abuse of Eminent Domain in England: A Comparative View

Tom Allen

Introduction

For an observer from England, one of the most interesting aspects of *Kelo v. City of New London*[1] is the attention and debate that it has provoked. While land use and development are frequently matters of intense public interest and debate in England, it is safe to say that the focus does not usually fall on the use or abuse of the power of eminent domain. Indeed, recent revisions of the statutory law on compulsory purchase raised very little public debate.[2] Yet, under the law of England and Wales,[3] the courts have no more power to control eminent domain than their American counterparts, and arguably they have even less. Moreover, there appears to be no greater reluctance to take property by compulsion. For example, recent plans for the regeneration of the Liverpool area called for the demolition of 19,758 housing units[4] and the construction of the Olympic site in London will require the purchase of

---

1   545 U.S. 649; 125 S. Ct. 2655 (2005).

2   Planning and Compulsory Purchase Act, 2004, C.5 (Eng.).

3   This chapter concentrates on the law of England, to the exclusion of Northern Ireland and Scotland. However, some aspects of the law on compulsory purchase apply throughout the United Kingdom, and hence some references are made to the United Kingdom instead of England.

4   NewHeartlands, Merseyside Housing Market Renewal Pathfinder February 2004 Prospectus Executive Summary (2004), 3 (available at http://www.newheartlands.co.uk/PAGES/PRESS_REL/executivesummary.pdf> ("NewHeartlands" is the "Pathfinder" for the Merseyside district. On its web site, <www.newheartlands.co.uk>, it describes itself as "a partnership spearheaded by three Merseyside local authorities – Liverpool, Sefton and Wirral, together with Local Strategic Partnerships (LSPs), the North West Development Agency and English Partnerships. It covers 123,000 properties in some of Merseyside's most disadvantaged communities." Only about 40 percent of the properties to be demolished are in owner-occupation: see NewHeartlands, Scheme Update 2005, Table 4.2. Demolition on this scale is not a new phenomenon: slum clearance levels ran at about 90,000 units annually before World War II. After dropping during the War, they recovered thereafter and remained high until the mid-1970s (see John English, Ruth Madigan, and Peter Norman, Slum Clearance: The Social and Administrative Context in England and Wales, 22–23 (1976)).

hundreds of businesses.[5] While many property owners threatened with compulsory purchase often sell voluntarily, it is only the threat of compulsion that extracts their "consent." Moreover, in England, as in the United States, land acquired by the actual or threatened use of eminent domain is often transferred to private developers, who then make a substantial profit from its use.

Despite these similarities in the use of eminent domain, the debate in England has been milder than in the United States. To be sure, there have been reports in the national media of growing opposition to some projects that rely on eminent domain[6] and there is some evidence that these protests are filtering through to the policy makers and politicians. In Newcastle upon Tyne, for example, the Liberal Democrats' victory in a recent local council election was partly due to a promise to shelve the old Labour council's "Going for Growth" program, which would have involved the demolition of large areas of the City.[7] Even so, the English debate, as far as it goes, does not focus as sharply on the rights of individual property owners, and the protests have tended to be local rather than national. There is no call for national legislation to give the courts greater power to restrain the use of eminent domain and there is virtually no debate on these issues in the legal academy.

This chapter therefore seeks to provide some possible explanations for the differences in the public debate over eminent domain. The first point to note is that there is a fundamental right to property in the English legal system. It comes from the European Convention on Human Rights (or, more accurately, the First Protocol to the Convention), which is now enforced by the courts throughout the United Kingdom. However, like the takings clause of the Fifth Amendment, the European right to property does not impose significant constraints on the purposes for which property may be taken. It appears that the concerns that are raised by *Kelo* and similar cases are addressed by other aspects of British and European law. This paper identifies some of these aspects. For example, English statutory law generally requires the acquiring body to cover some of the subjective losses suffered by the property owner. There are also administrative and legal controls on inter-governmental competition for investment that have the effect of avoiding some of the worst abuses of eminent domain. In addition, at the local level, the movement of industry or housing does not have the same impact on tax revenue that it does in many American municipalities and states, and consequently the fiscal incentive to attract or retain investment by offering cheap land assembly is often absent from the English scene. The chapter closes with a recognition that these factors are probably not enough, by themselves, to explain why eminent domain is not the focus of debate in England, and so it examines several aspects of English planning and regeneration laws that seem to have the effect of diverting attention to other aspects of state power over property.

---

5   Matthew Beard, Businesses on Olympic Site Fight To Avoid Eviction, THE INDEPENDENT (London, England), August 13, 2005, at 42.

6   The NewHeartlands report of 2005 refers to "persistent and extensive negative publicity from the national media." See NEWHEARTLANDS, SCHEME UPDATE, para 1.7.

7   "Lib Dems Scrap Demolition Plans," BBC News Service, June 14, 2004, *available at* http://news.bbc.co.uk/1/hi/england/tyne/3806827.stm.

Fundamental Rights and Property in the United Kingdom and Europe

While the legal system of the United Kingdom has no direct counterpart to the Bill of Rights or to the Fifth Amendment, the United Kingdom is a member of the Council of Europe and is bound by the European Convention on Human Rights and its Protocols.[8] Article 1 of the First Protocol[9] ("P1-1") contains a right to property, in the following terms:

> Every natural or legal person is entitled to the peaceful enjoyment of his possessions. No one shall be deprived of his possessions except in the public interest and subject to the conditions provided for by law and by the general principles of international law.

> The preceding provisions shall not, however, in any way impair the right of a State to enforce such laws as it deems necessary to control the use of property in accordance with the general interest or to secure the payment of taxes or other contributions or penalties.

Although the United Kingdom ratified the Convention in 1951[10] and the Protocol in 1952,[11] neither the Convention nor the Protocol were incorporated into domestic law until the passing of the Human Rights Act 1998.[12] The Act preserves Parliamentary supremacy, but it also provides that "[s]o far as it is possible to do so, primary legislation and subordinate legislation must be read and given effect in a way which is compatible with the Convention rights."[13] In addition, it makes it unlawful for a public authority to act in a way which is incompatible with a Convention right, unless legislation prevents it from doing so.[14] The Human Rights Act 1998 has become an important element of the British legal system, and the right to property has become a particularly fertile ground for challenges to legislative and administrative acts.[15]

For our purposes, it is the interpretation of the second sentence of P1-1 that is crucial. A "deprivation of possessions" corresponds to the American concept of a taking of property[16] and to the British idea of a compulsory purchase. As there is no mention of compensation, it leaves the degree of protection unclear. Plainly, the interpretation of P1-1 in a given case is bound to raise difficulties, but in some respects

---

8 Convention of the Protection of Human Rights and Fundamental Freedoms, Nov. 4, 1950, 213 U.N.T.S. 222.

9 213 U.N.T.S. 262.

10 The Convention came into force on September 3, 1953.

11 The Protocol came into force on May 18, 1954.

12 In force October 2, 2000. Human Rights Act, 1998, c. 42 (Eng.).

13 *Id.* s. 3. If interpretation does not resolve a conflict Convention rights, the court may issue a "declaration of incompatibility" under section 4 of the Act. While a declaration of incompatibility does not affect the validity of the legislation, section 10 provides that it does allow a Minister to invoke a rapid procedure for amending or repealing the legislation.

14 *Id.* s. 6.

15 For a general review on its impact on U.K. law, see Tom Allen, Property and The Human Rights Act of 1998 (2005).

16 The second sentence only covers outright expropriations of a full ownership interest; in most cases, a regulatory taking would fall under one of the other sentences: see *id.*, 86–91.

the task of the British courts is made easier by the availability of the extensive body of cases decided by the European Court of Human Rights.[17] While the Human Rights Act 1998 does not say that British courts are bound by the European case law, it does provide that the courts "must take [it] into account" where relevant.[18]

The Public Interest and Private Gain

In the vast majority of cases, there is no real dispute over the public interest requirement of P1-1. In cases involving the transfer of property from one private person to another, the Court of Human Rights allows States to frame the purpose of a taking so broadly that it is difficult to imagine how a redistribution would not serve a public interest in some way. This is shown by *James v. United Kingdom*,[19] which concerned legislation that allowed residential tenants on long leases to buy out their landlords. The landlords' real complaint concerned the level of compensation, but they also maintained that the legislation did not serve the public interest. This was not a general objection to all forms of property regulation: indeed, they accepted that the regulation of private tenancies might serve the public interest. However, they argued that expropriation was quite different than regulation.[20] In their view, this was a taking for a private purpose.

There were textual arguments that supported the landlords' position. The landlords maintained that the shift from the "public interest" to the "general interest" in the second and third sentences of P1-1 suggests that power to take property is narrower than the power to control property.[21] However, the Court dismissed this point, on the basis that:

> even if there could be differences between the concepts of "public interest" and "general interest" in Article 1 (P1-1), on the point under consideration no fundamental distinction of the kind contended for by the applicants can be drawn between them.[22]

The landlords also pointed out that the French version of P1-1 states that a deprivation is only permitted "*pour cause d'utilité publique*," which appears to restrict the power to take property more than the English version. Indeed, the French version seems closer to a "public use" requirement. The Court dismissed this argument as well. It stated that "public interest" and "*pour cause d'utilité publique*" have an "autonomous meaning."[23] In other words, they are not grounded on the meaning given to them in either English or French law, or in the law of any other Member State.

The Court accepted that this autonomous meaning would prohibit "a deprivation of property effected for no reason other than to confer a private benefit on a private

---

17 The Court of Human Rights is based in Strasbourg, and it hears applications from the Member States of the Council of Europe.

18 Human Rights Act § 2 (1).

19 98 Eur. Ct. H.R. (ser. A) (1986).

20 *James*, 98 Eur. Ct. H.R. (ser. A), para. 43.

21 *Id.*

22 *Id.*

23 *Id.*, para. 42.

party."[24] However, it did not accept that "the transferred property should be put into use for the general public or that the community generally, or even a substantial proportion of it, should directly benefit from the taking."[25] Moreover, it also accepted the United Kingdom's argument that "the compulsory transfer of property from one individual to another may, depending upon the circumstances, constitute a legitimate means for promoting the public interest."[26]

While this suggests that shifting property from one private person to another does not constitute a public interest if it is an end in itself, the facts of *James* suggest that the distinction between ends and means may be difficult to draw in practice. In relation to the public interest of the tenants' right to buy, the Court said that:

> the fairness of a system of law governing the contractual or property rights of private parties is a matter of public concern and therefore legislative measures intended to bring about such fairness are capable of being "in the public interest," even if they involve the compulsory transfer of property from one individual to another.[27]

The Court did not expand on its idea of fairness in property relations, except that it seems to be interchangeable with "social justice." Social justice itself has not been discussed in any detail, but it is clear that it is broadly interpreted and, in most cases, States should be able to point to some idea of fairness in support of redistribution of property. Indeed, fairness and social justice have also been found to be a legitimate objective in other cases, such as the restitution schemes intended to redress infringements of human rights under communist governments.[28] However, the Court has offered no further explanation of their meaning.

The *James* case is not directly comparable with *Kelo*, to the extent that the pursuit of fairness and social justice differs from economic development. However, the Court of Human Rights has also stated that economic policy may justify the transfer of property amongst private persons. For example, the Court has found that the public interest in managing the economy justifies consolidations of private agricultural land,[29] majority buy-out rules in company law,[30] and compulsory debt adjustment programs.[31] However, the Court has not examined the relationship between economic policy and the public interest in any detail. There is certainly nothing like a theory of economic efficiency in any of its judgments: in none of

---

24 *Id.*, para. 40.

25 *Id.*, para. 41.

26 *Id.*, para. 40.

27 *Id.*, para. 41; see also para. 45 ("a taking of property effected in pursuance of legitimate social, economic or other policies may be 'in the public interest,' even if the community at large has no direct use or enjoyment of the property taken.")

28 Zvolský and Zvolská v. Czech Republic, 2002-IX Eur. Ct. H.R. 163, paras 67–8; see also Pincová and Pinc v. Czech Republic, 2002-VIII Eur. Ct. H.R. 311.

29 See e.g., Erkner and Hofauer v. Austria, 117 Eur. Ct. H.R. (ser. A) (1987), Poiss v. Austria, 117 Eur. Ct. H.R. (ser A.) (1987), and Prötsch v. Austria, 1996-V Eur. Ct. H.R. 1812.

30 Bramelid and Malmström v. Sweden (1982) 5 Eur. H.R. Rep. 249, 256 (1982) (Commission Report).

31 See also Bäck v. Finland, Appl. No. 37598/97 (Eur. Ct. H.R. July 20, 2004), para. 53 and 60.

the cases has the State been expected to prove that the transfer of property actually produced an economic benefit.[32] Instead, it seems that it is enough that the State believed that the interference with property would have a positive impact on the economy (however that may be determined).

Plainly, the P1-1 public interest requirement, as interpreted by the Court of Human Rights, is very weak indeed. This is compounded by the tendency to subject the decisions of national authorities to a very low degree of scrutiny. This follows partly from the international character of the Court and the Convention: since the Convention was not intended to create a uniform set of national laws, or to require States to pursue similar social and economic policies, the Court has held that States have a "margin of appreciation" in relation to the setting and implementing national policies relating to property use and distribution.[33] For that reason, deference is especially high in relation to the public interest and programs relating to fairness, social justice and economic development. This also applies to the rationality of measures, as it often seems that it is enough for the State to claim that the taking of property was intended to serve a purpose that was in the public interest: it is not necessary to show that the taking actually served that purpose.[34] In *James*, for example, the Court did not subject the United Kingdom's claim that fairness justified the transfer of the freehold to tenants to any real scrutiny. It was enough that the fairness of the old system and the desirability of reform had been discussed by Parliament and the Government, and that they intended the Act to improve the system. Consequently, it would "respect the legislature's judgment as to what is 'in the public interest' unless that judgment be manifestly without reasonable foundation."[35] In *James*, it concluded that:

> The margin of appreciation is wide enough to cover legislation aimed at securing greater social justice in the sphere of people's homes, even where such legislation interferes with

---

32 In Lithgow v. United Kingdom, 102 Eur. Ct. H.R. (ser. A) (1986), para. 109, the applicants argued that an expropriation without compensation related to the actual value of the property could not be in the public interest. This was dismissed by the Court, but on the basis that the obligation to compensate could be derived from P1-1 as a whole; in other words, the Court did not consider the broader argument that some takings may be contrary to the public interest because they are economically inefficient. (In fairness to the Court, the shareholders did not seriously dispute the nationalization as such; it was only the amount of compensation that was important to them.)

33 See, e.g., *James*, 98 Eur. Ct. H.R. (ser. A); *Pincová*, 2002-VIII Eur. Ct. H.R.; *Zvolský*, 2002-IX Eur. Ct. H.R.

34 *Zvolský*, para. 68 (in justifying the interference with property, it was sufficient that the State "may have considered it necessary" in the interests of social justice. A clear example is provided by Mellacher v. Austria, 169 Eur. Ct. H.R. (ser. A) (1990), although it concerns rent controls rather than expropriation. Austria claimed that the rent controls served the public interest because they ensured that low-priced accommodation would be available; the landlords produced evidence that a sufficient quantity of reasonably-priced accommodation existed without controls. The Court rejected their evidence, solely on the basis that of a declaration contained in an "explanatory memorandum" produced by the Austrian Parliament that the legislation was necessary (at para. 47).

35 98 Eur. Ct. H.R. (ser. A), para. 46.

existing contractual relations between private parties *and confers no direct benefit on the State or the community at large.*[36]

It appears that the public interest requirement of P1-1, as interpreted by the Court of Human Rights, goes no further than the public use requirement of the Fifth Amendment.

While national courts must take the Court's case law into account,[37] the international context is plainly not relevant and so the margin of appreciation is not applied as such. However, the British courts have developed principles of judicial deference that are fairly close to those of the Court of Human Rights, especially in relation to the right to property. Consequently, it is unlikely that the national courts would find that a taking that is professed to further a public interest in economic development is incompatible with P1-1.[38] At least in this respect, the national courts are no more sympathetic to the individual owner than the Court of Human Rights, or the Supreme Court of the United States.

Compensation and the Purpose of the Taking

One aspect of the American debate concerns the relationship between compensation and the purpose of the taking, as perceptions of the justice and the potential for an abuse of power are affected by the extent of uncompensated losses and the surplus obtained by the taker.[39] In principle, these issues should also arise under P1-1. However, the second sentence of P1-1 does not mention compensation. This may seem to deny P1-1 of any significant substantive content (especially in the light of the interpretation of "public interest"), but the absence of any reference to compensation was no accident: the founding States of the Council of Europe found it impossible to reach agreement on a compensation entitlement.[40] However, in *Sporrong and Lönnroth v. Sweden*, the Court of Human Rights stated that an interference with property must strike a "fair balance" between "the demands of the general interest of the community and the requirements of the protection of the individual's fundamental rights."[41] In *James*, the Court stated that "compensation terms are material to the assessment whether a fair balance has been struck between the various interests at stake and, notably, whether or not a disproportionate burden

---

36 *Id.*, para. 47 (emphasis added).

37 Human Rights Act 1998, s. 2.

38 See, e.g., Wilson and others v. Secretary of State for Trade and Industry, [2004] 1 A.C. 816; Marcic v. Thames Water Utilities Ltd, [2004] 2 A.C. 42; R. (on the application of Alconbury Developments Ltd) v. Secretary of State for the Environment, Transport and the Regions, [2003] 2 A.C. 295; International Transport Roth GmbH v. Secretary of State for the Home Department, [2003] Q.B. 728 (C.A.).

39 For recent discussions, see Lee Anne Fennell, *Taking Eminent Domain Apart*, 2004 MICH. ST. L. REV. 957 (2004) and Charles E. Cohen, *Eminent Domain* after Kelo v. City of New London: *An Argument for Banning Economic Development Takings*, 29 Harv. J.L. & Pub. Pol'y 491, 536–43 (2006).

40 See ALLEN, PROPERTY, *supra* note 15, 13–22.

41 52 Eur. Ct. H.R. (ser. A) (1982), para. 69.

has been imposed on the person who has been deprived of his possessions."[42] It went on to say that "the taking of property without payment of an amount reasonably related to its value would normally constitute a disproportionate interference which could not be considered justifiable" under P1-1.[43]

This leads us to ask whether the Court's conception of "value" reflects the subjective value, to either the owner or the taker. Without much analysis, the Court has assumed that it is only the market value of the property that is relevant.[44] This may be surprising, given that the payment of compensation is supposed to balance the public interest against the interference with the individual's human rights interests, and the individual's interest under other Convention rights has a subjective element. For example, the State cannot justify an interference with freedom of expression on the basis only that an average or reasonable person would not have objected to it. In rare cases, it seems that the Court does allow some room to argue that the market value is not enough to strike a fair balance. One example is *Lallement v. France*,[45] where the applicant claimed that the compensation paid on the expropriation of part of his farm was inadequate because it became much less profitable to farm the remaining land. France argued that it should not be under a duty to compensate for the loss of profit, because the expropriating authority had offered to buy the entire farm at market value and the applicant only refused because he did not wish to move from the family home. The Court upheld the applicant's claim, and in doing so, it may have intended to say that the sentimental value of a home to its owner means that its loss should be treated differently, and more generously, than the loss of other property.[46]

Chassagnou v. France[47] provides another example. It concerned French laws which created communal hunting grounds by requiring owners of land below a certain size to transfer their hunting rights to approved hunting associations. While the owners became entitled to hunt on any land over which the association held hunting rights, they were also compelled to allow others to hunt on their own land.[48] France argued that the balance was fair, because the actual interference with the applicants'

---

42 *James*, 98 Eur. Ct. H.R. (ser. A), para. 36.

43 *Id.*

44 See ALLEN, PROPERTY, *supra* note 15, 131–9.

45 App. No. 46044/99 (Eur. Ct. H.R. April 11, 2002).

46 In *Lallement*, the value might not have been purely sentimental; for example, there may have been special adaptations for use of the applicant (or his family). However, judgment does not reveal anything further about the owner's desire to stay in the family home.

47 1999-III Eur. Ct. H.R. 21.

48 Under American takings law, this would probably be treated as taking, because the owners were permanently deprived of the right to exclude others from their land. Under P1-1, this was treated as a regulatory control on the use of the land because a deprivation of possessions is found only where there is an appropriation of the entire set of property rights (see ALLEN, PROPERTY, *supra* note 15, 86–93). Nevertheless, the content of the right is not radically different, because the substantive protection of P1-1 also applies to regulatory controls: they must be lawful, for a general interest (which in *James*, 98 Eur. Ct. H.R. (ser. A), was assimilated to the public interest), and most important, they must strike a fair balance between the public interest and the owner's fundamental rights.

land was slight[49] and, in any case, they were adequately compensated because they acquired the right to hunt on all of the local hunters' association's land.[50] However, the Court disagreed, because the applicants had ethical objections to hunting, which meant that the right to hunt on other land was worthless to them. As with *Lallement*, this case suggests that a subjective element – in this case the belief that hunting is wrong – should affect compensation and the balancing of interests.

There have also been faint suggestions that the purpose of the acquisition may support a claim based on the value to the taker. In *Motais de Narbonne v. France*,[51] a French municipality acquired property at fair market value for a land bank, for future development. After nineteen years, the former owner complained that the municipality still had no plans for the development of the land. The Court of Human Rights held that initial expropriation satisfied P1-1, but the failure to develop any plans for its use for such a protracted period violated it, and the municipality should have paid additional compensation to reflect the capital appreciation of the property over the period. The Court clearly believed that the municipality was engaging in a kind of speculation in land, and that it should not be permitted to retain that gain. Plainly, this is not the situation in *Kelo*, but there is still a suggestion that the value to the taker may be relevant in exceptional cases.

Although these cases suggest that there may be room to raise the compensation standard beyond the ordinary market value, they are not typical. If presented with a case on a situation similar to that of *Kelo*, the Court of Human Rights would probably reach the same conclusion as the Supreme Court. Indeed, it is unlikely that there would be any dissenting opinions on the issue, because the public interest would probably be described in terms of urban renewal and economic improvement. The transfer into private hands would be seen as a means of furthering the public interest; by the reasoning in *James*, it would follow that P1-1 would be satisfied.

Other Controls on the Use of Eminent Domain

As the preceding discussion demonstrates, the right to property in the United Kingdom does not provide British owners with better protection than American owners have under their constitutional law. Nevertheless, this has not provoked a similar degree of concern. Why is it that, in England, without a constitutional or international guarantee enforceable by the courts, the control of eminent domain seems to be less of a problem? In this section, we examine two aspects of English and European law that seem to avoid or ameliorate some potential abuses of eminent domain: the statutory rules on compensation, and the control on inter-governmental competition.

---

49 Hunting was only permitted for part of the year, and no closer than 150 meters from dwellings.

50 In addition, the Government claimed that the law allowed applicants to prevent hunting by enclosing their land or by acquiring enough additional land to be exempt from the law. However, the Court observed that these measures were not practical alternatives for the applicants, as they would have required considerable expense.

51 App. No. 48161/99 (Eur. Ct. H.R. July 2, 2002).

Compensation

British statutory law on compensation for expropriated land is more generous than P1-1 requires. In addition to the fair market value for the property, there is an obligation to make a "loss payment" in many cases. For owner-occupied homes, an additional amount of 10 percent of the value of the home is payable, subject to a minimum of £4,000 and a maximum of £40,000;[52] for businesses, the amount is 7.5 percent up to a maximum of £75,000.[53] A separate disturbance allowance is also payable where the compensation for the property is based on its existing use value (i.e. where the potential for enhancing the value by changing the use was ignored). In the case of a business that is forced to close as a result of the expropriation, the disturbance allowance takes the loss of goodwill into account.[54]

While Parliament remains free to authorize expropriation for less than market value compensation (subject to the constraints of P1-1),[55] the current system may explain why eminent domain is not as controversial as it is in the United States.[56] However, property owners are still left with uncompensated losses. Loss payments are calculated on a fixed scale and within a fixed range, and disturbance payments are not offered in every case.[57] For example, the local authority has the power to determine that a business should be extinguished rather than relocated, and to calculate the disturbance costs on that basis.[58] More generally, the objection that state power should not be used for private property is not met, as there is no rule that any part of the surplus should be paid over to the former owner. The American debate is not wholly about compensation for subjective loss, but also about the use of eminent domain by, or for the benefit of, private enterprises. This point is not addressed by the English statutory rules on compensation.

---

52 Land Compensation Act, 1973, ss. 29–30 (Eng.); Home Loss Payments (Prescribed Amounts) (England) Regulations 2006, S. I. 2006/ 1658, ¶ 2 (U.K.).

53 Land Compensation Act, s. 33A.

54 Land Compensation Act 1973, s. 38. There is also a duty to rehouse in cases of property occupied as a home in s. 39; s. 45 provides additional compensation for a disabled person.

55 See, e.g., *Lithgow*, 102 Eur. Ct. H.R.

56 Rob Imrie and Huw Thomas, *Law, Legal Struggles and Urban Regeneration: Rethinking the Relationships*, 34 Urban Studies 1401 (1997) (on the use of compulsory purchase in the Cardiff Bay development); Bob Sherwood, *Shadow Falls on Forgotten Face of Olympics: Many Businesses in the Designated Zone of the East End Have Not Been Offered Enough to Afford to Stay in the Area*, The Financial Times, June 5, 2006, 24; Martin Samuel, *What Paula Radcliffe Paused to do in the Streets of London, Bid Organisers are Doing to the Locals*, The Times (London), May 4, 2005, 64.

57 In addition, the Government recently rejected proposals for compensation on the basis of home-for-a-home valuations in areas where the market had been depressed relative to the rest of the country (i.e. where market value compensation would not provide sufficient funds to buy another house): see Allen, Property, *supra* note 15, 137–8.

58 For further examples, see Imrie & Thomas, *supra* note 56.

Controls over Inter-governmental Competition

It is still possible that the comparative generosity of compensation in the United Kingdom explains why expropriation raises fewer questions than in the United States. Nevertheless, it is worth pointing out that English public authorities are prevented from using cheap land assembly as a bargaining chip in negotiations with private businesses over decisions to locate (or relocate). This would rule out a transaction such as those discussed in notorious cases such as *Poletown Neighborhood Council v. City of Detroit*, where land that was assembled and prepared at a cost of over $200 million was sold to General Motors for about $8 million,[59] and *99 Cents Only Stores v. Lancaster Redevelopment Agency*, where land to be acquired by eminent domain at $3.8 million would have been resold for $1.[60] While *Poletown* was recently overruled,[61] and the taking in *99 Cents Only* was enjoined by the courts, the interesting point from a comparative perspective is that both cases turned on the scope of the public use requirement.[62] By contrast, in England, the legitimacy of this kind of taking would be framed differently, as explained in the next section. The section also shows that, in any case, there are unlikely to be significant tax benefits in the use of eminent domain powers as means of attracting or retaining businesses, or in the enhancement of land and property values in their areas. These have the cumulative effect of limiting the desirability, for both private developers and public authorities, of projects that would not be profitable without state support for cheap land assembly.

The Making and Confirmation of Compulsory Purchase Orders

In the United Kingdom, the power of compulsory purchase may only be granted by Parliament.[63] Local authorities have no independent power to acquire land. In the nineteenth century and earlier, compulsory purchase powers were ordinarily granted under private Acts of Parliament. The legislative process for considering private bills was quasi-judicial, and as a matter of practice it was necessary for the petitioner to demonstrate that the conferral of the power was in the public interest.[64] While the

---

59 410 Mich. 616, 304 N.W.2d 455 (Mich. 1981).

60 237 F. Supp. 2d 1123 (C.D. Cal. 2001), *appeal dismissed as moot*, 60 Fed. Appx. 123 (9th Cir. 2003).

61 County of Wayne v. Hathcock, 471 Mich. 445 684 N.W.2d 765 (Mich. 2004).

62 *Poletown* and *Hathcock, id.*, turned on the takings clause of the Michigan Constitution (Mich. Const. of 1963, art. 10, § 2: "Private property shall not be taken for public use without just compensation therefor being first made or secured in a manner prescribed by law. Compensation shall be determined in proceedings in a court of record.").

63 There may be some vestiges of the Royal Prerogative, but they are irrelevant in this context: see TOM ALLEN, THE RIGHT TO PROPERTY IN COMMONWEALTH CONSTITUTIONS (2000), 29–33.

64 RANDE KOSTAL, LAW AND ENGLISH RAILWAY CAPITALISM, 1825–1875, 112 (1994); see generally F.A. Mann, *Outlines of a History of Expropriation*, 75 L.Q.R. 188, 201 (1959); LAW COMMISSION OF ENGLAND AND WALES, TOWARDS A COMPULSORY PURCHASE CODE: (1) COMPENSATION, Law Com. No. 286, 8–9, 159–70 (2003); William B. Stoebuck, *A General Theory of Eminent Domain*, 47 WASH. L. REV. 553, 589–98 (1972).

public interest requirement was not examined or defined in any detail, it remained the case that its existence was not determined by local government, but by the central governing power.

Modern legislation provides local authorities with a broad range of powers for the compulsory acquisition of land for a variety of different purposes.[65] Private Acts are only used in exceptional circumstances: in the vast majority of cases, land is acquired under a compulsory purchase order ("CPO"). The process of obtaining a CPO begins with the making of the order by an "authorizing authority," which is normally the local authority. It must then be approved by a "confirming authority," and this is normally a designated minister of the government.[66] In most cases involving land development, it is the Deputy Prime Minister ("DPM"), in his or her capacity as First Secretary of State, who confirms the CPO. Objections may be made before confirmation, in which case a public inquiry may be called. The inquiry is chaired by a planning inspector appointed by the DPM. At the close of the inquiry, the inspector makes recommendations to the DPM, who may decide to confirm the order as it stands, or confirm it with modifications, or refuse confirmation. The local authority remains important in this process, as it is normally responsible for making the order, and in doing so it is accountable to the local electorate. However, the DPM (or other confirming authority) is not accountable to the local authority or the local electorate, but to Parliament and the national electorate.

The process makes it difficult to make an effective challenge in the courts based on public interest arguments. In essence, the property owner would need to show that the taking lay outside the scope of the statutory power. Since statutory powers are often drafted broadly, it would be difficult to show that this was the case. Indeed, section 226 of the Town and Country Planning Act 1990 authorizes local authorities to compulsorily acquire land for a project of development, re-development or improvement, so long as they believe that project would promote or improve the economic, social or environmental well-being of their area.[67] It is not necessary for the local authority to carry out the project: it may expropriate with the intention of transferring the land to a private developer.[68] Plainly, the breadth of section 226 makes it unlikely that a judicial challenge to a CPO would be successful. In practice, it would be more effective to direct the protest to the DPM at the point of confirmation (or to the planning inspector, if a public inquiry is called).

The breadth of section 226 does not mean that the public interest requirement is of no weight. Indeed, the scrutiny of the DPM may be quite close. The official guidance states that "[a] compulsory purchase order should only be made where there is a

---

65 See Office of the Deputy Prime Minister, Circular 06/04: Compulsory Purchase and The Crichel Down Rules (2004), 20–98 for a description of the most important powers relating to land acquisition (available at http://www.communities.gov.uk/embedded_object.asp?id=1162561).

66 Acquisition of Land Act 1981, c. 67 ss. 2, 7 (Eng.)

67 Town and Country Planning Act 1990, c. 8 s. 226(1) (1A). The acquisition in the Arsenal case was under s. 226 (see below).

68 Town and Country Planning Act 1990, s. 226(4) (Eng.).

compelling case in the public interest,"[69] and local authorities are expected to present a fairly detailed case for their confirmation. The "compelling case" rule goes beyond the relaxed public interest standard of P1-1. Moreover, the official guidance from the DPM advises local authorities that, where possible, they should rely on their specific powers instead of the general power, in the belief that this will force them to be more precise in specifying the reasons for acquisition.[70] Nevertheless, the choice of power could not be challenged in court: so long as the purpose of the CPO falls within the statutory power, it would not matter that there is a narrower power that would also authorize the taking. In any case, since the DPM's decision to confirm a CPO is often based on expert evidence of the impact of the project, a court would be reluctant to overturn it on the basis that the findings of fact were questionable or that the weight given to those facts was inappropriate.[71]

This is significant for two reasons. The first is that the DPM sees his role at least partly as the protection of individual property owners, as well as the protection of national interests in matters such as the preservation of heritage and environmental protection. This is a position that has evolved over time, and it is a matter of administrative practice rather than legislative command. Nevertheless, it is clear that property owners take the possibility of appeal seriously, as does the DPM.[72] For example, in relation to CPOs under section 226 of the Town and Country Planning Act 1990, the DPM has stated that factors relevant to the confirmation decision include, in addition to the "promotion or improvement of the economic, social or environmental wellbeing of the area," the degree of consultation with the local community, the financial viability of the project for which the land is acquired, and "whether the purpose for which the acquiring authority is proposing to acquire the land could be achieved by any other means."[73] While these factors are set in administrative policies, the failure to adhere to them would allow a court to set aside a decision by the DPM.[74]

---

69 OFFICE OF THE DEPUTY PRIME MINISTER, CIRCULAR 06/04: COMPULSORY PURCHASE AND THE CRICHEL DOWN RULES (2004), 7 (available at http://www.communities.gov.uk/embedded_object.asp?id=1162561).

70 *Id.*, 6.

71 See, e.g., Alliance Spring Co Ltd v. First Secretary of State, [2005] EWHC 18 (Admin).

72 See, e.g., "Residents Win Demolition Battle," BBC News Service, September 19, 2003 (available at http://news.bbc.co.uk/1/hi/england/lancashire/3123936.stm (last visited August 1, 2006) and Richard Girling, "Save Our Streets," SUNDAY TIMES MAGAZINE, September 19, 2004 http://www.timesonline.co.uk/newspaper/0,,2772-1251519_1,00.html (last visited August 1, 2006) (concerning the DPM's rejection of a CPO issued by Pendle Borough Council for the clearance of about 350 houses).

73 OFFICE OF THE DEPUTY PRIME MINISTER, CIRCULAR 06/2004, 23–4.

74 Although, as explained above, the courts would be reluctant to set aside a decision where it appeared that the DPM had at least considered arguments based on these factors, and the decision relied partly on expert evidence: see, e.g. *Alliance Spring, supra* note 71; London Borough of Bexley v. The Secretary of State for the Environments Transport and the Regions, Sainsburys' Supermarkets Limited v. The Secretary of State for the Environment, Transport

The second is the restriction on competition between local government. A recurring theme in the American use of eminent domain is the importance of competition, between municipalities and between states, for investment. This often puts private investors in a strong position to negotiate with local governments for concessions, especially in relation to land assembly. In the United Kingdom, the DPM is in a position to control this sort of negotiation.

This is demonstrated by the recent case involving the construction of a new stadium for the Arsenal Football Club. Toward the end of the 1990s, Arsenal decided that its stadium at Highbury, in the London Borough of Islington, was not large enough for its needs. Expansion on its existing site was not feasible. It considered relocating outside the borough, but reached an agreement with Islington to stay. Under the agreement, Islington sold Arsenal a substantial plot of land for the new stadium, but in exchange Arsenal agreed to construct housing and various amenities on the old site and on land surrounding the new stadium. Since some of the land covered by the plan was not owned by either Islington or Arsenal, Islington issued a CPO in June 2002 for its acquisition. The order was confirmed by the DPM, whose confirmation was upheld by the High Court in January 2005.[75]

The key point is that Islington conceded that the DPM's guidance meant that the CPO could not be made with the sole objective of persuading Arsenal to remain in the borough.[76] Instead, it argued that the stadium project provided an opportunity to regenerate an economically deprived area. As in *Kelo*, it was argued that compulsory powers should not be used for private profit; and, as in *Kelo*, the court held that the use of compulsion was legitimate where it was part of a larger plan that was in the public interest, even where a private party earns a substantial profit thereby. In the United Kingdom, this requirement has its source in policies set by the DPM, rather than rules developed by the courts.

As the CPO was confirmed, it may appear that there is little difference between the American and English approaches to these kinds of projects. However, the Islington-Arsenal agreement is much more balanced than some of the American agreements between local government and private investors, especially when compared with some of the American cases dealing with stadium construction.[77] While Islington

---

and the Regions, London Borough of Bexley, [2001] EWHC Admin 323; Tesco Stores Ltd v. Secretary of State for the Environment, Transport and the Regions, 80 P. & C.R. 427 (2000).

75 *Alliance Spring, supra*, note 71.

76 *Id.* at para. 17.

77 See Philip Weinberg, *Eminent Domain for Private Sports Stadiums: Fair Ball or Foul?* 35 ENVTL. L. 311 (2005); Peter Sepulveda, *The Use of The Eminent Domain Power in the Relocation of Sports Stadiums to Urban Areas: Is the Public Purpose Requirement Satisfied?* 11 SETON HALL J. SPORT L.137 (2001). A summary of the Islington-Arsenal agreement is available at www.islington.gov.uk/DownloadableDocuments/Environment/Pdf/section106finalterms.pdf (accessed July 28, 2006). As reported in *Alliance Spring*, at para. 5, Islington's CPO order stated that the development would include "a 60,000 capacity stadium, an education 'learning centre,' a replacement Arsenal Sports and Community Centre, a replacement waste and recycling centre, new and refurbished houses, new live-work units, new general business space, new shops, financial services and cafes/restaurants, new leisure space, two new gym/health clubs, two new nurseries, four new community health facilities

assembled the land for the project, Arsenal was still required to pay market value for it.[78] Arsenal also remained responsible for the construction works, and it did not receive any tax or other financial concessions to fund its construction. Clearly, Arsenal decided that the agreement worked to its benefit, and it made a considerable profit from the conversion of its old site.[79] However, while Islington worked hard to keep Arsenal from relocating to another borough, the control of the DPM limited the extent to which it could offer valuable concessions as an inducement to remain in the borough. This is the general pattern: local authorities are quite active in seeking to attract or retain investment in their areas, and competition between local governments is a part of British politics, but central administrative control limits the nature of competition.[80]

Dispositions of Land

The Islington-Arsenal transaction also raises a further point. In the case itself, no questions were asked about the initial sale of Islington's own land to Arsenal, but it would have been subject to the Council's obligations under section 123 of the Local Government Act 1972. This provision bars local authorities from disposing of land "for a consideration less than the best that can reasonably be obtained," unless they have the consent of the Secretary of State. The judicial interpretation of "consideration" is quite narrow. In *R. (on the application of Lemon Land Ltd) v. Hackney L.B.C.*,[81] Hackney London Borough Council indicated that it intended to accept the lower of two bids for land, on the basis that the low bidder's project would have created more jobs than the other bidder's project.[82] Nevertheless, the Court held that accepting the lower bid would violate the Act:

> Section 123(2) requires the Council to obtain the highest price that can be got for the land: less can only be accepted, however meritorious the reason for accepting less, if the Secretary of State accepts the political responsibility for the decision by giving his consent.[83]

---

and new publicly accessible open space of the land and new rights described in the Schedule hereto."

78 This is required under both national and European law, as explained in the next two sections.

79 £28.5 million in the 2004 and 2005 financial years (property sales are continuing): *see* ARSENAL HOLDINGS PLC, STATEMENT OF ACCOUNTS AND ANNUAL REPORT 2004/5, 7 (available at http://www.arsenal.com/userIncludes/docs/accounts2005.pdf).

80 See generally ALAN DEGAETANO AND JOHN S. KLEMANSKI, POWER AND CITY GOVERNANCE: COMPARATIVE PERSPECTIVES ON URBAN DEVELOPMENT (1999) (comparing political strategies of development in Birmingham, Boston, Bristol and Detroit).

81 [2001] EWHC Admin 336.

82 The low bid was for £1.65 million, and the proposed development would have created 322 jobs; the other bid was (ultimately) for £2.45 million but would have created between 160-200 jobs. Hackney argued that the value of the extra jobs outweighed the additional consideration.

83 [2001] EWHC Admin, para. 9; see also R. v. Pembrokeshire County Council ex p. Coker [1999] 4 All E.R. 1007.

By itself, without reference to the public interest or public use, this would rule out the transactions that were questioned in *Poletown Neighborhood Council v. City of Detroit*[84] and *99 Cents Only Stores v. Lancaster Redevelopment Agency*, where public authorities sold land to private companies for a fraction of their cost.[85]

The overall picture is clear: without the consent of the DPM, the powers of local authorities relating to the acquisition and disposition of land are quite narrow. The DPM is therefore in a position to protect property owners, to a greater extent than the courts. But why has Parliament taken the view that the DPM should have this power over local authorities? And why does the DPM take an active role in exercising this power, instead of merely rubber-stamping local authority proposals? That does not mean that it cannot be justified: indeed, it may be the case that successive governments have feared that a failure to control local authorities would lead to the kind of criticisms now heard in the United States regarding eminent domain. More generally, there have been long-standing concerns over the financial discipline of local authorities, especially since the election of Mrs. Thatcher's Conservative government. This applies more to controls on expenditure relating to the acquisition and disposal of assets, rather than the safeguarding of individual rights threatened by CPOs, but the effect is to control some of the excesses that have been so controversial in the United States.

The control over inter-governmental competition is reproduced under European law, in the form of controls on "state aids" that affect the common market. Under Article 87 of the EC Treaty, state aid comprises any aid granted by a State or from State resources that "distorts or threatens to distort competition by favouring certain undertakings or the production of certain goods" and affects trade between the Member States.[86] The European Commission has the power to require a State to recover or modify "state aid."[87]

These provisions have been applied to the sale of public land to a private company on favorable terms. For example, in 1991, the Commission decided that the sale of public land by the Derbyshire County Council to Toyota, for the construction of a new plant, was an improper state aid because the sale price of £18.3 million was below an independent valuation of £22.5 million.[88] The imbalance between the price and value of the land is plainly not as dramatic as it was in *Poletown*[89] or *99 Cents Only Stores*.[90] Indeed, the United Kingdom maintained that the transaction was not a state aid, because the price was the best that could be obtained, and hence Derbyshire had complied with section 123 of the Local Government Act 1972. Derbyshire claimed

---

84 304 N.W.2d 455.

85 237 F. Supp. 2d 1123.

86 *Id.*

87 Treaty Establishing the European Community, Nov. 10, 1997, arts. 87, 88, 1997 O.J. (C 340) 3.

88 Commission Decision of 31 July 1991(concerning aid provided by the Derbyshire County Council to Toyota Motor Corporation, an undertaking producing motor vehicles), [1992 O.J. (L 006) 36.] While the Commission accepted that there was no intent to undervalue the property, and that Toyota had not sought state aid, it held that Derbyshire had failed to undertake a sufficiently detailed valuation of the property.

89 304 N.W.2d 455.

90 237 F. Supp. 2d. 1123.

it hoped to break even on the deal and the best estimate of cost of its acquisition of the land by CPO was about £13.4 million. Nevertheless, the Commission ordered the United Kingdom to recover the £4.2 million undervalue on the sale from Toyota.[91] Plainly, the focus of the Derbyshire-Toyota case is different than in *Poletown* and *99 Cents Only Stores*: the legitimacy of aid is the question, rather than the purpose of the initial expropriation. However, the EC law prevents the kind of concessions to private enterprise that occur in cases like *Poletown* and *99 Cents Only Stores*. Moreover, it even discourages businesses from negotiating for these kind of concessions: in the Derbyshire-Toyota case, Toyota was required to return the amount of the undervalue, which may have left it with property that it might not have bought at the price that the Commission determined to be appropriate.

The focus on competition means that Article 87 does not operate as a substitute for a more rigorous public interest/public use requirement for expropriations. Moreover, there are several important loopholes and exemptions from Article 87. There is, for example, a requirement that the aid was granted directly by the State, or that it came from State resources.[92] A concession or exemption from ordinary regulatory laws does not constitute state aid unless it involves a transfer of state resources. This is not interpreted with rigidly – a tax exemption would constitute a state aid – but nonetheless there must be some kind of financial burden on the State.[93] For this reason, a grant of planning permission would not be treated as a state aid, even if it increases the value of land, because it involves no transfer of a state resource and represents no burden on the state treasury. For example, questions were recently asked about the city of Madrid's role in the financial recovery of the Real Madrid football team.[94] To help Real Madrid clear a substantial debt, the City granted it permission to change the use of a training ground to permit development, and then agreed to buy it from Real. With permission for the change of use, the land was worth considerably more than a training ground. This enabled Real Madrid to earn a substantial profit on the ground. The Commission concluded that, although Real Madrid plainly received a financial advantage as a result of the permission to develop the property, the grant of permission did not constitute the transfer of a financial resource. Accordingly, there was no question of a state aid.[95]

---

91 The Commission subsequently released an official communication, in which it stated that the sale of publicly held land or buildings should either by through an open bidding process, or at a price set by independent valuation; in addition, there could be no special conditions unique to the buyer. See Commission Communication on State aid elements in sales of land and buildings by public authorities, 1997 O.J. (C 209) 3.

92 There are also important exemptions for aid in support of the regeneration of economically depressed areas. See below note 121.

93 CONOR QUIGLEY AND ANTHONY COLLINS, EC STATE AID LAW AND POLICY (2003), 53–7 (taxation) and 26–48 (sources of state aid).

94 *See, Answer given by Mr Monti on behalf of the Commission to a Written Question by Pere Esteve and Camilo Nogueira Román*, 2003 O.J. (161 E) 57 (Jul. 10, 2003).

95 The purchase of the land by Madrid is, apparently, the subject of a separate investigation: *EU to Look Into Real Property Deal*, THE TIMES, March 4, 2004, 47. There is no record of a decision on this issue. One might question this approach, at least in the British context. The grant of planning permission is a direct conferral of a valuable right, since the

This suggests that a direct conferral of the power of compulsory acquisition on a private developer would be treated differently that the sale of land already held by a public body. As long as there is no financial burden on the State, Article 87 does not apply.[96] This, of course, makes it relatively easy to avoid the rules. Indeed, in the Derbyshire-Toyota case, the United Kingdom would have avoided the state aid rules if the power of compulsory acquisition had been conferred directly on Toyota. While Toyota would have been responsible for compensating the owners, there would have been no question of Article 87 applying because none of the State's financial resources would have been used. Indeed, Article 87 would have been avoided even if Toyota had been given the power to acquire property below its market value.[97] Again, Article 87 is not a substitute for a stronger public interest/public use requirement, although it seems to have the same effect in some cases.

The Incentive to Compete

A further factor to consider is the lack of financial pressure on local authorities. While local authorities still seek to attract or retain investment in their areas (as in the Derbyshire-Toyota case), the reasons for doing so are not as narrowly focused on fiscal considerations as they seem to be in the United States.[98] Local authorities in England have little financial incentive to use compulsory purchase (or other powers) to raise property values in their area, or to attract or retain businesses that produce value-added or other taxes. With the exception of the local council tax, taxes in England and Wales are set centrally.[99] The council tax itself is property-based, but the impact of increases in values on revenue is limited by national rules that ensure that the highest tax bills are no more than three times the lowest, regardless of the actual difference in the value of the property. In any case, the council tax produces

---

state has held the right to develop on land since 1947 (see below). Nevertheless, the decision that there was no state aid in Real Madrid's case suggests that the abstract right to develop land is not, by itself, a state resource. The situation would probably different if the British development charge had never been abolished, because the grant of an exemption from paying the charge would be state aid.

96 See Case C-379/98, Preussen Elektra AG v. Schleswag AG, 2001 ECR I-02099 (Price controls imposed to support the renewable energy industry did not constitute state aid, because state itself did not provide aid. The renewable energy industry received an economic advantage from the price controls, but at the cost of the third party purchaser rather than the state.) (*Preussen Elektra* was cited in support of the Commission decision on Real Madrid.)

97 Although, in that case, it is possible that P1-1 would be breached.

98 DeGaetano & Klemanski, Power and City Governance, *supra* note 80; for American examples, see Nicole Stelle Garnett, *The Public-Use Question as a Takings Problem*, 71 Geo. Wash. L. Rev. 934, 957–8 (2003).

99 For comparative reviews of local government taxation and revenue, see Tony Travers, International Comparisons of Local Government Finance: Propositions and Analysis (available at http://www.lyonsinquiry.org.uk/docs/051215%20research%20report%20travers.pdf) (last visited July 28, 2006); John Loughlin and Steve Martin with assistance from Suzannah Lux, Options for Reforming Local Government Funding to Increase Local Streams of Funding: International Comparisons (available at http://www.lyonsinquiry.org.uk/docs/051215%20research%20report%20cardiff.pdf) (last visited July 28, 2006).

a relatively small proportion of local authority revenue, as about 75 percent of their budget is obtained directly from the central government. In addition, a national system on revenue equalization "seeks to achieve a very high level of equality in services ... against a background of quite significant variation in needs and resources around the country."[100] While this protects each local authority from insolvency[101] and ensures that they can provide services that are at a level comparable to other authorities, it also reduces the incentive to increase council tax receipts by attracting or retaining investment.[102] At the same time, it gives the central Treasury a strong incentive to exercise control over local expenditure. If, for example, a local authority squandered valuable resources in an effort to attract business from a neighboring authority, the Treasury could find itself under a financial burden to make up any losses that occurred.[103]

The English systems therefore gives local authorities broad powers to take property, but leaves them without a fiscal incentive to do so, and in any case it subjects them to controls that limits their power to offer concessions or advantages to private developers. As explained below, there may be other financial incentives: in particular, there are substantial funds available for regeneration. However, these are specific programs, and the rules on distributing the funds are set up and administered

---

100 LYONS INQUIRY INTO LOCAL GOVERNMENT, CONSULTATION PAPER & INTERIM REPORT (2005), 78 (available at http://www.lyonsinquiry.org.uk/docs/051215%20interim%20report. pdf; TRAVERS, INTERNATIONAL COMPARISONS, *id.* at 3 ("European states, including the UK, differ from the United States in maintaining a commitment to similar levels of service across the national territory and in avoiding the "post-code lottery" *referring to* JULIA DARBY, ANTON MUSCATELLI AND GRAEME ROY, FISCAL FEDERALISM AND FISCAL AUTONOMY: LESSONS FOR THE UK FROM OTHER INDUSTRIALISED COUNTRIES (2002) (available at http://ideas.repec.org/p/gla/ glaewp/2002_12.html> (also noting the strict borrowing controls over local governments in the U.K.); LOUGHLIN & MARTIN, OPTIONS, *id.* at 29; MATTHEW GREEN AND ADAM MARSHALL, ECONOMIC DEVELOPMENT TOOLS – INTERNATIONAL COMPARISONS (2005) (available at http:// www.ippr.org.uk/uploadedFiles/cfc/research/projects/centre_for_cities/web_annex_3_ international_-comparisons.pdf) (last visited July 28, 2006).

101 GREEN & MARSHALL, ECONOMIC DEVELOPMENT, *supra* note 100.

102 See LYONS INQUIRY, CONSULTATION, *supra* note 100, 79: "The grant given to a local authority takes into account the business rates it receives and the amount of council tax it can collect locally. There is little financial gain for a local authority if the number of businesses or houses, or the population of its area increases, or if the success of the local economy or popularity of the area leads to an increase in the value of land and property in it. This means there is little financial incentive for authorities to promote economic development and provides no financial reward for creating a successful and prosperous area, or resources to help respond to residents' concerns."

103 Even at the national level, the incentive to increase land values is limited. While capital gains tax, inheritance tax and stamp duties on land transfers are linked to the value of land, but the potential increase in tax revenue does not appear to be significant enough to have a real impact on policy. In any case, compulsory purchase for resale to private investors would be a cumbersome way of realizing a gain from an increase in property values. It would generally be much easier to grant planning permission to change the use of agricultural land to industrial or residential land.

by the central authorities. The general picture remains one in which local authorities depend on central government.

While the controls on inter-governmental competition indirectly provide property holders with more protection than P1-1 in at least some circumstances, it would overstate matters to say that they resolve all the problems that are the subject of debate in the United States. In the United Kingdom, the threat of an abuse of power still exists. The Government's proposals for clearing large areas of a number of urban centers, on the grounds of "market failure" and "market renewal," have been very controversial.[104] In Newcastle upon Tyne, the local Labour council was voted out of office partly because its clearance plans were highly unpopular,[105] and criticisms of these programs are increasingly heard in the local and national media.[106] However, the debate on these issues is framed differently in the United Kingdom. The focus tends to fall on the planning system and urban regeneration programs generally, rather than the protection of individual rights or use of eminent domain for private profit. The next section considers two factors that contribute to this: the structure of the planning system, and the focus of urban regeneration programs.

The Planning System

In the United States, the focus on the debate on the public use requirement is squarely on eminent domain as a source of private profit. While the English rules on the public interest requirement are no stricter than the American rules, and the English rules on compensation go no further in terms of clawing back the surplus gained by the taker on the purchase, this point has not been as controversial. However, in the English system, it is often the grant of permission to develop land that has the most dramatic impact on land values, rather than the assembly of the land.

The modern planning system was created by the enactment of the Town and Country Planning Act 1947.[107] The Act nationalized the right to develop land and created a centralized system for authorizing development. Consequently, virtually any development that requires a CPO also requires planning permission. Most

---

104   The proposals were contained in OFFICE OF THE DEPUTY PRIME MINISTER, SUSTAINABLE COMMUNITIES: BUILDING FOR THE FUTURE (2003) (available at http://www.communities.gov.uk/index.asp?id=1139870). For criticisms, see, e.g., ANNE POWER, SUSTAINABLE COMMUNITIES AND SUSTAINABLE DEVELOPMENT: A REVIEW OF THE SUSTAINABLE COMMUNITIES PLAN (2004) (available at http://sticerd.lse.ac.uk/dps/case/CR/CASEreport23.pdf). Allan Cochrane, *Devolving the heartland: Making Up A New Social Policy for the "South East"* 26 CRITICAL SOCIAL POLICY 685, 691 (2006) ("With the exception of the Thames Gateway, where regeneration and development are combined, this programme clearly owes little to any concern for the inner cities or other traditional targets for urban policy" (references omitted).) Mike Raco, *Sustainable Development, Rolled-out Neoliberalism and Sustainable Communities*, 37 ANTIPODE 324 (2005).

105   "Lib Dems Scrap Demolition Plans," *supra* note 7.

106   See, e.g., "Residents Win Demolition Battle," *supra* note 72; Girling, "Save Our Streets," *supra* note 72; *MP Attacks House Demolition Plans*, BBC News Service, Feb. 16, 2006 (available at http://news.bbc.co.uk/1/hi/england/merseyside/4721370.stm.).

107   c. 51 (Eng.).

acquiring authorities wait until planning permission has been granted before making the CPO (or seeking confirmation). Indeed, it is likely that the DPM would refuse to confirm a CPO for a development that has not yet obtained planning permission.[108]

The importance of planning law means that it often overshadows the process of making or confirming the CPO. Since questions regarding the impact and public interest of the proposed development are normally examined in detail as part of the planning review, a grant of planning permission often resolves issues that might otherwise fall for consideration in relation to compulsory purchase. To be sure, the grant of planning approval does not mean that CPO in support of the development must be granted: when dealing with a CPO confirmation, the DPM asks both whether the overall scheme is desirable, and whether there is a case to justify the acquisition of private interests.[109] In practice, however, it seems that the grant of planning approval is usually conclusive, and the payment of compensation is seen as providing the property owner with the protection that it needs.[110]

By itself, this probably diverts some attention from the making and confirmation of the CPO.[111] It also diverts attention from the CPO because the enhancement of value to land does not occur primarily through the assembly of land, but through the grant of planning permission. Recent figures show that the average value of mixed use agricultural land in England was just over £7,000 per hectare,[112] but for residential "bulk" land it is £2.6 million per hectare.[113] Clearly, the grant of planning permission has a dramatic impact on land values. Of course, the assembly of land is also important, and the CPO is valuable as a means of avoiding holdouts. However, in practice, it seems that CPOs are not used to drive down prices but to ensure that timetables are met, and thereby to control the overall costs of the project.[114] Predictability of cost makes the scheme more attractive to potential suppliers of private finance. Accordingly, although land agents can be very aggressive in using

---

108 OFFICE OF THE DEPUTY PRIME MINISTER, CIRCULAR 06/2004, 8; see, e.g., Department for Transport, London Underground (Camden Town Station) Order, June 20, 2005 (available at http://www.dft.gov.uk/stellent/groups/dft_about/documents/page/dft_about_038374.hcsp).

109 *Id.*, 7.

110 See *Alliance Spring, supra* note 71, [2005] EWHC at para. 16: "In considering whether to confirm the CPO the Secretary of State has judged the desirability of the overall scheme not solely on the basis that there is a planning approval, but also whether there is a compelling case in the public interest to justify acquiring private interests. Whilst the fact that planning permission for the proposals has been granted does not automatically mean that the CPO should be confirmed, the Secretary of State is satisfied that the provisions of s. 226(1) and (2) have been met and that it is in the public interest that the development should proceed."

111 Or the loss to be made by the local authority, if the intention is to sell the land on at a loss (as in *Poletown, supra* note 59 (304 N.W.2d 455)).

112 Bare and with vacant possession.

113 VALUATION OFFICE AGENCY, PROPERTY MARKET REPORT JANUARY 2005 (2005) (http://www.voa.gov.uk/publications/property_market_report/pmr-jan-06/index.htm.) (last visited July 28, 2005).

114 Stanley McGreal, Alastair Adair, Jim Berry, Bill Deddis, and Suzanne Hirst, *Accessing Private Sector Finance in Urban Regeneration: Investor and Non-Investor Perspectives*, 17 J. OF PROPERTY RESEARCH 109 (2000).

CPOs to negotiate lower prices and force quick sales,[115] it seems that the private developers do not focus on CPOs or land assembly as a primary source of profit.[116] Consequently, the sense that the power of eminent domain is being abused, for the sake of private interests, is not as prevalent in the United Kingdom as it seems it is in the United States.

The Impact of Regeneration

CPOs are used extensively in England, and their use is often controversial, but middle class homeowners are rarely the target. The most extensive use of compulsory purchase is made in areas that would probably be characterized as slums or blighted areas in most American states.[117] In *Kelo*, the City of New London may have been experiencing economic decline, but the properties in question were not slums and were not in an area of blight. While eminent domain in Britain is sometimes used in such areas, and against middle class homeowners, there is certainly not the same threat to their security that American homeowners seem to fear. This removes one particularly vocal group from the political scene, both locally and nationally.

As explained above, the English system leaves local authorities with little or no financial incentive to raise land values through redevelopment, with or without private capital. In general, extensive redevelopment can proceed only with funding from central authorities. For example, slum clearance and reconstruction projects received central support of various kinds from the Victorian period and throughout the last century.[118] This continues to be the pattern, as it is primarily in relation to regeneration projects that we see a high degree of central support and an extensive use of the CPO. Under the most recent regeneration initiatives, about £2 billion is being channeled through regional development agencies.[119] Local authorities bid for

---

115   See, e.g., Imrie & Thomas, *supra* note 56, on the Cardiff Bay developments.

116   McGreal et al, *supra* note 114, 122–5.

117   Although some interpretations of statutory references to "blight" in the United States are very broad: see generally Colin Gordon, *Blighting the Way: Urban Renewal, Economic Development, and the Elusive Definition of Blight*, 31 FORDHAM URB. L.J. 305, 307 (2004) ("'blight' has lost any substantive meaning either as a description of urban conditions or as a target for public policy.") and Wendell E. Pritchett, *The "Public Menace" of Blight: Urban Renewal and the Private Uses of Eminent Domain*, 21 YALE L. & POL'Y REV. 1 (2003) ("Legislatures have created long lists of criteria that redevelopment agencies are required to use to determine whether an area is blighted. These criteria, however, remain vague and subject to broad interpretation by redevelopment authorities, to which courts have granted great deference.").

118   See generally ENGLISH, MADIGAN & NORMAN, SLUM CLEARANCE, *supra* note 4; J.A. YELLING, SLUMS AND REDEVELOPMENT: POLICY AND PRACTICE IN ENGLAND, 1918–45, WITH PARTICULAR REFERENCE TO LONDON (1992); J.A. YELLING, SLUMS AND SLUM CLEARANCE IN VICTORIAN LONDON (1986).

119   See generally Department of Trade and Industry (U.K.), Regional Development Agencies, http://www.dti.gov.uk/regional/regional-dev-agencies/index.html (last visited July 31, 2006).

regeneration funds, usually in partnership with other local or regional authorities.[120] The scheme is designed with the European rules on state aids in mind, and in recognition of the availability of exemptions for regeneration aid. The Commission has adopted a system for identifying "assisted areas," where states may implement regional support schemes.[121] Separate exemptions are also available for aid given in deprived urban areas.[122] Clearly, it is unlikely that these exemptions would be available in areas of mid-value homes, and the national scheme is only targeted at poorer areas.

This, by itself, affects the debate in Britain. Many of the residents of areas of regeneration are unlikely to protest as vociferously as middle-class homeowners. Indeed, in many areas, many of them are regarded as marginal or virtually invisible populations.[123] Moreover, their protests do not always focus on the rights of property owners, since many of them are tenants or family members of tenants. Where there is a concern over the destructive aspects of regeneration, the real question is not the fairness of expropriating the minority of owner-occupiers, but the effect on the community as a whole.

In any case, many clearance schemes have received local support. However, this is often due to the perception that clearance provides opportunities, particularly

---

120 Indeed, some of the larger schemes have bypassed local authorities altogether. In the 1980s and 1990s, the Conservative government set up "urban development corporations" to manage regeneration. These corporations were run by appointed (i.e. unelected) boards, and were given substantial budgets and powers over planning and compulsory purchase. They were frequently criticized for failing to consult with local populations and local (elected) authorities, and, as they focused on engaging private business in redevelopment, some of the criticisms raised concerns that appear on the American scene: see, e.g., PATSY HEALEY, SIMIN DAVOUDI, SOLMAZ TAVSANOGLU, MO O'TOOLE, AND DAVID USHER, REBUILDING THE CITY: PROPERTY-LED URBAN REGENERATION (1992). (*See also* Mark Kleinman, *Include Me Out? The New Politics of Place and Poverty*, 21 POLICY STUDIES 49 (2000) and Stuart Cameron, *Gentrification, Housing Redifferentiation and Urban Regeneration: 'Going for Growth' in NewcastleUpon Tyne*, 40 URBAN STUDIES 2367, 2373 (2003) on parallels with current U.K. policies and earlier American blight and poverty policies.) In that sense, local bodies do compete for investment capital, but the competition is for public investment rather than private. That is not to say that relationships between local bodies and private investors are not important, as the strength of a bid for regeneration funds depends partly on the degree of involvement of private investors.

121 See QUIGLEY & COLLINS, EC STATE AID, *supra* note 93, 125–44.

122 *Id.* at 151–5.

123 Richard Cowell and Huw Thomas, *Managing Nature and Narratives of Dispossession: Reclaiming Territory in Cardiff Bay*, 39 URBAN STUDIES 1241 (2002); Stuart Cameron, *Gentrification, Housing Redifferentiation and Urban Regeneration: 'Going for Growth' in NewcastleUpon Tyne*, 40 URBAN STUDIES 2367, 2372 (2003); POWER, SUSTAINABLE COMMUNITIES, *supra* note 104, at 21; SOCIAL EXCLUSION UNIT, A NEW COMMITMENT TO NEIGHBOURHOOD RENEWAL: NATIONAL STRATEGY ACTION PLAN (2001), 5 ("Seventy per cent of ethnic minority citizens in the United Kingdom live in the 88 most deprived local authority wards"). This point has attracted (some) attention in the media: see, e.g., Save our Homes (available at http://www.theasiannews.co.uk/news/s/191/191605_save_our_homes.html) (first published Feb. 25, 2005) ("ASIAN and white residents in Oldham have branded a council plan to demolish their terraced homes to make away for new housing as 'ethnic cleansing.'").

for those outside regeneration areas. Programs often concentrate on "improving" the social mix of the inhabitants.[124] This becomes apparent with the regeneration solutions that are put forward for the most deprived areas, as they concentrate on making them attractive to a different class of owners and occupiers. This, it seems, can only be achieved by clearing the area and dispersing the current residents.[125]

Current policy in the United Kingdom focuses on the demand for housing in the area, as shown by vacancy rates and housing prices. This is taken as proof of market failure, and hence a need for intervention to achieve a market renewal.[126] However, it is not really explained why demolition and reconstruction provide a more cost-effective means of market "renewal" than other regeneration programs,[127] but it clearly represents the most emphatic possible statement that the social factors that made the old neighborhood unattractive to many potential buyers have been addressed. For example, the new developments generally offer very little housing that the former residents could afford. While some housing is designated as affordable social housing, there is unlikely to be enough to re-house anything more than a

---

124 Cowell & Thomas, *supra* note 123, and Cameron, *supra* note 123. This has received (some) attention in the national media; see, e.g., *MP Attacks House Demolition Plans*, *supra* note 106 (reporting that "Jane Kennedy, the Labour MP for Wavertree, said: 'It breaks my heart that people are being pushed out because they don't fit the mould of the kind of residents the council wants to bring into this area.'")

125 In some of the areas to be cleared, it has been said that the housing stock is old and no longer suits the current demand, but this does not explain why the market would fail to correct any such deficiencies. In Liverpool, for example, it is said that there is an over-supply of terraced housing. Whether this is a cause or effect of decline is unclear: it might be said that much of the housing built before World War II was designed for a different way of life, and yet it is not the case that older housing is generally undesirable. In neighborhoods that are not suffering economically, older houses often command a premium over newer houses. See generally POWER, SUSTAINABLE COMMUNITIES, *supra* note 104 at 21, 22 (value of heritage); ODPM: HOUSING, PLANNING, LOCAL GOVERNMENT AND THE REGIONS COMMITTEE, EMPTY HOMES AND LOW DEMAND PATHFINDERS, 2004–5, HC 295-I, 10–11; Office of the Deputy Prime Minister, The Government's Response to the ODPM: Housing, Planning, Local Government and the Regions Select Committee's Eighth Report on Empty Homes and Low Demand Pathfinders, 2005, Cm. 6651, 6–7.

126 See OFFICE OF THE DEPUTY PRIME MINISTER, SUSTAINABLE COMMUNITIES, *supra* note 104; *see also* OFFICE OF THE DEPUTY PRIME MINISTER, HOUSING MARKET ASSESSMENT MANUAL (2004) <http://odpm.gov.uk/embedded_object.asp?id=1140536>, which goes into considerable depth in advising local authorities on the identification of areas of low demand, but suggests that they rely almost entirely on surveys of housing demand; "low demand" is not lack of potential buyers, but the lack of right kind of buyer. (The web site of the Office of the Deputy Prime Minister states that "[a]lthough this report was commissioned by the Office, the findings and recommendations are those of the authors and do not necessarily represent the views of the Office of the Deputy Prime Minister." The authors are not named.) The emphasis on "market failure" is also seen in the European rules on state aids: *see* EUROPEAN COMMISSION, STATE AID CONTROL AND REGENERATION OF DEPRIVED URBAN AREAS: VADEMECUM (2006), 1, 5–6.

127 POWER, SUSTAINABLE COMMUNITIES, *supra* note 104, at 12 (the cost of demolition has not been fully considered).

fraction of the existing residents.[128] With clearance, there is certainly no effort to save the community, as the residents are dispersed as a result of the redevelopment. The emphasis lies on re-integrating the area with the rest of the urban geography, rather than the re-integration of the people and community that live in the area.[129] Plainly, this can threaten those who live within the area, and hence there is a growing emphasis on consultation with local residents. However, there is no threat to the middle-class homeowner who lives outside these areas.

Conclusions

Many American commentators share a belief that eminent domain is being used excessively, and in a manner that treats some citizens quite unfairly and others very generously. While England does have a fundamental right to property, with a public interest requirement, it does no more to protect owners from an abuse of power than the takings clause in the United States. Yet this has not been a cause for concern, at least to the same extent as it is in America. This is not to say that there is no debate in England: CPOs are frequently challenged, and large-scale clearance projects are often the topic of discussion in the local and national media. However, the focus is not usually on the distinction between the public interest in takings and the private profit that it seems to produce.

From the American point of view, the English "solution" for controlling the abuse of eminent domain would not fit within its constitutional structure, as it would involve stripping local and state authorities of much of their power in favor of federal institutions.[130] This leads to the Supreme Court and federal takings law, but the *Kelo* judgment indicates that it is unlikely to provide a real control. In England, the acceptance of central control over compulsory purchase fits easily with the strong public expectation that public services should be provided at an equal level throughout the country.[131] This carries over to all issues relating to land use, as questions of planning, economic regeneration, and the protection of heritage and the environment are perceived to have a strong national aspect. However, the English system has virtually eliminated both the power and the incentive for local authority competition, without considering how it may produce benefits in some situations.

---

128 For example, in the development of the new Arsenal football stadium, only 25 percent of the new housing units were to be designated as affordable housing. [BBC News,] "Poor People Skills Threaten Urban Renewal" Tues BBC News Tuesday, 8, March, 2005 http://news.bbc.co.uk/1/hi/programmes/file_on_4/4327431.stm: "The managing director of Liverpool's New Heartlands project, Pauline Davies, said: 'This isn't a housing renewal programme, it is a market renewal programme.'"

129 Cowell & Thomas, *supra* note 123, at 1252, point out that the regeneration of Cardiff Bay, and its Butetown area, was sold partly on the basis that it would make the community of Butetown "safe for respectable Cardiff."

130 Local, in this sense, includes both municipal/county bodies as well as the states themselves.

131 See Travers, International Comparisons, *supra* note 100 and Darby, Muscatelli and Roy, Fiscal Federalism, *supra* note 100.

By contrast, in the United States, efforts to find any effective means of controlling it have failed, with the consequent problem that intrusions on the right to property have become more difficult to control.

Chapter 6

Federalism and Localism in *Kelo* and *San Remo*

Marc R. Poirier[1]

Introduction: An Emerging Account of Property, Regulation and Reviewing Courts

In 2005 the United States Supreme Court rendered three opinions that, taken together, offer an ever more coherent account of the Fifth Amendment's Takings Clause. They present an integrated concept of the interaction of private property expectations, government actions affecting private property, and the review of those government actions by the state and federal courts. This newly reasserted account is an alternative to the nearly absolute property rights account so copiously expressed in academic and political writings of the past two decades, and evident in the opinions of certain Justices, notably Justice Scalia.[2] One important aspect of this emerging coherent account is a species of functional federalism, and by the same token a concern for localism in state and local decisions about land use, natural resources and environmental externalities.[3] These themes of federalism and localism will be

1   The author thanks Ben Barros, Mark Fenster, Rachel Godsil, Robin Paul Malloy and Charles Sullivan for providing helpful suggestions on a draft of this chapter. He appreciates his thoughtful conversations with Ahmed Bulbulia, Rachel Godsil, Ed Hartnett, Louise Halper and Larry Solan. He also thanks research assistants John Devendorf and Michelle Ghali for their able assistance.

2   See Laura S. Underkuffler, Tahoe's *Requiem: The Death of the Scalian View of Property and Justice*, 21 CONST'L COMMENTARY 727 (2004) (describing a Scalian view of property and analyzing its demise in the analysis of the majority opinion in *Tahoe-Sierra Preservation. Council v. Tahoe Reg'l Planning Agency*, 535 U.S. 302 (2002)). See also Joseph William Singer, *The Ownership Society and Takings of Property: Castles, Investments, and Just Obligations*, 30 HARV. ENVT'L L. REV. 309 (2006) (outlining two ownership models of property, one the lord of the castle, the other the manager of investment property, and arguing that the Court in *Lingle v. Chevron U.S.A. Inc.*, 544 U.S. 528 (2005), has rejected them in favor of a third model of property that incorporates social obligations). Foremost among the many academic and practitioner exponents of a nearly absolute view of property is Richard Epstein. See, e.g., RICHARD A. EPSTEIN, TAKINGS: PRIVATE PROPERTY AND THE POWER OF EMINENT DOMAIN (1985).

3   We must set aside federal control of federal lands and of property or property-like interests specifically delegated to Congress by the Constitution, such as navigable waters, copyrights and patents. These are different matters. See Melvin R. Durchslag, *Forgotten Federalism: The*

the focus of this chapter, with special emphasis on *Kelo v. City of New London*[4] and on one aspect of *San Remo Hotel v. City and County of San Francisco.*[5] *Lingle v. Chevron U.S.A. Inc.*[6] marks a different, although equally important, part of this emerging account; but an exploration of *Lingle* is beyond the scope of this chapter.[7] Suffice it to say here that in all three 2005 Takings Clause cases, a resolution of a Takings Clause claim in federal court is rebuffed, leaving the private property owners and those in similar situations to state and local administrative and legislative processes and state courts.

The Supreme Court's federalism and localism expressed in *Kelo* may be undermined in Congress. Congress cannot displace the Court's interpretation of "public use" as a matter of constitutional interpretation, of course. But it may be able to use its authority under the Spending Clause to impose restrictions on state and local uses of eminent domain, and thus implement the "use by the public" interpretation which was advocated by the losing petitioners in *Kelo*. And Congress can certainly restrict the federal government's own uses of eminent domain. It has

---

Takings Clause and Local Land Use Decisions, 59 MD. L. REV. 464, 465 n.7 (2000) (outlining types and sources of federal and state, as opposed to local, land use regulation).

    4   Kelo v. City of New London, 545 U.S. 469 (2005) (interpreting the "public use" phrase of the Takings Clause broadly to allow various public purposes for eminent domain as determined by state law; and refusing to impose a heightened standard of judicial review on state and local government determinations of the public benefits of the use of eminent domain).

    5   San Remo Hotel v. City and County of San Francisco, 545 U.S. 323, 339 (2005) (discussing Williamson County Regional Planning Comm'n v. Hamilton Bank, 473 U.S. 172 (1985) and reaffirming the validity of the *Williamson County* requirement that has applied takings compensation claims against state and local governments must be litigated first in state rather than federal court); but see *id.* at 340 (Rehnquist, J., concurring) (suggesting that this part of *Williamson County* "may have been mistaken").

    6   Lingle v. Chevron U.S.A. Inc., 544 U.S. 528 (2005).

    7   *Lingle* clarifies regulatory takings doctrine by holding that one of the tests for regulatory takings articulated in *Agins v. City of Tiburon*, 447 U.S. 255 (1980) – whether a challenged government action "substantially advances a legitimate state interest" – is not properly part of a challenge to regulation under the Takings Clause after all. *Lingle*, 544 U.S. at 540–45 (clarifying Agins v. City of Tiburon, 477 U.S. 255, 260 (1980)). (I say that *Lingle* "clarifies" rather than "overrules" the *Agins* test because *Lingle* also holds that this test was always only dictum and was never applied by the Supreme Court. Some lower courts were misled. *Lingle* at 545–48.) In so doing *Lingle* eliminates what appeared to be a federal doctrinal hook for Takings Clause claims. The practical consequence of the holding in *Lingle* is to steer challenges to state and local land use and environmental regulation even more straightforwardly into state legal and administrative remedies. *Lingle* also provides a foundational explanation of the difference between the purpose of the Takings Clause – to protect property owners from undue loss – and substantive due process review, which polices the means/end fit in challenges to legislation and regulation. *Id.* at 536–40. See, e.g., D. Benjamin Barros, *At Last, Some Clarity: The Potential Long-Term Impact of* Lingle v. Chevron *and the Separation of Takings and Substantive Due Process*, 69 ALB. L. REV. 343, 344 (2005) (*Lingle* "has tremendous potential to clarify takings doctrine").

already done so for one funding cycle.[8] Potentially much more important, in 2005 the House of Representatives passed a Private Property Rights Protection Act.[9] If some such bill were enacted into law, it would prohibit a state or a political subdivision of a state from using eminent domain for economic development in any fiscal year in which it receives federal economic development funds.[10] The prohibition would also kick in if condemned property is at any subsequent time used for economic development.[11] The penalty for violating this prohibition is draconian: the loss of two years of federal funding for economic development.[12] This Act would create a private right of action in federal or state court, and would waive (or attempt to waive) the states' Eleventh Amendment immunity from suit in federal court.[13] Attorneys fees, court costs and expert costs would be available to a prevailing plaintiff.[14] When an eminent domain action is challenged, the governmental entity would have to prove by clear and convincing evidence that the condemnation was not for economic development.[15] This last provision reverses a longstanding approach to burdens of proof and standards of judicial review where socioeconomic legislation is concerned.

---

8   Pub. L. No. 109–115 Sec. 726 (2005), an appropriations act, limits the use of any fund authorized in it for eminent domain only to "public use" narrowly defined. (Condemnations are allowed for use by the public, common carriers, public utilities and brownfields remediation, and for the immediate removal of threats to public health and safety.) This act also provides for a twelve month study of state-by-state approaches to "public use", to be done by the General Accountability Office working with property rights advocates. President Bush also recently issued an Executive Order commanding federal agencies to apply the "use by the public test" when exercising eminent domain. Exec. Order No. 13, 406 (June 23, 2006), 71 Fed. Reg. 36,973 (June 28, 2006). The Order is riddled with exceptions and deals principally with agencies that are almost never involved in the kind of local land use issues at stake in *Kelo*, so it is for practical purposes likely to be meaningless. Yet it is symbolic of the ongoing political marketability of public fear of the abuse of eminent domain power.

9   Private Property Rights Protection Act of 2005, H.R. 4128, 109th Cong. (2005).

10   H.R. 4128, 109th Cong. Sec. 2(a) (2005).

11   H.R. 4128, 109th Cong. Sec. 2(a) (2005). The same prohibition would apply to federal government condemnations. H.R. 4128, 109th Cong Sec. 3 (2005).

12   H.R. 4128, 109th Cong. Sec. 2(b) (2005). The governmental entity is given an opportunity to cure by returning all condemned property, replacing all property destroyed, and paying any other damages. H.R. 4128, 109th Cong. Sec. 2(c) (2005). "Economic development" is defined in the bill as "taking private property … and conveying or leasing [it] … to another private person or entity for commercial enterprise carried on for profit, or to increase tax revenue, tax base, employment, or general economic health … " H.R. 4128, 109th Cong. Sec. 8(1) (2005). Exceptions similar to those in the already-enacted appropriations bill would apply. H.R. 4128, 109th Cong. Secs. 8 (1)(A)-(F) (2005). "Economic development funds" are defined as "any funds distributed to or through States or political subdivisions of States under Federal laws designed to improve or increase the size of the economies of states or of political subdivisions of States." H.R. 4128, 109th Cong. Sec. 8(2) (2005). The bill does not specify what funds those are.

13   H.R. 4128, 109th Cong. Sec. 4(a) (2005).

14   H.R. 4128, 109th Cong. Sec. 4(c) (2005).

15   H.R. 4128, 109th Cong. Sec. 4(a) (2005).

It also reverses *Kelo*'s specific holding on the proper standard for judicial review of "public use" determinations.

The ongoing possibility that similar legislation will be introduced at the behest of property rights advocates makes it important as a practical matter to appreciate and defend the federalism and localism in *Kelo*, *San Remo* and *Lingle*. To be sure, these opinions sound themes of judicial restraint vis-à-vis legislatures generally.[16] At this juncture however, it is most important to emphasize federalism in the direction of localism. This will help us to justify allowing states to address individually the post-*Kelo* political furor over eminent domain abuse. It may help to dissuade Congress from imposing on the states a "one-size-fits-all" constraint, one that would interpret "public use" in a way that reins in state and local governments' options to address eminent domain abuse, and that might cripple states and local governments that have depended on eminent domain as one of the tools available to manage urban decline. Exploring federalism and localism in the 2005 Takings Clause decisions will illuminate the relationship between the substantive provisions of local land use and environmental law and appropriate jurisdiction over regulation, in terms of local knowledge, local norms and local political and governmental processes. To those of us with a theoretical bent, the 2005 account also provides support for the general contention that property rights are best understood as always evolving and negotiated, so that we must incorporate social relations into our understanding of property. Here, in particular, as to land use as well as many natural resource and environmental concerns, the jurisdictional focus is properly local and regional because of the scale of the interests at issue; and this localism is achieved through functional federalism.

Kelo also reproduces a strategy of deference to state and local governmental processes that was deployed recently in *Tahoe-Sierra* and *Palazzolo*. Justice O'Connor's concurring opinion in *Palazzolo v. Rhode Island,* construing the majority opinion, rejected the temptation to establish a bright line rule protecting property owners' expectations, much to the dismay of her colleague, Justice Scalia.[17]

---

16 A recent article by Mark Fenster also analyzes the 2005 Takings Clause cases as a set which contains a unified approach to property and regulation. He proposes to understand the Court's new account in terms of Hart and Sacks' legal process theory. Mark Fenster, *The Takings Clause, Version 2005: The Legal Process of Constitutional Property Rights*, 9 U. PA. J. CONST. L. 667 (2006) (discussing legal process theory, as reflected in HENRY M. HART, JR. & ALBERT M. SACKS, THE LEGAL PROCESS (William N. Eskridge, Jr. & Philip P. Frickey eds., 1994), as the source of the understanding of the Takings Clause that is emerging in the 2005 cases). Fenster explores a federalism analysis of the underlying approach, but finds it "incomplete." While I do agree with Fenster that the three 2005 cases are about property and legal process, I suspect that Fenster means something slightly different and narrower by federalism than I do. There are plenty of different meanings of the term to go around. To me, for the reasons explored herein, federalism and localism are the more important themes. And based on a conversation with Fenster, he sees my focus on localism as squarely encompassed within his focus on institutionalism and legal process. We are not really in disagreement.

17 Palazzolo v. Rhode Island, 533 U.S. 606, 616–19 (2001) (O'Connor, J., concurring) (clarifying that it may sometimes but not always be relevant to a regulatory takings claim that a law or regulation was enacted prior to a property owner's acquisition of property, in

Tahoe-Sierra Preservation Agency v. Tahoe Regional Planning Agency similarly
rejected various bright-line arguments, based on *Lucas*, as applied to the temporary
takings claim at issue in that case. *Kelo* does the same. All three of these opinions
– *Kelo*, *Palazzolo* and *Tahoe-Sierra* – reject a substantive bright line rule offered
by property rights advocates to constrain government actions affecting property as
a matter of federal constitutional law. In so doing, these decisions leave these and
similar challenges to be resolved in state judicial and administrative fora.[18] Resorting
to constitutional balancing tests that are implemented by the states and involve
assessments of state and local law and circumstance is, as Stewart Sterk has recently
argued, in and of itself a form of federalism in takings doctrine,[19] another argument
explored more fully in the discussion below.

What We Might Mean by Federalism and Localism

Federalism is "such a big topic, one can't possibly hope to grasp more than a small
part of the beast."[20] Fortunately, many aspects of it are not especially relevant to
the elements I wish to emphasize here. Let us first boldly set aside all arguments
about how the Constitution categorically restricts the powers of Congress, or of state
legislatures, or of impositions that Congress might make on states. Let us set aside
discussions of whether those restrictions are or ought to be judicially enforceable.

---

terms of legitimate expectations); cf. *Palazzolo*, 533 U.S. at 619–20 (Scalia, J., concurring)
(vehemently disagreeing with Justice O'Connor's expressed view on the meaning of the
Court's opinion and insisting on a bright-line rule about expectations). Justice Stevens in
Tahoe-Sierra incorporated approvingly Justice O'Connor's concurrence in *Palazzolo*. Tahoe-
Sierra Preservation Council v. Tahoe Reg'l Planning Agency, 535 U.S. 302, 336–7 (citing and
quoting *Palazzolo*, 533 U.S. at, 616–19 (2001) (O'Connor, J., concurring)).

18 *Kelo* allowed challenged condemnations for economic development to go forward;
these had been initiated and reviewed by local and state legislative bodies and when challenged
were reviewed by the trial court and the highest court of the state. *Tahoe-Sierra* allowed a
temporary moratorium on development imposed by a bi-state regional agency for a specific
duration; the moratorium was intended to facilitate the agency's deliberation on how best to
protect a valuable natural resource, Lake Tahoe. *Palazzolo*, after striking a per se rule holding
that the state could always and unilaterally change subsequent owners' property expectations
by changing the legal rule, remanded to the state courts. There the Rhode Island Superior
Court upheld the permit denial after all, both on the basis of a background principle of state
law – as a public nuisance affecting water quality, the state could ban the development – and
through the application of the *Penn Central* ad hoc balancing test. Palazzolo v. State, 2005
WL 1645974, 4–5 (R.I. Super. 2005) (finding the development would be a public nuisance
because of its effects on water quality, and applying the background principles test of *Lucas v.
South Carolina Coastal Council*, 505 U.S. 1003 (1992)); *id.* at 8–14 (applying the three factors
of the ad hoc balancing test articulated in *Penn Central Transp. Co. v. New York City*, 438
U.S. 104, 124 (1978)); cf. Erin Ryan, Palazzolo, *The Public Trust, and the Property Owner's
Reasonable Expectations: Takings and the South Carolina Marsh Island Bridge Debate*, 15
SOUTHEASTERN ENVT'L L.J. 121 (2006).

19 Stewart E. Sterk, *The Federalist Dimension of Regulatory Takings Jurisprudence*, 114
YALE L.J. 203, 243–51 (2004).

20 Larry Kramer, *Understanding Federalism*, 47 VAND. L. REV. 1485, 1485 (1994).

With the important exception of *Williamson County* and its consequences, let us eschew procedural aspects of federal rights such as standing, implied rights of action, abstention and attorneys fees. Let us set aside almost all aspects of the parity debate, that is, whether federal rights of citizens, or more broadly defined "rights of belonging," ought to be enforceable in federal court.[21]

Where both eminent domain and regulatory takings are concerned, I am more interested in what I shall call "permissive federalism." That is, even though a federal institution might be able to impose a uniform rule on the states, it chooses not to do so. In the event of *Kelo*, the institution was the United States Supreme Court. (Post-*Kelo* it might be Congress.) If one were to make a distinction between formal (constitutional) and functional issues of federalism,[22] I am most interested here in pragmatic, functional arguments about fairness and levels of governance. Frank Michelman's articulation of the federalism within *Lucas*, taking off from Justice Black's "Our Federalism" in *Younger v. Harris*, provides a fair approximation:

> "Our Federalism" names a certain disposition on the part of federal judges regarding their dealings with state law and state courts. It encompasses three related concerns: (i) a concern to keep clear the demarcations between federal law and state law, and between federal and state adjudicative provinces; (ii) a concern to maintain within the federal judiciary a deportment of respect for the competence and responsibility of the state judiciaries; and (iii) a more general concern to maintain within the federal judiciary a posture of judicial restraint.[23]

---

21 Some classic considerations of parity include Erwin Chemerinsky, *Parity Reconsidered: Defining a Role for the Federal Judiciary*, 36 UCLA L. REV. 233 (1988); Burt Neuborne, *Toward Procedural Parity in Constitutional Litigation*, 22 WM. & MARY. L. REV. 725 (1981); Burt Neuborne, *The Myth of Parity*, 90 HARV. L. REV. 1105 (1977). Recent important entries include Denise C. Morgan & Rebecca E. Zietlow, *The New Parity Debate: Congress and Rights of Belonging*, 73 U. CINN. L. REV. 1347 (2005), and the essays in AWAKENING FROM THE DREAM: CIVIL RIGHTS UNDER SIEGE AND THE NEW STRUGGLE FOR EQUAL JUSTICE (Denise C. Morgan, Rachel D. Godsil & Joy Moses eds., 2006).

22 This distinction is articulated in Edward Rubin, *The Myth of Accountability and the Anti-Administrative Impulse*, 103 MICH. L. REV. 2073, 2084 (2003) (footnotes omitted) ("Arguments for federalism can be either formal, that is, based on an interpretation of the Constitution, or functional, that is, based on pragmatic considerations that emerge from concerns about fair or effective governance.")

23 Frank I. Michelman, *Property, Federalism, and Jurisprudence: A Comment on Lucas and Judicial Conservatism*, 35 WM. & MARY L. REV. 301, 303 (1993) (referring to *Younger v. Harris*, 401 U.S. 37, 44 (1971) and analyzing *Lucas v. South Carolina Coastal Council*, 505 U.S. 1003 (1992)). In *Younger v. Harris*, Justice Black wrote that "Our Federalism" requires neither blind deference to the states nor centralization of control of every important issue in the federal government. It is rather a system in which there is "sensitivity to the legitimate interests of both state and National Governments, and in which the National Government, anxious though it may be to vindicate and protect federal rights and federalism interests, always endeavors to do so in ways that will not unduly interfere with the legitimate activities of the States" 401 U.S. at 44.

Others concerned with federalism, localism and the Takings Clause also move directly to functional issues within federalism.[24]

In a different (but helpful and not dissimilar) context, Anuj Desai catalogs the values inherent in federalism.[25] One is geographic diversity. This justifies variation among jurisdictions in order to adapt law to local conditions, as well as to different citizen preferences and perhaps to different moral or ethic norms. At times I will refer to this rationale as involving local knowledge. A dynamic version of the geographic diversity justification assumes that citizens may move from one jurisdiction to another as a means of expressing their preferences. Experimentation is a second rationale. States try out different legal and policy solutions to address an issue, and then adopt approaches from other states that have proved themselves. The classic Supreme Court expression of this rationale is Justice Brandeis' dissent in *New State Ice Co. v. Liebemann*:

> There must be power in the States and the Nation to remould, through experimentation, our economic practices and institutions to meet changing social and economic needs. ... It is one of the happy incidents of the federal system that a single courageous State may, if its citizens choose, serve as a laboratory; and try novel social and economic experiments without risk to the rest of the country.[26]

Evidently, the process of experimentation is also inherently dynamic. A third federalism rational sometimes invoked is communitarian – the idea is that smaller communities are tighter and foster a better sense of belonging. A related but distinct rational is the idea that political participation is easier in a smaller jurisdiction rather than a larger one, at least for the average citizen. Information is better, costs are less. There are also arguments that federalism prevents the abuse of power, by diffusing sovereignty.[27]

Concerning localism, I am likewise not interested here in formal legal arguments about how states may be constrained by their state constitutions vis-à-vis local

---

24 See, e.g., Durchslag, *supra* note 2, at 490–91.

25 Anuj C. Desai, *Filters and Federalism: Public Library Internet Access, Local Control, and the Federal Spending Power*, 7 U. PA. J. CONST. L. 1 (2004). Desai argues that it would have been best to allow local governments – here public libraries – to reach varying accommodations between internet filters and concerns about exposure of patrons to internet pornography. Instead the field of argument was polarized between two one-size-fits-all solutions – a First Amendment prohibition on filters altogether, and a Congressionally mandated (via the spending clause) imposition of filters.

26 New State Ice Co. v. Liebemann, 285 U.S. 262, 311 (1932) (Brandeis, J., dissenting) (footnotes omitted).

27 Desai, *supra* note 24, at 48–55. Similar catalogs can be found in Matthew D. Adler & Seth F. Kreimer, *The New Etiquette of Federalism*: New York, Printz, and Yeskey, 1998 SUP. CT. REV. 71, 77–82; and Erwin Chemerinsky, *The Values of Federalism*, 47 FLA. L. REV. 499 (1995). Desai goes on to articulate some of the principal counterarguments to these justifications for federalism. States acting on their own may impose externalities on others. Interstate competition can lead to a race to the bottom. Federalism can lead to inefficiencies for actors in multiple jurisdictions. Desai, *supra* note 24, at 55–57.

governmental entities, or vice versa.[28] As with federalism, I am interested in the functional virtues and vices of local government control vis-à-vis higher levels of governmental decision making. These could be both state and federal. Important themes again include the facilitation of citizen participation at a local level; greater awareness of and responsiveness to local conditions (in terms of resources available, congestion and other externality issues, public welfare, pre-existing expectations of the citizenry, and the potential for or evidence of government abuse); an ability to experiment; a consequent ability to compete for residents along the model developed by Charles Tiebout; and an ability practically to handle a large number of low-level disputes.[29] Some of these themes are identical in their general nature to those made for functional justifications of federalism. At the same time, differences in scale may indicate important differences between local and state level governments or even between different types of local government.[30]

Edward Rubin and Malcolm Feeley argue that many persuasive policy reasons advanced under federalism are in fact about the advantages of decentralization, which they view as an entirely different matter.[31] Policy arguments often made in the

---

28 See generally Richard Briffault, *Our Localism, Part I – The Structure of Local Government Law*, 90 COLUM. L. REV. 1 (1990). To a very great extent localism is not formally required, but appears as the result of a kind of "permissive localism" through state delegation of important powers and a willingness to allow local governments to exercise those powers. Richard Briffault, *Our Localism, Part II – Localism and Legal Theory*, 90 COLUM. L. REV. 346, 354 (1990) (local power "emerg[es] out of the standard state practices of delegating revenue-raising, regulatory and expenditure authority to localities and of not interfering with the local exercise of that authority" (footnote omitted)) [*hereinafter* Briffault, *Our Localism, Part II*].

29 Several of these themes are developed in Carol Rose's writings. See, e.g., Carol M. Rose, *Takings, Federalism, Norms*, 105 YALE L.J. 1121 (1996) (reviewing WILLIAM A. FISCHEL, REGULATORY TAKINGS: LAW, ECONOMICS, AND POLITICS (1995)) [*hereinafter* Rose, *Takings, Federalism*]; Carol M. Rose, *The Ancient Constitution vs. The Federalist Empire: Anti-Federalism from the Attack on "Monarchism" to Modern Localism*, 84 NW. L. REV. 74 (1989); Carol M. Rose, *Planning and Dealing: Piecemeal Land Controls and Problems of Local Legitimacy*, 71 CAL. L. REV. 837 (1983).

30 See, e.g., Briffault, *Our Localism, Part II, supra* note 27, at 354 (1990) (examining the consequences on the functions of localism of difference in scale and function between city and suburb); Todd E. Pettys, *The Mobility Paradox*, 92 GEO. L. J. 384 (2004) (arguing that as the scale of the regulatory jurisdiction increases the costs of exit increase, so that the salutary effect of Tiebout competition diminishes); Rose, *Takings, Federalism, supra* note 28 (challenging Fischel's assertion that political process defects are more likely to occur at the local level than at the state and federal levels, and also asserting that opportunities for local participation in political processes are greater at the local level).

31 Edward L. Rubin & Malcolm Feeley, *Federalism: Some Notes on a National Neurosis*, 41 UCLA L. REV. 903, 914 (1994). "Decentralization is a managerial concept; it refers to the delegation of centralized authority to subordinate units of either a geographic or a functional character." *Id.* at 910. "Subsidiarity" is also occasionally invoked to encompass generally the same idea. See, e.g., Jared Bayer, *Re-Balancing State and Federal Power: Toward a Political Principle of Subsidiarity in the United States*, 53 AM. U. L. REV. 1421 (2004). Federalism, in contrast, is "a structuring principle for the system as a whole." Rubin & Feeley, *supra*, at 911.

name of federalism, but that Rubin and Feeley contend are really about the benefits of decentralization, include enhanced public participation, providing citizen choice through competition among jurisdictions, achieving economic efficiency through competition among jurisdictions, and encouraging experimentation.[32] It is by now a familiar list.

The Court in *Kelo* and *San Remo* uses the vocabulary of federalism, of respect for state and local governmental approaches to property rights and land use disputes, in the service of decentralization. Generally speaking, in practice the two overlap: "[s]tates fulfill the important governmental function of facilitating decentralization ... "[33] Differences in analytical terminology do not undermine what I view as important to say here about the 2005 decisions – that the 2005 cases direct the supervision of property and land use processes away from inflexible federal standards and away from federal courts to state and local fora and processes, which can then apply both federal and state law, in light of local knowledge, often under balancing tests. Further exploration of conceptual and terminological distinctions around federalism, localism, decentralization and subsidiarity are beyond the scope of this chapter.

Federalism and Localism in *Kelo*

Kelo v. City of New London[34] is easily read as a decision about the relative institutional competence of courts and legislatures. It reiterates the principle, well-established in *post-Lochner* jurisprudence, that the role of the courts should be limited when reviewing socioeconomic decisions of legislatures.[35] Two passages from *Kelo* also directly evidence federalism and localism concerns. In one key passage, which concludes the majority opinion's review of precedent on the meaning of "public use," Justice Stevens writes:

> Viewed as a whole, our jurisprudence has recognized that the needs of society have varied between different parts of the Nation, just as they have evolved over time in

---

32 Rubin & Feeley, *supra* note 30, at 914–26 (1994). *But cf.* Roderick M. Hills, Jr., *Is Federalism Good for Localism? The Localist Case for Federal Regimes*, 21 J. L. & POL. 187 (2005) (arguing that decentralization is indeed valuable, but that federalism is the best governmental structure for achieving it).

33 Rubin & Feeley, *supra* note 30, at 908.

34 *Kelo*, 545 U.S. 469 (2005).

35 In introducing its review of precedent the Court refers to a "longstanding policy of deference to legislative judgments" in determining public purpose. It parses *Berman v. Parker*, 348 U.S. 26 (1954), *Hawaii Housing Authority v. Midkiff*, 467 U.S. 229 (1984), and *Ruckelshaus v. Monsanto Co.*, 467 U.S. 986 (1984), in this light. *Kelo*, 545 U.S. at 462–83. In a subsequent section of the opinion, in which the Court rejects petitioners' argument that the Court must require "reasonable certainty" that the anticipated public benefits will actually materialize, the Court again turns to this rationale for rejecting heightened review. *Id.* at 487–8 (quoting *Midkiff*, 467 U.S. at 242). It rejects a demand to scrutinize closely which parcels are required for the project in similar language. *Id.*, at 488–9 (quoting *Berman*, 348 U.S. at 35–6). And it also cites to *Lingle*'s rejection of the "substantially advances" test as improperly importing the wrong level of judicial supervision of legislative judgments. *Id.* at 488.

response to changed circumstances. Our earliest cases in particular embodied a strong theme of federalism, emphasizing the "great respect" that we owe to state legislatures and state courts in discerning local public needs. For more than a century, our public use jurisprudence has wisely eschewed rigid formulas and intrusive scrutiny in favor of affording legislatures broad latitude in determining what public needs justify the use of the takings power.[36]

This passage reflects four correlated themes. The first is one of judicial deference. In this passage in particular, it might appear from the third sentence standing alone that the Court means deference of the judiciary to legislative judgments.

Notably, however, in the above-quoted paragraph deference is not articulated in terms of the institutional capacities of the coordinate branches. It is articulated in the context of a recognition that "the needs of society have varied between different parts of the nation" and that state governments must "discern[] local public needs." In other words, the Supreme Court's historic deference ("eschew[ing] rigid formulas and intrusive scrutiny") is explicitly linked here to localism, as manifested through the freedom that federalism gives to the states (and if the states allow it, to localities) to respond to different geographic and historic circumstances and to "discern[] local public needs." Earlier in its account, the Court also flagged this theme of localism, explaining that a rigid "use by the public" test, applied by many state courts in the mid-19th century, "proved to be impractical given the diverse and always evolving needs of society."[37] So localism is the second theme of the quoted passage. It is a separate reason for Supreme Court deference in applying the "public use" provision to local land use decisions involving private property.

Third, it is significant that the second sentence of this passage addresses the whole state governmental process – "state legislatures and state courts" – as governmental processes capable of discerning local public needs and traditionally meriting deference. Thus, the passage suggests an active role for state courts, presumably in disciplining state and local legislative and administrative processes through judicial review on constitutional and statutory bases.

Fourth, the Court describes its past jurisprudence as deferential to states in two ways. One is by avoiding "intrusive scrutiny," and can be linked to the first theme, judicial deference in socioeconomic matters. The other is by avoiding "rigid formulas." Rigid formulas imposed by the United States Supreme Court presumably could too much constrain state governmental processes. As discussed further below, one can parse constitutional balancing tests – especially in the property area – as a way of relegating the primary responsibility to state governmental processes. One can also conclude that, by its reference to flexibility, the Court understands dialogue and flexibility among the coordinate branches of state government to be necessary to allow state governmental processes to address local public needs which might require the exercise of eminent domain in different geographical and cultural circumstances and as times change.

---

36 *Kelo*, 545 U.S. at 482–3 (footnote and citations omitted).

37 *Id.* at 479 (footnote omitted). This passage links localism to the fourth theme I will identify, avoidance of rigid tests in order to facilitate flexibility.

The next section of the *Kelo* majority opinion, applying the precedent summarized to the New London case at hand, casts the Court's rejection of the petitioners' proposed bright line precisely in terms of deference to state and local processes.[38] "Public use" as "use by the public" is held to be the wrong test because it is too rigid. The Court of course agrees throughout its opinion that eminent domain may not be used to transfer private property from citizen A to citizen B for the sole purpose that citizen B will put it to more productive use.[39] But the Court distinguishes the situation here. The New London condemnations involve a usual exercise of government power in developing and applying an integrated development plan, not an "unusual" and "suspicious" exercise of governmental power over private real estate.[40] No restrictive categorical test is appropriate, for we are looking at the ordinary workings of local governmental power.

Justice Kennedy's concurrence is quite explicit on a related point. He rejects the need for delineating any narrowly drawn category of eminent domain actions that might merit heightened scrutiny, given the nature of the government processes established by the facts here.[41] Justice Kennedy also specifically relies on the scrutiny of local government processes that was provided in the proceedings below by the trial court and the Connecticut Supreme Court.

The other passage from *Kelo* that I wish to examine is found at the conclusion of the majority opinion. It is about the political aftermath of *Kelo*. It gestures broadly to state responsibility and opportunity to address the public's concerns about governmental abuse of eminent domain:

> We emphasize that nothing in our opinion precludes any state from placing further restrictions on its exercise of the takings power. Indeed, many states already impose "public use" requirements that are stricter than the federal baseline. Some of these requirements have been established as a matter of state constitutional law, while others are expressed in state eminent domain statutes that carefully limit the grounds upon which takings may be exercised. As the submissions of the parties and their amici make clear, the necessity and wisdom of using eminent domain to promote economic development are certainly matters of legitimate public debate.[42]

Essentially, this passage points out that as a result of the Court's hewing to prior precedent in *Kelo*, the federal Constitution establishes a very tolerant "baseline" for "public use." But states are free to impose a more stringent standard if they wish, or to address the underlying concern for governmental abuse of eminent domain in other ways. If states do not like the result in *Kelo*, they may adjust restrictions on eminent domain at the state level. Moreover, both state legislatures and state courts may be

---

38 *Id.* at 483–4 (The City's determination is "entitled to our deference," " [g]iven the comprehensive character of the plan, the thorough deliberation that preceded its adoption, and the limited scope of our review … ").

39 *Id.* at 477–8, 486–7.

40 *Id.* at 487 ("an unusual exercise of government power would certainly raise a suspicion that a private purpose was afoot").

41 *Id.* at 490–93 (Kennedy, J., concurring). Justice Kennedy of course joined the majority opinion at its fifth vote, but also added "further observations." *Id.* at 490.

42 *Id.* at 489.

involved in this response. (I read the opinion's reference to "state constitutional law" to include state court interpretations of state constitutional provisions, as well as the possibility of amending a state's constitution.) This passage expresses three of the four correlated themes we found in the earlier passage: (1) federal judicial restraint; (3) involvement of all parts of the state governmental process; and (4) rejection of bright-line rules imposed as a matter of federal constitutional law. Moreover, its federalism may well be informed by (2) localism, insofar as much of the "public debate" is expected to occur state by state in light of local conditions and political preferences.

Justice Stevens stood by this formulation when, soon after *Kelo* came down, he spoke to the Clark County (Nevada) Bar Association. He indicated that he did not agree necessarily as a policy matter with the latitude afforded condemnation in the *Kelo* decision's reading of "public use," though it was consistent with precedent; but that state and local governmental processes could respond to *Kelo* appropriately at the state level.[43]

Some of the early public use precedents relied on by the *Kelo* majority themselves express a considerable deference to state legislative and judicial processes. To be sure, they are informed by the localism of a different era, and as pre-New Deal cases derive from a different understanding of the roles of state and federal governments and of the place of the federal constitution and the federal courts in constraining states.[44] And they inevitably reflect the political and theoretical push-and-pull of their times.[45] So it would be easy to put too much weight on them standing alone. But the Court's references to them in *Kelo* undeniably play up their federalism and localism. And the themes are relevant to early twenty-first century fights over private property and government constraint every bit as much as to the late nineteenth and early twentieth conceptions of the relative role of state and federal judiciaries in implementing constitutional restrictions on eminent domain.

Clark v. Nash is the most interesting of the cases *Kelo* cites. It involved a Utah statute permitting condemnation by an individual for the purpose of transporting water across another's land to his land for irrigation or for mining. The United States Supreme Court said that while this justification might not be a permissible public use in most states, this conclusion would "depend upon a number of considerations

---

43   Hon. John Paul Stevens, *Judicial Predilections*, 6 NEV. L.J. 1, 3–4 (2005) (address to the Clark County Bar Association on August 18, 2005); see also Linda Greenhouse, *Justice Weighs Desire v. Duty (Duty Prevails)*, N.Y. TIMES, Aug. 25, 2005, at A1.

44   See, e.g., Bradley C. Karkkainen, *The Police Power Revisited: Phantom Incorporation and the Roots of the Takings Muddle*, 90 MINN. L. REV. 826, 835 (2006) (arguing that until the mid-twentieth century the federal constitutional constraint on states was understood to be the Fourteenth Amendment's Due Process clause, not the Fifth Amendment's Takings Clause selectively incorporated).

45   See Eric R. Claeys, *Public Use Limitations and Natural Property Rights*, 2004 MICH. ST. L. REV. 877, 905–908 (discussing the emergence of a "public usefulness" interpretation of "public use" as the result of Progressive and Legal Realist movements). See generally RICHARD A. EPSTEIN, HOW PROGRESSIVES REWROTE THE CONSTITUTION (2006).

relating to the situation of the State ... "[46] The Court specifically mentioned soil and climate as well as economic conditions. These factors might make a valid public use what would otherwise be an invalid private use.[47] Institutionally, the Court wrote, "we are always, where it can fairly be done, strongly inclined to hold with the state courts, when they uphold a state statute providing for such condemnation."[48] It then elaborated on the theme of local knowledge:

> Those facts must be general, notorious and acknowledged in the State, and the state courts may be assumed to be exceptionally familiar with them. They are not the subject of judicial investigation as to their existence, but the local courts know and appreciate them. They know and understand the situation which led to the demand for the enactment of the statute, and they also appreciate the results upon the growth and prosperity of the State ... This court has stated that what is a public use may frequently and largely depend upon the facts surrounding the subject, and we have said that the people of a State, as also its courts, must in the nature of things be more familiar with such facts ... than can any one be who is a stranger to the soil of the State, and that such knowledge and familiarity must have their due weight with the state courts.[49]

What a rich passage! It presents a variation of the same four correlated themes as in *Kelo*. First, *Clark v. Nash* expresses federal judicial restraint and deference. Second, this deference is justified in the name of localism.[50] Here the localism is explicitly about local geographic conditions and economic conditions, as well as about deference to local governmental processes. Third, the deference is accorded to state courts as well as state legislatures. Indeed, state courts are portrayed as at the top of the power and policy pyramid, policing the state legislature. Fourth, the Supreme Court has eschewed general rules that might apply in most of the country out of deference to local governmental processes that reflect local circumstances.

The localism here runs deep. It is local knowledge of both the natural resources and of how they play out in the economy of the state. Moreover, instead of doing the fact-finding and policy making, the Court presumes that those with links to the state – its people and its courts – will be more familiar with the crucial and particular facts than outsiders. Thus, federal court deference is justified in terms not just of respect for coordinate state structures but of respect for the local knowledge that normally will be reflected in the workings of those structures but not of a judicial reviewer foreign to it.

Two further points about *Clark v. Nash*. The United States Supreme Court does indicate some reserved authority to deal with the unusual situation that does not merit deference, for it calls for deference to state courts "where it can fairly be done." Moreover, it recognizes that differences in local conditions may affect

---

46 Clark v. Nash, 198 U.S. 361, 367 (1905).

47 *Id.* at 368.

48 *Id.*

49 *Id.* at 368–9 (citation omitted).

50 The case precedes *West Coast Hotel v. Parrish*, 300 U.S. 379 (1937), and *United States v. Carolene Prod. Co.*, 304 U.S. 144 (1938), by some three decades. We see deference expressed in *Clark* as that of the federal judiciary to the state legislative and judicial process, not as general deference of the judicial branch to the legislature.

various aspects of a state's property and natural resource law, making it different from that of sister states elsewhere in the country. The principle is not limited just to public use determinations. The Court notes that the arid western states altered eastern water law to suit their own circumstances, thereby treating notions of private and public differently with respect to this natural resource.[51]

Strickley v. Highland Boy Gold Mining Co.,[52] also relied on in *Kelo*, was handed down the year after *Clark v. Nash*. *Strickley* relied on *Clark*. The issue in *Strickley*, also coming out of Utah, was whether a mining company could under state law condemn a right of way for an aerial tram to gets its ore to railroads in the valley, or whether that was a prohibited private use of the eminent domain authority. The Court stated in *Strickley* that *Clark* acknowledged "the inadequacy of 'use by the general public' as a universal test." It recognized that "there might be exceptional times and places in which the very foundations of public welfare could not be laid without requiring concessions from individuals to each other upon due compensation which under other circumstances would be left wholly to voluntary consent." The Fourteenth Amendment did not prevent a state from requiring such a concession of the basic rights of private property, so long as the state court allowed it. It was "a local affair."[53] Ultimately it was up to the legislature and the Supreme Court of Utah to determine the public welfare of the state.

We see once again (1) federal court deference (2) in the name of local conditions and knowledge (3) as expressed by a state governmental process involving both the legislature and ultimately the state courts, such that (4) a general federal constitutional rule was unnecessary. Other early public use decisions cited by the Court in *Kelo* in support of the first passage quoted above are similar and need not be explored at length. These include *Hairston v. Danville & Western Ry. Co.*[54] and *O'Neill v. Leamer*.[55]

Elsewhere in *Kelo* the Court cites an early leading public use case, *Fallbrook Irrigation Dist. v. Bradley*. This case involved a challenge to California's irrigation laws where property was to be forfeited for non-payment of assessments. The United States Supreme Court inquired into whether the irrigation law was for public use, as part of its inquiry into whether the owner was deprived of property without due process of law. It indicated that this determination depended on local circumstances, such as aridity, and that "declarations and acts and decision of the people and

---

51 It is not clear to me what the Court's precise point is beyond this. Perhaps the Court means that the state, having privatized water ownership, has a more plausible argument that privatizing the eminent domain power to compel access to water is still a public use in some broad sense. There is no other way to conceptualize a specific party's right to access to water located elsewhere in a prior appropriation state except as a private right, yet access to water is still important to the public as a whole.

52 Strickley v. Highland Boy Gold Mining Co., 200 U.S. 527 (1906).

53 *Id.* at 531.

54 Hairston v. Danville & Western Ry. Co., 208 U.S. 598 (1908) (affirming a condemnation of land for a railroad spur based on deference to the courts of Virginia as to public use, given local conditions).

55 O'Neill v. Leamer, 239 U.S. 244 (1915) (affirming a Nebraska scheme for drainage districts, including eminent domain authority, based on local conditions and with deference to the state court's involvement in the scheme).

legislature and courts of California" while not determinative, would be accorded "very great respect."[56] *Kelo* also relies on *Dayton Gold & Silver Mining Co. v. Seawell*,[57] a state case which upheld condemnation of a strip of land to enable a mine to do business as a public use in light of the resources and economic conditions of the State of Nevada in the 1870s.[58] So these precedents also demonstrate the four intertwined themes I have outlined.

Kelo's result also demonstrates another aspect of federalism, one that is inherent in current regulatory takings doctrine as parsed by Stewart Sterk. To be sure, Sterk acknowledges that the Supreme Court has deployed categorical rules in regulatory takings to address several problematic cross-cutting issues; but these rules can then be applied by state courts without further interference from the federal courts.[59] But Sterk argues that the substantive balancing tests that are most often applied to resolve regulatory takings challenges systematically leave stand the decisions made by state courts on review of state and local government actions, and essentially defer to their understanding of all the local factors involved.[60] Sterk points out that the Court has never accepted certiorari of a case where a state court found a regulatory taking under *Penn Central*'s analysis. In such cases, the Court effectively defers to the state court's disciplining of state or local government actions. In contrast, where the Court has agreed to consider regulatory takings challenges to state and local regulations on the merits, it either finds *Penn Central* satisfied, effectively deferring to the past state court determination; or it remands for further consideration, deferring to a future state court determination.[61]

Kelo too expresses a deference to local legislative and judicial processes. The state Supreme Court approved of New London's proposed condemnations as part of a legitimately public development plan, one that fit within the state provisions for such activity as well as state and federal constitutional provisions.[62] In not overruling the state court's federal constitutional determination, the United States Supreme Court allowed the remainder of the decision, implementing Connecticut state land use and local government law and policy, to stand.[63]

---

56 Fallbrook Irrigation Dist. v. Bradley, 164 U.S. 112, 159–160 (1896).

57 Dayton Gold & Silver Mining Co. v. Seawell, 11 Nev. 394 (1876).

58 *Id.*

59 Sterk, *supra* note 18, at 243–51. Sterk discerns five categorical rules, some of them addressing procedure, standard of review or remedy. They include: requiring money damages as the remedy for regulatory takings; requiring a showing of rough proportionality in the exactions context; requiring compensation for the loss of all economically valuable use due to regulation; requiring compensation for permanent physical occupation; and barring any per se rule that a post-acquisition change in law automatically vitiates a takings claim due to altered expectations by property owners. *Id.* at 243–4.

60 *Id.* at 251–4.

61 *Id.* at 251–2.

62 Kelo v. City of New London, 843 A.2d 500 (Conn. 2004), *aff'd*, 545 U.S. 469 (2005).

63 The public use precedents of *Berman v. Parker*, 348 U.S. 26 (1954) and *Midkiff* are not so straightforward examples of federal deference to state judicial review as Sterk's claims for regulatory takings precedents are. I believe the comparison still stands, however.

Support for applying Sterk's thesis to public use also comes from two studies of the state and federal courts' application of the public use doctrine to invalidate exercises of eminent domain. These show that state courts have, occasionally, found attempts to use eminent domain out of bounds. Thomas Merrill's classic analysis of public use challenges to eminent domain actions found that while federal courts had never overturned condemnation based on the public use restriction in the period from 1954–1985, state courts did, from time to time, at the rate of about one in six.[64] A follow-up study for 1986–2003 confirmed that a minority of state courts have invalidated state and local condemnations as not involving public use, at about the same rate.[65] To me the significant fact here is that there continues to be a recognizable minority of state appellate courts that *do* enforce the public use doctrine as a constraint. In judicial review of administrative agency action, agencies win most of the time. In judicial review of state and local government action pursuant to a public use clause, I do not see why our expectations should be any different. The fact is, occasionally state supreme courts do and have reversed legislative actions as violations of the public use constraint in state or federal law. As Merrill observed, "[S]tate courts are much less deferential to legislative declarations of public use than one would expect in light of *Poletown, Oakland Raiders* and *Midkiff*."[66] The

---

In *Midkiff*, the Supreme Court reversed a lower court decision holding the Hawaii land ownership redistribution scheme unconstitutional. But that decision was by the Ninth Circuit, not a state supreme court; the case came up through the federal district court. Midkiff v. Tom, 702 F.2d 788 (9th Cir. 1981), *rev'd*, Hawaii Hous. Auth. v. Midkiff, 467 US. 229 (1984). So the Supreme Court decision in *Midkiff* reinstated Hawaii's redistributive land use scheme, imposing a deferential standard of federal review on a wayward federal circuit.

As for *Berman*, it is hard to parse in terms of deference to state and local governmental processes, for different reasons. *Berman* involved Supreme Court review of a decision by a three federal judge panel, upholding an act of Congress acting in its capacity as the legislature of the District of Columbia. Schneider v. District of Columbia, 117 F.Supp. 705 (D.D.C. 1953), *aff'd*, Berman v. Parker, 348 U.S. 26 (1954). But the District is not a state, and at that time it did not elect its legislature or executive. It was basically run by members of Congress until 1973. See, e.g., Clarke v. United States, 886 F.2d 404, 406–07 (D.C. Cir. 1989), *vac. as moot*, 915 F.2d 699 (D.C. Cir. 1990) (there was no representative government in the District until 1973). And the judges who sat on the case below were federal (two from federal district court, one from the federal Court of Appeals for the District of Columbia Circuit). They were not judges linked by their past to the District of Columbia.

64 Thomas W. Merrill, *The Economics of Public Use*, 72 CORNELL L. REV. 61, 96 (1986) (roughly one in six challenges in state appellate courts to condemnation based on public use were sustained during the 1954–1985 period).

65 Corey J. Wilk, *The Struggle Over the Public Use Clause: Survey of Holdings and Trends, 1986–2003*, 39 REAL PROP. & TR. J. 251, 258 (2004) (18 percent finding of no public use for state courts). Wilk also identified a few lower federal court decisions in his study period that had invalidated state and local condemnations based on the lack of public use. *Id.* at 270–71 (discussing 99 Cents Only Stores v. Lancaster Redevelopment Agency, 60 Fed. Appx. 123 (9th Cir. 2003), Daniels v. Area Plan Comm'n of Allen County, 305 F.3d 445 (7th Cir. 2002) and Cottonwood Christian Center v. Cypress Redevelopment Agency, 218 F.Supp. 2d.203 (C.D. Cal. 2002) (preliminary injunction)).

66 Merrill, *supra* note 63, at 65.

Supreme Court has not reversed any of these more stringent public use cases from state courts, in effect deferring to state court policing of state and local government implementation of the eminent domain power, whether via the federal public use clause or for other reasons and doctrines.[67]

Federalism and Localism in *San Remo*

San Remo Hotel v. City and County of San Francisco[68] concerns whether and when federal courts must apply a general preclusion principle that prevents relitigation in federal court of issues of law or fact litigated and resolved in state court.[69] One of the reasons someone desiring to pursue a federal takings claim in federal court might find herself in state court instead is *Williamson County Regional Planning Comm'n v. Hamilton Bank.*[70] That case holds that a constitutional claim for uncompensated deprivation of property by a state or local government does not ripen until the property owner has pursued without success all avenues provided by the state to obtain compensation.[71] But in pursuing state avenues of redress first, the claimant is very likely to litigate issues of fact and law the first time in state court and then not be permitted to litigate them again in federal court. Consequently, "*Williamson County* all but guarantees that claimants will be unable to utilize the federal courts to enforce the Fifth Amendment's just compensation guarantee"[72] against state and local entities.

---

67 To be sure, the deference to legislative determinations expressed in *Berman v. Parker* (and reiterated in *Hawaii Housing Authority v. Midkiff*) may well have encouraged some state courts to approach eminent domain for purposes of urban renewal with greater deference, as Wendell Pritchett argues. Wendell E. Pritchett, *The "Public Menace" of Blight: Urban Renewal and the Private Uses of Eminent Domain*, 21 YALE L. & POL'Y REV. 1 (2003). But state courts and legislatures have also remained free to rein in permissive interpretations. The most celebrated recent example is the Michigan Supreme Court's overruling of its earlier permissive understanding of the eminent domain power under the state constitution. County of Wayne v. Hathcock, 684 N.W. 2d 765 (Mich. 2004) (overruling Poletown Neighborhood Council v. City of Detroit, 304 N.W.2d 455 (Mich. 1981)). Wilk describes some other recent examples. Wilk, *supra* note 64, at 267–9. Wilk also describes recent state cases invalidating condemnations based on various statutory limitations rather than ever reaching the public use question. *Id.* at 271–4.

68 San Remo Hotel v. City and County of San Francisco, 545 U.S. 323 (2005). The underlying, long-running substantive dispute was whether a city and county ordinance could impose a heavy cost on a single room residential hotel if it sought to convert to more upscale tourist clientele.

69 Full faith and credit are required by 28 U.S.C. Sec. 1738, implementing Article IV sec. 1 of the United States Constitution.

70 Williamson County Regional Planning Comm'n v. Hamilton Bank, 473 U.S. 172 (1985).

71 *Id.* at 194–7. Williamson County also requires that a plaintiff get a final decision from the state or local governmental entity involved before bringing a lawsuit. *Id.* at 185–94. That part of *Williamson County* was not at issue in *San Remo*, nor did Chief Justice Rehnquist question its continued validity in his *San Remo* concurrence.

72 *San Remo*, 545 U.S. at 342 (Rehnquist, C.J., concurring).

Chief Justice Rehnquist, troubled, wrote a concurring opinion in *San Remo* joined by three other Justices. He asked "why federal takings claims in particular should be singled out to be confined to state court, in the absence of any asserted justification or congressional directive."[73] He concluded that "the justifications for [*Williamson County*'s] state litigation requirement are suspect, while its impact on takings plaintiffs is dramatic."[74] He indicated that in an appropriate case *Williamson County*'s requirement to seek final compensation first in state court should be reconsidered.

Justice Stevens, writing the opinion of the Court in *San Remo*, responded to this argument, albeit very briefly. Stevens pointed out that "[s]tate courts are fully competent to adjudicate constitutional challenges to local land-use decisions. Indeed, state courts undoubtedly have more experience than federal courts do in resolving the complex factual, technical, and legal questions related to zoning and land-use regulations."[75] This is indeed terse, but it expresses clearly a localist concern, and reflects the information rationale for federalism and localism. State courts know how to do these things. Let them. Stevens' response in *San Remo* also resonates with his separate concurrence in *Williamson County* itself, where he expressed confidence in the general good faith of zoning boards and other local governmental entities and indicated that the touchstone of whether a constitutional violation occurred was whether the process involved was fair.[76]

The federalism/localism defense of *Williamson County* is only marginally addressed in the majority opinion in *San Remo* and, as Rehnquist points out, *Williamson County*'s continued vitality was not argued by the parties.[77] Getting rid of *Williamson County*'s restrictions on access to federal courts has, nevertheless, long been part of the property rights agenda.[78] For Rehnquist to raise it so vigorously

---

73   *Id.* (footnote omitted).

74   *Id.*

75   *Id.* at 339 (Stevens, J.) (majority opinion).

76   *Williamson County*, 473 U.S. at 205.

77   *Id.* at 342. Several amici in San Remo did urge the reversal of the *Williamson County* state compensation litigation requirement. Others briefs briefly argued both that *Williamson County*'s second requirement was correct, and that the Court should not address it.

78   See, e.g., J. David Breemer, *You Can Check Out But You Can Never Leave: The Story of* San Remo Hotel – *the Supreme Court Relegates Federal Takings Claims to State Courts Under a Rule Intended to Ripen the Claims for Federal Review*, 33 B.C. ENVTL. AFF. L. REV. 247 (2006); J. David Breemer, *Overcoming* Williamson County*'s Troubling State Procedures Rule: How the England Reservation, Issue Preclusion Exceptions, and the Inadequacy Exception Open the Federal Courthouse Door to Ripe Takings Claims*, 18 J. LAND USE & ENVT'L L. 209 (2003); Madeline J. Meacham, *The* Williamson *Trap*, 32 URB. LAW. 239 (2000). *But see* Douglas T. Kendall, Timothy J. Dowling & Andrew W. Schwartz, *Choice of Forum and Finality Ripeness: The Unappreciated Hot Topics in Regulatory Takings Cases*, 33 URB. LAW. 405 (2001) (outlining the procedures and related controversies); Kathryn E. Kovacs, *Accepting the Relegation of Takings Claims to State Courts: The Federal Courts' Misguided Attempts to Avoid Preclusion under* Williamson County, 26 ECOLOGY L.Q. 1 (1999) (approving of the effective relegation of state and local takings claims to state and local courts); Max Kidalov & Richard H. Seamon, *The Missing Pieces of the Debate Over Federal Property Rights Legislation*, 27 HASTINGS CONT'L L.Q. 1 (1999) (analyzing federal property

suggests this part of the agenda remains on some Justices' minds. One lower court has already interpreted Rehnquist's concurrence as questioning the continuing validity of the second prong of *Williamson County*.[79]

We might do a head count in order to ascertain how seriously *Williamson County* is imperiled, in light of Chief Justice Rehnquist's invitation for an appropriate petition for certiorari. Two of the Justices signing on to Rehnquist's concurrence, Justice O'Connor and Rehnquist himself, are no longer on the Court. They have been replaced by Chief Justice Roberts and Justice Alito. Does this bode ill for *Williamson County*? Not necessarily. While on the Third Circuit, then-Judge Alito was part of a panel that issued a per curiam opinion quoting *San Remo* to the effect that state courts were fully competent to adjudicate constitutional challenges to local land use decisions.[80] And in 2004 Alito authored an opinion clarifying the standard that the Third Circuit would apply in determining whether to take garden variety land use cases where plaintiffs claimed local governments had acted so arbitrarily as to violate the federal constitution's substantive due process provision. In *United Artists Theatre Circuit, Inc. v. Township of Warrington, Pa.*, he wrote that "[l]and-use decisions are matters of local concern" and expressed a strong reluctance to see federal courts cast as "a zoning boards of appeal."[81]

United Artists brought the Third Circuit into line with a number of other federal circuits which, for more than thirty years, have generally refused to treat abuses of ordinary land use and zoning processes as rising to the level of a violation of substantive due process. To be sure, the issue of what abuses of land use and zoning amount to substantive due process violations is doctrinally distinct from the *Williamson County* requirement of state court litigation of compensation claims, though the issues are often presented in the same cases.[82] The underlying federalism and localism concerns are so similar that it is worth taking a moment to look at one

---

rights legislation and arguing that Congress does not have the authority to eliminate either of *Williamson County*'s requirements); Thomas E. Roberts, *Ripeness and Forum Selection in Fifth Amendment Takings Litigation*, 11 J. LAND USE & ENVT'L L. 37 (1995).

79 See Nahas v. City of Mt. View, 2005 U.S. Dist. LEXIS 34718 at n. 4 (N.D. Cal. 2005).

80 Ash v. Redevelopment Authority, 143 Fed. Appx. 439 (3d Cir. 2005).

81 United Artists Theatre Circuit., Inc. v. Township of Warrington, Pa., 316 F.3d 392, 402 (3d Cir. 2004) (Alito, J.) (overruling the "improper motive" standard of *Bello v. Walker*, 840 F.2d 1124 (3d Cir. 1988), and replacing it with a "shocks the conscience" standard derived from *County of Sacramento v. Lewis*, 523 U.S. 833 (1998)). *United Artists* cited a leading decision on this issue, *Creative Environments, Inc. v. Estabrook*, 680 F.2d 822 (1st Cir. 1982), which itself was quoting Justice Marshall's dissent in *Village of Belle Terre v. Boraas*, 416 U.S. 1, 12 at 13 (1974). The underlying dispute in *United Artists* involved a township's delay in issuing a permit to United Artists to construct a movieplex, while the application of a competing movieplex builder was allowed to go forward. The town was only big enough to support one movieplex.

82 Courts have differed on whether either of the *Williamson County* requirements should apply to federal constitutional challenges in the zoning and land use area that are based on provisions other than the Takings Clause. The Takings Clause may be different. One could plausibly argue that the *Williamson County* state litigation requirement derives from the text of the Fifth Amendment itself, as until compensation for a taking has been denied there is

or two of these cases. And indeed, they have been relied on by commentators to support the *Williamson County* test.[83]

In *Village of Belle Terre v. Boraas*, Justice Thurgood Marshall wrote, in an often-quoted passage, that the role of the Supreme Court "should not be to sit as a zoning board of appeals."[84] He emphasized that zoning is a "complex and important function of the state" and "may be the most essential function performed by local government." He stressed the need for wide latitude and continued deference by reviewing courts to local legislative judgments, citing *Berman* and *Euclid*.[85] To be sure, Marshall was in dissent here, and was arguing that the exclusionary regulations at issue trampled on fundamental rights and therefore deserved to be reviewed and reversed. Nevertheless, his words are emblematic of the approach generally taken by the federal courts – hands off (or mostly off) to federal court review of local land use decisions, out of deference to state and local government.

Lower federal court decisions, typically although not always dealing with substantive due process claims, have sometimes amplified on the reasons why. Workload is one standard reason – federal courts could not handle all that volume.[86] But garden-variety land use disputes are also typically viewed as fundamentally state and local, not federal, unless there is some truly troubling abuse of governmental authority.[87] Judge Easterbrook's formulation is especially clear:

> Federal courts are not boards of zoning appeals. This message, oft-repeated, has not penetrated the consciousness of property owners who believe that federal judges are more hospitable to their claims than are state judges. Why they should believe this we haven't a clue; none has ever prevailed in this circuit, but state courts often afford relief on facts that do not support a federal claim. Is it that they have omitted the steps necessary to obtain review in state court and hope for the best in a second-chance forum? Well, we are not cooperating. Litigants who neglect or disdain their state remedies are out of court, period.[88]

---

no constitutional tort. See, e.g., Kidalov & Seamon, *supra* note 77, at 35–41 (*Williamson County*'s requirements derive from the constitutional text; Congress cannot alter them).

83 See, e.g., Kovacs, *supra* note 77, at 43–6.

84 Village of Belle Terre v. Boraas, 416 U.S. 1 at 12, 13 (1981) (Marshall, J., dissenting).

85 Village of Euclid v. Ambler Realty Co., 272 U.S. 365 (1926).

86 See, e.g., Coniston Corp. v. Village of Hoffman Estates, 844 F.2d 461, 465 (7th Cir. 1988) (Posner., J.) ("This case presents a garden-variety zoning dispute dressed up in the trappings of constitutional law … . If the plaintiffs can get us to review the merits of the Board of Trustees' decision under state law, we cannot imagine what zoning dispute could not be shoehorned into federal court in this way, there to displace or postpone consideration of some worthier object of federal juridical solicitude.").

87 As one leading case put it, "The conventional planning dispute – at least when not tainted with fundamental procedural irregularity, racial animus, or the like – which takes place within the framework of an admittedly valid state subdivision scheme is a matter primarily of concern to the state and does not implicate the Constitution. … A federal court, after all, 'should not sit as a zoning board of appeals.'" Creative Env'ts, Inc. v. Estabrook, 680 F.2d 822, 832 n. 9 (1st Cir. 1982) (quoting Village of Belle Terre v. Boraas).

88 River Park, Inc. v. City of Highland Park, 23 F.3d 164, 165 (7th Cir. 1994).

Courts occasionally also explain that state judges are closer to the subtleties of the matter than federal judges would be. One federal appellate court wrote, "Federal judges lack the knowledge of and sensitivity to local conditions necessary to a proper balancing of the complex factors that are inherent in municipal land use decisions."[89] Another wrote, "In the vast majority of instances, local and state agencies and courts are closer to the situation and better equipped to provide relief. We have left the door slightly ajar for federal relief in truly horrendous situations."[90]

In terms of the four elements outlined in my earlier discussion of *Kelo*, we can discern the following, both in *Williamson County* and in the lower federal courts' reluctance to entertain run-of-the-mill zoning and land use cases under various federal constitutional claims: (1) federal judicial restraint, indeed (under *Williamson County*) a general requirement of trying claims in state court first;[91] (2) hints of localism, both in terms of local knowledge and efficiency; and (3) an expectation of involvement of all parts of the state governmental apparatus. The fourth consideration may be trickier to identify, but to the extent that federal constitutional principles such as balancing are applied in light of local knowledge and often in tandem with state and local tests, the work is done by the state courts and not the federal courts.

Federalism and Localism as an Essential Part of an Evolutionary Theory of Private Property and Public Constraint

A great deal can be said, I believe, to justify and expand on the federalism and localism themes in the 2005 Takings Clause cases. I can only sketch out some of the possibilities here.

First, let us put these themes into their general context. The Court seems to be well along in abandoning an absolutist, Scalian view of property.[92] This clears the way for a more explicit adoption by the Court of a general account of property and its relationship to government as evolutionary.[93] The Court might now begin

---

89 Gardner v. City of Baltimore Mayor and City Council, 969 F.2d 63, 68 (4th Cir. 1992) (Wilkinson, J.) (quoting Sullivan v. Town of Salem, 805 F.2d 81, 82 (2d Cir. 1986)).

90 Nestor Colon Medina & Sucesores v. Custodio, 964 F.2d 32, 45 (1st Cir. 1992).

91 Facial takings claims do not trigger the *Williamson County* requirement. Yee v. City of Escondido, 503 U.S. 519 (1992). Many courts also find that if state court litigation is futile it will not be required.

92 Underkuffler, *supra* note 1 (*Tahoe-Sierra* demonstrates the demise of a Scalian view of property) Singer, *supra* note 1, at 327 (*Lingle* demonstrates that a case by case approach to regulatory takings has clearly won out, as foreshadowed in O'Connor's opinion in *Palazzolo* and in *Tahoe-Sierra*).

93 Justice Kennedy struggled with the idea of evolving property norms in his concurrence in *Lucas*. Ultimately he concluded that legislative enactments do sometimes legitimately influence property expectations, and that one cannot cabin the current understanding of property norms within a wholly pre-existing body of common law. *Lucas*, 505 U.S. at 1032 (Kennedy, J., concurring). It is an old idea in our jurisprudence. See, e.g., *Hudson Water Co. v. McCarter*, 209 U.S. 349, 355 (1908) (Holmes, J.) ("The limits set to property by other public interests present themselves as a branch of what is called the police power of the State. The boundary at which the conflicting interests balance cannot be determined by any general

to acknowledge more openly that, whatever the conventional view of property as relatively absolute, it is in fact routinely negotiated and readjusted along important dimensions, as an operational matter.[94]

Once we acknowledge, as I believe the Court is currently doing, that property inevitably involves change and transition, and that private property and regulatory or informal constraints are two sides of the same coin, we can explore in a more nuanced, sensible and explicit way what it means for regulatory takings to be about transition management.[95] The overall problem is to allow appropriate change and not to disappoint or injure property owners unfairly.[96] Specific subsets of regulatory takings can also usefully be examined relying on the understanding that the basic issue is managing property processes.[97]

---

formula in advance, but points in the line, or helping to establish it, are fixed by decisions that this or that concrete case falls on the nearer of farther side.")

94 Laura Underkuffler has argued that we operate with two views of property, a conventional view tending towards an absolute account, and a operational view that reflects our true social practice of renegotiations. See LAURA S. UNDERKUFFLER, THE IDEA OF PROPERTY: ITS MEANING AND POWER 37–51 (2003); see also Marc R. Poirier, *The Virtue of Vagueness in Takings Doctrine*, 24 CARDOZO L. REV. 93, 187–90 (2002) (exploring why it is socially useful not to describe property rights as unstable and negotiable, even though to some extent they are).

95 See, e.g., Holly Doremus, *Takings and Transitions*, 19 J. LAND USE & ENVT'L L. 1 (2003) (proposing doctrinal reforms in light of an understanding of regulatory takings as management of transitions); Daniel J. Hulsebosch, *The Tools of Law and the Rule of Law: Teaching Regulatory Takings after Palazzolo*, 46 ST. LOUIS U. L. REV. 713 (2002) (analyzing regulatory takings doctrine as managing the fairness of transitions in property regimes); Poirier, *supra* note 93 (analyzing regulatory takings doctrine in light of an underlying premise that property regimes are regularly renegotiated); Carol M. Rose, *Property and Expropriation: Themes and Variation in American Law*, 2000 UTAH L. REV. 1 (analyzing regulatory takings doctrine in light of an underlying premise that property regimes are regularly renegotiated); T. Nicolaus Tideman, *Takings, Moral Evolution, and Justice*, 88 COLUM L. REV. 1714 (1988).

96 Susan Ayres, *The Rhetorics of Takings Cases: It's Mine v. Let's Share*, 5 NEV. L.J. 615 (2005) (applying the ancient Greek concept of *kairos* (fairness, beauty) to regulatory takings fairness issues); Rose, *supra* note 94, at 22. A classic and highly influential exploration of the relationship of fairness and utility, especially on the issue of disappointed expectations, is Frank I. Michelman, *Property, Utility, and Fairness: Comments on the Ethical Foundations of "Just Compensation" Law*, 80 HARV. L. REV. 1165 (1967).

97 See, e.g., Mark Fenster, *Takings Formalism and Regulatory Formulas: Exactions and the Consequences of Clarity*, 92 CAL. L. REV. 609 (2004) (examining the effects of different approaches to exactions on the regulatory process); Marc R. Poirier, *The NAFTA Chapter 11 Expropriation Debate Through the Eyes of a Property Theorist*, 33 ENVT'L L. 851 (2003) (comparing sovereign governmental judicial mechanisms and international arbitrations as fora for resolving international regulatory takings disputes); Poirier, *supra* note 93, at 175–8 (identifying specific resource use conflicts in which clear property rules have evolved through dialogic conversations among stakeholders); Danaya C. Wright, *A New Time for Denominators: Toward a Dynamic Theory of Property in the Regulatory Takings Relevant Parcel Analysis*, 34 ENVT'L L. 175 (2004) (arguing that the specifics of the property owner's holdings and behavior are central to a proper application of the relevant parcel issue).

The expectations inquiry is central, especially given the current state of doctrine. With a few recognized categorical exceptions, regulatory takings typically now relies on an ad hoc, all things considered *Penn Central* test.[98] This test is, as Stewart Sterk points out, typically administered by the state courts in matters involving local land use and environmental regulation.[99] As Patrick Hubbard has argued, "the *Penn Central* approach provides a pragmatic process for an open, public resolution of the conflict between rights and regulations within a specific factual context."[100] Moreover, the antecedent inquiry into background principles of nuisance and property law that was established in *Lucas* also directs the application of regulatory takings law to state-based expectations about the limits of private property, as defined by state law and ascertained by state processes.[101] The centrality both of expectations and of preexisting state law in regulatory takings analysis can be properly relabeled as a correct attention to these formal and informal property norms as they evolve.

I see localism at work here, focused through federalism. It is but a small step to justify the processes of, in the first place, property transitions and, in the second place, control and supervision of property transitions, not only in terms of respect for coordinate branches of government but also of an acknowledgment of the signal importance of local knowledge. Expectations about local land use, local property law and practices, and so on can occur and be shared at different geographic and territorial scales, of course. But as they develop, evolve and are renegotiated, we can expect that the informal social processes leading to this productive movement and tension will typically be local where local resources are concerned. The whole notion that property law varies from state to state in response to local conditions (eastern and western water law is a classic example) also supports the argument that local knowledge is an essential component in the production, reproduction and evolution of norms both of private property rules and of formal and informal governance. Depending on circumstance, these shared norms may well be relatively local in scale. For example, Giulianna Ruiz argues that visual cues about land use inform understandings about expectations in the context of regulatory takings.[102] I have argued that territorially based review of takings challenges to regulations is superior to aterritorial arbitration in the NAFTA expropriations context, in part because of the greater likelihood that territorially-based processes will be infused

---

98 Lingle v. Chevron U.S.A. Inc., 544 U.S. 528, 538 (2005) (outside of two "relatively narrow categories" of categorical rules and the "special context of land-use exactions, ... regulatory takings challenges are governed by the standards set forth in *Penn Central Transp. Co. v. New York City*, 438 U.S. 104 (1978))" (parallel citations omitted).

99 Sterk, *supra* note 18. See discussion in Part II *supra*.

100 F. Patrick Hubbard, Palazzolo, Lucas *and* Penn Central: *The Need for Pragmatism, Symbolism, and Ad Hoc Balancing*, 80 NEB. L. REV. 465, 517 (2001).

101 See Michael C. Blumm & Lucus Ritchie, Lucas's *Unlikely Legacy: The Rise of Background Principles as Categorical Takings Defenses*, 29 HARV. ENVT'L L. REV. 321 (2005). Frank Michelman explored this tension in his critique of *Lucas*. Michelman, *supra* note 22.

102 Giulianna K. Ruiz, Student Comment, *Informing Expectations Through Visual Cues: Creating the Assurance of Justice in Regulatory Takings Jurisprudence*, 36 SETON HALL L. REV. 1309 (2006).

with information about local conditions.[103] By relying on vague ad hoc tests that are then implemented locally by courts within the fora where the resources are at issue, the Court places supervision of the process of renegotiation of property in proximity to the norms, parties and resources affected.

This is entirely appropriate. As Melvyn Durchslag writes:

> [W]hen the Takings Clause is applied to local land use regulation, it must be tempered with a concern for federalism. ... [T]he Court must apply the same version of "Our Federalism" to the Takings Clause as it does to the Liberty Clause. I do not reach this conclusion easily because I do not ordinarily advocate that basic liberties be modified in the name of federalism values. But ... land use regulation is a, if not the, leading candidate for an exception.[104]

Kelo is of course not about regulatory takings. It asks whether the Fifth Amendment's "public use" wording constrains the use of eminent domain power in the economic development context in which New London sought to apply it, or whether to constrain such exercises through a heightened standard of review. But insofar as the challenge to economic development condemnations at bottom expresses a fear of government majoritarian excesses,[105] the situation that motivates *Kelo* and the post-*Kelo* political reaction is not so different from a well-recognized rationale for concern about regulatory takings challenges, especially at the local level.[106] One can understand the fundamental concern about abuse of eminent domain, like that

---

103   Poirier, *supra* note 96, at 184–86 (discussing Eric T. Freyfogle, *Owning the Land: Four Contemporary Narratives*, 13 J. LAND USE & ENVTL. L. 279, 286–303 (1998)). Insofar as territorially based jurisdictions have better access to conflicts that involve local knowledge about competing resource uses and values, they may well evidence a land ethic or natural use approach to property, as described by Eric Freyfogle, and thus they may be relatively more sympathetic to restrictions on absolute property rights in the service of other uses of the resource.

104   Durchslag, *supra* note 2, at 473 (footnotes omitted).

105   Whatever the validity of imputing a broad limitation to the words of the constitutional text, the political motivation these days is clearly a concern about local governmental excess and abuse. On the historical intent, see, e.g., John Fee, *Reforming Eminent Domain*, in EMINENT DOMAIN USE AND ABUSE: *KELO* IN CONTEXT 125, 127–9 (Dwight H. Merriam & Mary Massaron Ross eds., 2006) (arguing that the constitutional text and historical precedent do not support a narrow reading of "public use"); Matthew P. Harrington, *"Public Use" and the Original Understanding of the So-Called "Takings" Clause*, 53 HASTINGS L.J. 1245 (2002) (arguing that the original understanding of "taken for public use" was not intended to impose a limitation of the use of eminent domain); but see Claeys, *supra* note 44, at 896–901 (arguing that the original intent was more likely "use by the public" than "public usefulness").

106   See, e.g., WILLIAM A. FISCHEL, REGULATORY TAKINGS: LAW, ECONOMICS, AND POLITICS (1995) (arguing that regulatory takings constraints may be justified to rein in local government's potential for majoritarian abuses of powerless minority property owners). But see Rose, *Takings, Federalism, supra* note 28 (disagreeing that local governments are especially susceptible to process abuse, and arguing that local governments have the advantage of easier participation). See generally William Michael Treanor, *The Original Understanding of the Takings Clause and the Political Process*, 95 COLUM. L.

of regulatory takings, to be about political process.[107] Local knowledge is relevant to state and local government decisions as whether and how to approach economic redevelopment of urban centers in the first place, including whether to allow and apply eminent domain in this context. Also, after *Kelo*, just as a state's property law may vary in response to local conditions as well as reflecting inherited traditions, so its response to the legitimate concerns with abuse expressed in *Kelo* can take different forms. The approaches advocated by the petitioners in *Kelo* – a clear prohibition of economic development condemnations attached to an interpretation of the "Public Use" clause in the federal constitution, and/or a heightened burden of proof for economic development condemnations – are but two among several possible approaches. States may statutorily or constitutionally rein in the eminent domain power at the state level, for example. They also may address both local majoritarian excess, and the possibility of abuse of power through favoritism to developers, by deploying a variety of administrative law reforms. These could involve transparency, public notice, structure of hearings, tighter evidentiary requirements, stronger rights to appeal and grounds for appeal, shifts in burden of proof, broadening the scale and number of governmental approvals required for condemnation, and so on.[108] State legislatures or courts may also respond to *Kelo* by attending to the issue of just compensation, increasing it in beyond fair market value in one way or another

---

REV. 782 (1995) (the original understanding of the takings clause was to protect against process defects).

Other possible process problems can be identified. At a larger scale of government a different process defect is plausible, in which concentrated and focused minority interests prevail over diffuse majority interests. And there is also always the possibility that particular uses of eminent domain may be corrupt or at least tainted by informal quid-pro-quos. This is undeniably sometimes the case – the problem is not majoritarian use of power but abuse of power by government officials. Other process theorists have puzzled over what the possibility of public choice process defects means for regulatory takings doctrine. See, e.g., Daniel A. Farber, *Economic Analysis and Just Compensation*, 12 INT'L REV. L. & ECON. 125 (1992); Daniel A. Farber, *Public Choice and Just Compensation*, 9 CONST. COMMENTARY 279 (1992); Saul Levmore, *Just Compensation and Just Politics*, 22 CONN. L. REV. 285 (1990); Glynn S. Lunney, Jr., *A Critical Reexamination of the Takings Jurisprudence*, 90 MICH. L. REV. 1892 (1991); Marc R. Poirier, *Takings and Natural Hazards Policy: Public Choice on the Beachfront*, 46 RUTGERS L. REV. 243, 327–38 (1993) (discussing public choice analysis of takings doctrine).

107 Nicole Stelle Garnett, *The Public-Use Question as a Takings Problem*, 71 GEO. WASH. L. REV. 934 (2003); Clayton P. Gillette, Kelo *and the Local Political Process*, 34 HOFSTRA L. REV. 13, 13 (2005) (eminent domain and *Kelo* in particular are issues of political process). Cf. Richardson v. City and County of Honolulu, 124 F.3d 1150, 1168 (9th Cir. 1997) (O'Scannlain, J., concurring in part and dissenting in part) (arguing that increased scrutiny should be given to condemnations); Merrill, *supra* note 63 (arguing that careful scrutiny of eminent domain under the public use doctrine is appropriate when various conditions make bargaining to a fair price unlikely and the process inefficient).

108 See, e.g., Gillette, *supra* note 106, at 20 (noting administrative law reforms as a response to *Kelo*). In addition to administrative reforms directed specifically at eminent domain abuse, broader reforms of state and local government contracting processes and campaign finance and conflict of interest laws might also be called for.

to make it reflect the loss of homes, the need for compensation that approximates replacement value, or simply to make it more expensive and therefore less common that economic development condemnations will occur.[109]

Allowing a state to choose how it approaches the problem foregrounded in *Kelo* is a matter not only of respect for coordinate state governments, but also a matter of recognizing the importance of local knowledge. By this I intend local knowledge as to the physical and economic conditions of the urban cores most likely to be candidates for economic redevelopment, and also of a particular state's traditions and persistent problems concerning land use. As an example, the Public Advocate of the State of New Jersey issued a report in May 2006 containing detailed recommendations for statutory responses to abuse of eminent domain in the economic development context.[110] The Public Advocate does not recommend adopting a "use by the public standard," which as a matter of New Jersey law would require a state constitutional amendment, in any event. Referring to the inclusion of blight as a public use in the state constitution, he observes that the statutory bases for authorizing use of eminent domain have been broadened excessively, drifting away from their constitutional mooring, and that they need to be reined in. The Public Advocate also recommends a host of administrative reforms, as well as a new approach to compensation in economic development condemnations. These recommendations are made explicitly against the backdrop of New Jersey's situation as a densely populated, highly urbanized state,[111] and one that has articulated ongoing public policy concerns about affordable housing and about ethics in government.[112] Many of the recommendations are included in the leading bills currently pending in the state legislature. With those

---

109   See, e.g., D. Benjamin Barros, *Home as a Legal Concept*, 46 SANTA CLARA L. REV. 255, 298–300 (2006) (exploring the possibility of increasing compensation for condemnation of homes); David L. Callies & Shelley Ross Saxer, *Is Fair Market Value Just Compensation? An Underlying Issue Surfaced in* Kelo, in EMINENT DOMAIN USE AND ABUSE: *KELO* IN CONTEXT 137 (Dwight H. Merriam & Mary Massaron Ross eds., 2006); Gillette, *supra* note 106, at 20–22 (suggesting revisiting the issue of compensation as a way of reducing abuses of eminent domain for economic development); Fee, *supra* note 104, at 132–5 (addressing the problem of unjust compensation in eminent domain); James E. Krier & Christopher Serkin, *Public Ruses*, 2004 MICH. ST. L. REV. 859, 865–73 (exploring the possibility of adjusting compensation in economic redevelopment condemnations). See generally Christopher Serkin, *The Meaning of Value: Assessing Just Compensation for Regulatory Takings*, 99 NW. U.L. REV. 677 (2005).

110   New Jersey Department of the Public Advocate, *Reforming the Use of Eminent Domain for Private Redevelopment in New Jersey* (May 18, 2006), available at http://www.state.nj.us/publicadvocate/reports/pdfs/PAReportOnEminentDomainForPrivateRedevelopment.pdf [hereinafter *Public Advocate's Report*].

111   New Jersey is the most densely populated state in America. New Jersey also has some of the most aggressive land preservation and smart growth policies in the nation, with large areas such as the Highlands and Pinelands protected from overdevelopment and a range of programs designed to channel growth into cities and towns that have already been developed. As a result, the prosperity of New Jersey's communities is more reliant on redevelopment than perhaps any state in the nation. *Id.* at 4 (footnote omitted).

112   *Id.* at 2–3 (specific discussion in summary of proposal of affordable housing concerns and ethics in government concerns).

bills stalled as of late 2007, the New Jersey Supreme Court stepped in, limiting to some extent the availability of eminent domain to put property to more productive, as a misreading of the state constitutional authorization to use eminent domain to redevelop "blighted areas."[113] In short, New Jersey's response to *Kelo* will be tailored to local circumstance in ways that a one-size-fits-all federal constitutional interpretation would not be.

The Public Advocate's report briefly alludes to this local knowledge, noting that its approach is different from that of South Dakota, which did adopt a "use by the public" approach.[114] South Dakota is a different place than New Jersey in a host of respects – size, population density, population composition, urbanization, and sprawl among them. (I will not venture into comparisons of South Dakota's state and local government practices with those of New Jersey, which are notorious.) It is understandable that New Jersey's approach to concerns about eminent domain abuse would be different than South Dakota's, and the difference is wholly justifiable in terms of local knowledge.[115]

Of the other federalism and localism values identified at the outset of this chapter, I should say at least a word or two about experimentation. Experimentation is an inevitable corollary to an evolutionary notion of property. Allowed to do so, different jurisdictions will try out different approaches to property. Whether this is a formal or informal response to geographic and cultural difference (local knowledge)

---

113   Gallenthin Realty Development, Inc. v. Borough of Paulsboro, 924 A.2d 447 (N.J. 2007). *Gallenthin* is now being explored by New Jersey's lower courts in various factual contexts, both as to what constitutes blight and as to scope of review of eminent domain determinations. See, e.g., Cramer Hills Residents Ass'n, Inc. v. Primas, 928 A.2d 61 (N.J. Super. Ct. App. Div. 2007); Fanaro v. Borough and Council of Bound Brook, 2007 WL 3354308 (N.J. Super. Ct. App. Div.); Arborwood I, II, III Condominium Ass'ns v. Borough of Lindenwold, 2007 WL 3005954 (N.J. Super. Ct. App. Div.); Evans v. Township of Maplewood, 2007 WL 2227123 (N.J. Super. Ct. L. Div.); see also Howard D. Geneslaw & Shepard A. Federgreen, *The New Rules of Redevelopment: Courts More Skeptical of "Area in Need of Redevelopment" Designations*, 190 N.J.L.J. 402 (2007); Brian S. Montag & Dawn M. Monsen, *A Narrower Definition of Blight: Courts Will Be Taking a Harder Look at Evidence in Support of a Blight Definition*, 190 N.J.L.J. 614 (2007); William J. Ward, *Reversal of Blight: New Crop of Cases Face* Gallenthin's *Substantial, Credible Evidence Test*, 190 N.J.L.J. 666 (2007). The author would like to acknowledge written work in progress by student Constance DeSena; it helped him focus on the importance of the *Gallenthin* case.

114   *Public Advocate's Report, supra* note 109, at 4. Actually it appears that South Dakota re-adopted a "use by the public" test, as case law had already established it there. Benson v. State of South Dakota, 710 N.W.2d 131, 146 (S.D. 2006) (noting that South Dakota's longstanding interpretation of "public use" in its state constitution is stricter than the federal definition and requires "use by the public"; and specifically referencing *Kelo*'s indication that states were free to impose interpretations of "public use" stricter than the federal base line).

115   For a detailed exposition of the unique circumstances of land use and urban redevelopment in New Jersey, and an argument that this requires flexibility in the use of condemnation for economic development, see Brief for K. Hovnanian Companies, LLC, in support of Respondents, Kelo v. City of New London, 545 U.S. 469 (2005) (No. 04-108).

or is the result of random variation (slippage)[116] or a calculated attempt to garner economic advantage[117] will depend. To the extent that experimentation is understood to lead towards an eventual more uniform adoption of whatever the "best" approach to a problem is, experimentation and geographic and cultural diversity might be thought to be at odds. They are not. They can be reconciled if one takes seriously the evolution idea within an evolutionary notion of property. The general theory of evolution in the biological context starts from random variation, and posits that some of these differences will survive where they provide an adaptive advantage to local ecological conditions. In other words, over the longer term uniformity will occur where it is successful (appropriate) and diversity will also occur where it is successful (appropriate).

In the public use context, I venture to suggest that we should be entering a phase (thanks to the outcome in *Kelo*) of true experimentation. That is, despite the pressure for a uniform solution from property rights advocates, we should in fact hope to see over the next few years a variety of different state-based solutions. Differing approaches to compensation, administrative reforms, and even the definition of blight, in states that allow condemnation to address it, may all turn out to be of more general applicability. They could also lead to further reforms in other types of eminent domain proceedings. (For example, perhaps condemnation of primary residences should always receive some kind of compensation above and beyond fair market value. *Kelo* could be the leading edge of such a reform.)[118] A one-size-fits-all imposition of "use-by-the-public" as a restriction on eminent domain will stifle this type of beneficial and informative variability.

Local political participation is another underlying value of federalism and localism that I have not yet touched on. Public access to the ongoing processes of adjustments of property rights as well as to the process of supervising the shaping seems to be a basic, if often unarticulated, element of the evolutionary understanding of property. Especially if property is indeed a special and fundamental right because it is so basic to life,[119] then the processes of its management should be widely accessible. Where local resources and property are at issue, this means local political participation. Conceptually, federalism and localism serve this end.[120]

---

116   Steven Winter uses the term "slippage" to describe the gaps and discrepancies in the evolving practice of social norms that inevitably arise over time, even among those who begin with a shared norm. Steven L. Winter, *Contingency and Community in Normative Practice*, 139 U. PA. L. REV. 963, 996–9 (1991).

117   E.g., Abraham Bell & Gideon Parchomovsky, *Of Property and Federalism*, 115 YALE L.J. 72 (2005).

118   Barros, *supra* note 108, at 295–300 (exploring the possibility, in light of *Kelo*, that eminent domain systematically undercompensates homeowners).

119   Laura S. Underkuffler, *Property: A Special Right*, 71 NOTRE DAME L. REV. 1033, 1039–40 (1996).

120   Timothy Dowling argues that grassroots organizations often benefit directly from eminent domain used in support of redevelopment projects, so long as their participation is properly structured; and that a flat ban on eminent domain for economic development would destroy this potential benefit to impoverished communities. Timothy J. Dowling, *How to Think*

To be sure, if these local political processes are exclusionary or otherwise biased, more is required. As I have suggested elsewhere, the unity between substance and access to process is a favorite theme of environmental justice advocates, who typically emphasize the importance of both process and outcome.[121] They seem to believe (perhaps over-optimistically) that participation in regulatory processes, properly structured, can help to achieve the substantive ends they think are fair. Hence they critique regulatory process every bit as much as substantive discrimination. Indeed, William Treanor observed that the concern about process defects that underlies regulatory takings doctrine is quite similar to the concerns expressed by environmental justice advocates.[122] We could add eminent domain abuse to the list.

Generally speaking, where more than one person has an important interest in a resource, looking to private property rights alone is never enough, despite the rhetoric of property rights advocates. This is because, as a fundamental matter, property rights are not like classic negative liberty rights. As centrally important as they are to human well-being, claims of property rights are very, very likely to involve allocation and redistribution, as between individuals, not just to be about protecting individuals from the state.[123] This is nowhere truer than where interests in land and related natural resources are involved. However a private property owner uses her/his land and natural resources, her/his actions affect the neighbors and the whole community. Negative and positive externalities are practically inevitable.

About Kelo *after the Shouting Stops*, in EMINENT DOMAIN USE AND ABUSE: *KELO* IN CONTEXT 321, 329–33 (Dwight H. Merriam & Mary Massaron Ross eds., 2006).

121 Poirier, *supra* note 96, at 890–92 (describing environmental justice advocates' links between process and substantive result). See, e.g., Robert W. Collin & Robin Morris Collin, *The Role of Communities in Environmental Decisionmaking: Communities Speaking for Themselves*, 13 J. ENVT'L L. & LITIG. 37, 88–9 (1998) (communities must be included in environmental decision making to redress substantive inequities in environmental problems); Eileen Gauna, *The Environmental Justice Misfit: Public Participation and the Paradigm Paradox*, 17 STAN. ENVT'L L.J. 3, 5 (1998) (administrative process that fail effectively to incorporate public participation fail to achieve equity in environmental practice); Carmen G. Gonzalez, *Beyond Eco-Imperialism: An Environmental Justice Critique of Free Trade*, 78 DENV. U. L. REV. 979, 1013–14, 1016 (2001) (local participation in environmental decision making is essential in order to capture the complexity of the issues and design more effective responses).

122 Treanor, *supra* note 105, at 873–7.

123 Laura S. Underkuffler, *When Should Rights "Trump"? An Examination of Speech and Property*, 52 MAINE L. REV. 311, 322 (2000) ("The classic liberal model of individual rights ... does not describe – or justify – the protection of property."); Underkuffler, *supra* note 118, at 1046 ("Property rights are not, in fact, private interests which the state neutrally abides. Property rights are collective, enforced, even violent decisions about who shall enjoy the privileges and resources of this society.") It is a fundamental error of property rights advocates to understand property protection as just another constitutional right, rather than one with very a different genesis and implications. Compare Frank I. Michelman, *Liberties, Fair Values, and Constitutional Method*, 59 U. CHI L. REV. 91 (1992) and Underkuffler, *supra*, at 322 with Richard A. Epstein, *Property, Speech, and the Politics of Distrust*, 59 U. CHI. L. REV. 41 (1992). Part of what informs the zeal of property rights advocates to press for uniform national solutions to property conflicts is at bottom just this fundamental misunderstanding of the nature of property.

Consequently, property rights cannot be understood as pre-social and inherently deserving of protection against any coerced renegotiation. To do so would mean that an initial allocation should be protected no matter the changes in use, scarcity, preferences, technology, social mores or any other background condition.

To conclude. Myrl Duncan, one of the theorists who argue that property evolves, puts it in these terms: property is a public conversation and not a Lockean soliloquy.[124] If we understand that we are always having conversations about property, we have to ask whose living room the conversations are in, and who is invited. All societal discourses about property and resources are situated, not only culturally and historically, but also geographically. They have ubiety.[125] Both the participants and the resources at stake have a territorial dimension. That territoriality will likely inform the processes of renegotiating property, as the green property and land ethics folks assert.[126] Where state and local land use and resource regulation are concerned, and also where local problems of urban revitalization are concerned, the property process is particularly localized in its concerns. The federalism and localism in the 2005 Takings decisions recognize this. These decisions answer the question of whose living room we should sit in when we have property conversations. It is the living room of those most affected.

I wish that I could end this chapter on this relatively upbeat note. But I cannot. Assume that I am correct in reading the 2005 Takings Clause cases, in conjunction with *Palazzolo* and *Tahoe-Sierra*, as recognizing the central role of open, public resolutions of conflicts between property rights and regulation or eminent domain within specific factual contexts and at an appropriate level of scale and government. Congress may not be headed in that direction. The House of Representatives in 2005 would have upset the balance of "Our Federalism" in local land use matters by nationalizing an important and currently flexible and deferential constitutional interpretation of "public use" in *Kelo*.[127] It may or may not be legitimate as matter of spending clause authority for Congress to do this. But the proposed Act expressed a fundamental misunderstanding of the nature of property rights in land. It discouraged potentially informative and beneficial experimentation. It flew in the

---

124 Myrl L. Duncan, *Property as a Public Conversation, Not a Lockean Soliloquy: A Role for Intellectual and Legal History in Takings Analysis*, 26 ENVTL. L. 1095 (1996). Susan Ayres recently employed the same trope, analyzing property rhetoric in terms of a tension between "it's mine" and "let's talk" approaches. Ayres, *supra* note 95. And Frank Michelman has argued more generally that balancing tests "solicit future conversation[s]." Frank I. Michelman, Foreword: *Traces of Self-Government*, 100 HARV. L. REV. 4, 34 (1986).

125 That is, they depend on a particular place, and the geographic situatedness of that place shapes their basic characteristics. See Poirier, *supra* note 96, at 884–5 and n.166 (contrasting territorially-based national sovereigns and interest-based merchant and investor communities that are not territorially based).

126 See *id.* at 884–93 (2003) (arguing that environmental and land use regulations have territorial dimensions that will be better acknowledged in territorially based tribunals than in territorial arbitration panels).

127 See Dowling, *supra* note 119, at 322 (a one-size-fits-all national restriction on eminent domain contravenes basic principles of federalism).

face of respect for local knowledge and local political process. It overreacted to tales of local government eminent domain abuse, preferring to abolish a governmental mechanism altogether rather than to allow localities to explore various methods for improvement. (Imagine if Congress were to respond to examples of widespread abuse in local government police departments by using the spending power to ban police departments.) It would have displeased a lot of federal judges, who clearly do not want their role to include sitting as zoning boards of appeals and probably would not relish routinely reviewing the actions of redevelopment commissions either.

In a host of ways, the Private Property Rights Protection Act misfired, and similar future legislation will misfire because it misunderstands the federalism and localism of land use and urban development processes – both in initial administrative and legislative processes, and in state court judicial and constitutional control of those processes. Congress should take its cue from the 2005 Takings Clause decisions and "Our Federalism" as expressed in them. It should let the federalism and localism approved explicitly and implicitly in *Kelo* and the other 2005 Takings Clause decisions run its course.

Chapter 7

Just Compensation in an Ownership Society

Rachel D. Godsil and David Simunovich

Introduction

Homeownership has been accorded a hallowed status in American society.[1] We
consider homeowners to take better care of their property, play more active roles in
local governance and schools, vote more frequently, participate in local community
building, and in general to constitute more active citizens.[2] For the vast majority
of Americans, their home is their single most valuable asset as well as the locus
of their family and community. As Margaret Radin famously articulated, the home
is part of "the way we constitute ourselves as continuing personal entities in the
world."[3] It is now widely recognized that homeownership is characterized by
genuine psychological and emotive attachments that possess real, though perhaps
not quantifiable, value to the homeowner.[4]

In addition to its psychological dimensions, homeownership has significant
financial benefits. It permits the owner to leverage capital, which can help to buy
investment properties, start a new business, send a child to college, or save for
retirement.[5] Because we value homeownership and homeowners, the government
entitles homeowners to a generous array of benefits, including the mortgage tax
deduction and protection from creditors. For many, the step of becoming a homeowner
is among the most significant of their lives.

Following the ravages of Hurricane Katrina and the Supreme Court's recent
decision in *Kelo v. City of New London*,[6] however, homeownership is seen as
dangerously precarious. The possibility of losing one's home as a result of natural

---

1   D. Benjamin Barros, *Home as a Legal Concept*, 46 Santa Clara L. Rev. 255–6
(2006).

2   Eduardo Penalver, *Property as Entrance*, 91 Va. L. Rev. 1889, 1949 (2005).

3   Margaret Radin, *Property and Personhood*, 34 Stan. L. Rev. 957, 959 (1982).

4   Timothy Sandefur, Cornerstone of Liberty: Property Rights in 21st Century
America 5–10, 21–30 (2006) (recounting a variety of reasons why owners develop special bonds
to a home they live in, and why that relationship should be protected by the government).

5   Hernando DeSoto, The Mystery of Capital: Why Capitalism Triumphs in the
West and Fails Everywhere Else 6 (2000). Throughout his book, DeSoto demonstrates the
transformative power of asset ownership in a functioning capitalist society, and the necessity
for an ordered, coherent property system to facilitate wealth accumulation.

6   Kelo v. City of New London, 545 U.S. 469 (2005).

disaster compounded by governmental neglect or an express political decision that one's home will garner more social utility as a shopping mall seems quite real to many Americans. This attention has resulted in a spate of legislative enactments and even a few state constitutional amendments prohibiting the use of eminent domain for all but the most traditional public uses. However, most states have not yet adopted such draconian statutes, and even in states with limiting legislation or constitutional provisions, government still retains the power of eminent domain for a wide spectrum of uses.

Is the current public anxiety about the potential government abuse warranted? Have property rights become meaningless?

Despite the media hype, for most homeowners, *Kelo* changed very little. Property rights have never been as static and "secure" as many presume. As law students learn their first year, ownership is not a single concept. Rather, property rights consist of a bundle of rights or entitlements to occupy and use property, to exclude others from it, and to transfer the property to others. Property rights are (and have always been) limited by the interests of others in countless respects. Neighbors may sue in nuisance to limit offensive conduct, local government can limit uses under zoning and land use regulations, and, most dramatically, government may require sale of land for its own use. This last limit, the government's power of eminent domain, is the primary source of the public's current anxiety.

The media's overheated rhetoric notwithstanding, the use of eminent domain is not widespread.[7] And, in the unlikely event that the government requires one's home for a highway or a park or to spark economic activity, most homeowners will be well compensated and easily able to purchase another home. Many will argue that their home is not fungible, easily replaced by another. Indeed, Radin classes homes within the category of personhood property along with family albums, diaries, and heirlooms.[8] Even if this is so, however, we would argue that more significant than the loss of an individual home is the loss of one's status as a homeowner. For some, the "fair market value" of their home (all the government is generally required to compensate), will not be enough to allow them to purchase another home. In these circumstances, the government's use of eminent domain will have the effect of casting families from the "ownership society" and causing them to lose access to the range of benefits afforded property owners.[9] This injury, to us, seems to meet the

---

7   Among the most vocal critics of the use of eminent domain, Dana Berliner, documents a recent five year period which included 10,282 actual or "threatened" takings across all fifty states and the District of Columbia. Dana Berliner, Public Power, Private Gain: A Five-Year, State-By-State Report Examining the Abuse of Eminent Domain (2003). While this number is not insignificant, it is approximately forty properties per state per year. This amounts to a tiny fraction of properties in each state – and this number includes "threatened" as well as actual takings.

8   Radin, *supra* note 3, at 967.

9   Our argument is focused upon the loss of homeowner status, but is not intended to suggest that renters may not experience losses from the use of eminent domain that are substantial and worth compensating. However, this issue is beyond the scope of our chapter.

Supreme Court's maxim that fair market value should apply unless "its application would result in manifest injustice to owner or public."[10]

The harm of losing one's status as homeowner has a far-reaching impact at both the individual and collective levels. Property ownership ties one to the larger community in myriad ways. Homeowners – even those with the same income, education, and other socio-economic characteristics – tend to be both more civically active and more apt to engage in market transactions linked to their homes.[11] This involvement often stems from their financial obligations and vulnerability, but it has the effect of creating stronger and more cohesive communities which has salutary effects both for their community and themselves. According to Carol Rose, "[d]espite its appeal to self-interest, commerce also carries a culture; it inculcates rules, understandings, and standards of behavior enforced by reciprocity of advantage. To do business, one must learn the ways and practices of others."[12] Losing this link to the larger market and community is likely to harm a family and its long-term prospects far more even than the emotional loss of the home.

This harm is particularly acute if the affected homeowner is black or Latino. African Americans and Latinos are significantly less likely than whites to own their homes. In 2005, 75 percent of whites owned their homes compared to 49 percent of Latinos and 48 percent of blacks.[13] The dramatic racial differences in homeownerships are not accidental. They can be traced back to the federal government's post-World War II policies including the Veteran Administration and Federal Housing Administration's refusal to extend mortgage guarantees to black families and the concurrent private sector lending discrimination.[14] While these disparities appear stark, they actually reflect the highest homeownership rate for blacks and Latinos, and the smallest racial gap in our country's history.[15]

Past discrimination is not the only cause of racial disparities in homeownership rates and thus the significance of harm to a black or Latino family if homeownership status is lost. Thomas Shapiro has found that blacks are rejected for home mortgages at a sixty percent higher rate than equally creditworthy whites.[16] While the advent and enforcement of the Community Reinvestment Act,[17] which requires banks doing business in urban communities to meet the credit needs of those communities, has had some effect, Shapiro concludes that financial institutions simply redefine "objective" criteria that result in blacks being denied credit at substantially higher rates. In addition, blacks and Latinos tend to have significantly less family wealth to rely upon for down payments and the like so often have to pay higher interest

---

10 United States v. Commodities Trading Corp., 331 U.S. 121, 123 (1950).

11 Penalvar, *supra* note 2, at 1950.

12 CAROL M. ROSE, PROPERTY AND PERSUASION 147 (1994).

13 U.S. Census Bureau, Homeownership Rates by Race and Ethnicity of Householder: 1994 to 2005.

14 MELVIN L. OLIVER & THOMAS M. SHAPIRO, BLACK WEALTH/WHITE WEALTH: A NEW PERSPECTIVE ON RACIAL INEQUALITY 30 (1995).

15 Thomas M. Shapiro, *Race, Homeownership and Wealth*, 20 WASH. U. J.L. & POL'Y 53 (2006).

16 *Id.* at 68.

17 12 U.S.C. § 2901 (2000).

rates and costs. Accordingly, re-achieving homeownership status will be less likely for a black family who loses the family home to eminent domain than a similarly situated white family, and the "injustice" of the inadequate compensation is even more acute.

Indeed, even the symbolic significance of homeownership may have unique salience for blacks and Latinos in light of the United States' history of exclusion. As Irma Muñoz, a Senior Manager with Fannie Mae, described:

> I would give speeches on wealth building and about the impact that home ownership has on communities, but I never truly understood what I was saying until very recently. Two years ago, my siblings and I bought our parents their first home in the United States. Soon after they moved in, we were having dinner together. I had never seen as much peace in my parents' eyes as I saw that night. I had never seen them as happy as they were. Home ownership did that for them. After they became homeowners, they became voters. They are involved in the community. They participate in the school system. They advocate for other Latinos in the area. And after September 11, my parents' house instantly had an American flag on the garage door.
>
> My parents feel fully like a part of this country. Home ownership was the catalyst to make sure that they felt like part of the United States.[18]

Some may contend that the government should not be forced to exceed fair market value simply because a particular home is worth so little on the market that its fair market value is inadequate to cover the purchase of another home. This argument is based upon the premise that the government need only place the property owner in as good a position as she was prior to the exercise of eminent domain. However, the Constitution requires that those whose property is taken shall receive "just compensation." Further, this argument presupposes that the government had no role in determining the value of the property, and that distributive justice concerns cannot be taken into account in determining the "justness" of compensation. Neither assumption is accurate. As we will discuss, government activity tends to be integral to determining the market value of property. In addition, as we suggest above, the status of homeowner has value independent of the specific monetary value of the specific property. Accordingly, for compensation to be "just" when the government exercises its power of eminent domain, it must both recognize its own role in setting property value and compensate to ensure that property owner status is retained.

Many have argued that whatever compensation condemnees receive, it is certainly not "just."[19] In response, scholars have proposed a panoply of alternatives.

---

18 *Sixth Annual Harvard Latino Law and Policy Conference: Latino Leadership and Collective Power*, 7 Harv. Latino L. Rev. 75, 93 (2004).

19 See generally Michael DeBow, *Unjust Compensation: The Continuing Need for Reform*, 46 S.C. L. Rev. 579 (1995); Thomas Merrill, *Incomplete Compensation for Takings*, 11 N.Y.U. Envtl. L.J. 110 (2002). But see Abraham Bell, *Not Just Compensation*, 13 J. Contemp. Legal Issues 29 (2003) (arguing for downward adjustment in compensation to combat moral hazard); Nicole Stelle Garnett, *The Neglected Political Economy of Eminent Domain*, 105 Mich. L. Rev. 101, 104 (2006) (noting that many scholars have "overstate[d] the compensation problem").

The theories of compensation have included the need to fully compensate property owners for their loss, discourage inefficient takings, mitigate what would otherwise be an onerous individual burden to bear for the public benefit, and the introduction of elements of distributive justice into a process that has disproportionately burdened stigmatized groups.[20]

This chapter will evaluate these many proposed standards suggested to replace the fair market standard. Unlike many other commentators, we are not taking the position that compensation should be a tool to impede the use of eminent domain. Rather, for purposes of this chapter, we accept that the government may have good reason to use its power either for a specific public use such as a school or highway or to revitalize an economically distressed municipality. We will note when a particular proposed compensation scheme would seem likely to be so expensive as to render impossible the government's use. In other words, we are not attempting to manipulate compensation to render the use of eminent domain prohibitively expensive. It is our intention to evaluate compensation schemes to ensure a degree of compensation that protects against the loss of homeowner status.[21]

The Jurisprudence of Just Compensation

The power of eminent domain is of ancient origin.[22] Prior to the American Revolution, the colonies appear to have taken for granted the power of government to compel certain uses of land and sometimes to condemn land for government-chosen uses.[23] The framers of the Constitution recognized the necessity of retaining this power, but tempered it with the requirement that private property shall not be taken for public use without "just compensation."

The Court has long acknowledged the inherent difficulty in adhering to this constitutional mandate. In *Kimball Laundry v. United States*, the Court acknowledged that:

---

20 Stigmatized group in this context refers to "minority groups in the United States victimized by social stigma" which includes racial and ethnic minorities, and more broadly, the poor, the elderly, and politically disempowered groups. See Shavar Jeffries, *The Structural Inadequacy of Public Schools for Stigmatized Minorities: The Need for Institutional Remedies*, 34 HASTINGS CONST. L.Q. 1, 2 n.1 (2006).

21 Eminent domain also works particular harms on renters; however, it is not the scope of this piece to address displacement policy relating to non-owner occupants. It should be noted, however, that under the Uniform Relocation Assistance and Real Property Acquisition Policies for Federal and Federally Assisted Programs ("URA"), *infra*, renters receive significant relocation assistance. 49 C.F.R. § 24.202(a) (2007).

22 The term "eminent domain" was not coined by the Romans; however, evidence suggests that compulsory takings did exist in some form at this early point in history. Matthew P. Harrington, *"Public Use" and the Original Understanding of the So-Called "Takings" Clause*, 53 HASTINGS L.J. 1245, 1249 n.10 (2002) (*citing* J. Walter Jones, *Expropriation in Roman Law*, 45 L.Q. 512, 521 (1929); Errol E. Meidinger, *The "Public Uses" of Eminent Domain: History and Policy*, 11 ENVTL. LAW. 1, 8 (1980)).

23 John F. Hart, *Colonial Land Use Law and Its Significance for Modern Takings Doctrine*, 109 HARV. L. REV. 1252, 1282–3 (1996).

[f]or purposes of the compensation due under the Fifth Amendment, of course, only that "value" need be considered which is attached to "property," but that only approaches by one step the problem of definition. The value of property springs from subjective needs and attitudes; its value to the owner may therefore differ widely from its value to the taker.[24]

To avoid the definitional conundrum, the Court adopted a fair market standard of compensation, noting that:

[m]ost things, however, have a general demand which gives them a value transferable from one owner to another. As opposed to such personal and variant standards as value to the particular owner whose property has been taken, this transferable value has an external validity which makes it a fair measure of public obligation to compensate the loss incurred by an owner as a result of the taking of his property for public use.[25]

While acknowledging that the property owner would suffer real and uncompensated loss, the Court reasoned that, like the losses due to the exercise of the police power, such was the burden of citizenship.

In other cases the Court has suggested that its case law demands that just compensation makes the owner "whole,"[26] and restores the owner to "the same position monetarily" that the owner would have occupied but for the taking.[27] The Court held in *Monongahela Navigation Co. v. United States* that "compensation must be a full and perfect equivalent for the property taken."[28] The *Monongahela* position was reaffirmed in *Seaboard Airline* and *Miller*, when the Court held that eminent domain compensation should put an owner "in as good a position pecuniarily as he would have been had his property not been taken."[29] However, the Court has never deviated from its conclusion that compensation is just so long as it reflects the fair market value of the property on the date the property is taken.[30]

Fair market value is presently held to be "what a willing buyer would pay in cash to a willing seller at the time of the taking."[31] Courts have repeatedly held that while the legislature, or any other government actor, may offer a specific amount of money to a property owner, the determination of whether the compensation is "just"

---

24 Kimball Laundry v. United States, 338 U.S. 1, 5 (1949).

25 *Id.*

26 United States v. 564.54 Acres of Land, 441 U.S. 506, 516 (1979) (quoting Olsen v. United States, 292 U.S. 246, 255 (1934)).

27 United States v. Reynolds, 397 U.S. 14, 16 (1970).

28 148 U.S. 312, 326 (1893).

29 United States v. Miller, 317 U.S. 369, 373 (1943) (citing *Monongahela Navigation Co.*, 148 U.S. at 327); Seaboard Air Line Ry. Co. v. United States, 261 U.S. 299, 304 (1923) (citing *Monongahela Navigation Co.*, 148 U.S. at 327).

30 Kirby Forest Indus. v. United States, 467 U.S. 1, 10 (1984). Assessing compensation awarded on the date the property is actually taken creates a problem known as condemnation blight, discussed below, where the condemner artificially lowers its acquisition costs through announcement of plans to condemn a predetermined area. Bell, *supra* note 19, at 67.

31 *564.54 Acres of Land*, 441 U.S. at 511 (quoting *Miller*, 317 U.S. at 374).

remains a judicial question.[32] Fair market value, therefore, must be measured against the just compensation requirement, and a court may properly adjust an award up or down, so as to ensure that "compensation is 'just' both to a [property owner] and to the public that must pay the bill."[33]

As noted above, commentators challenge whether the fair market value standard sufficiently compensates the owner so as to satisfy the just compensation requirement. The *Kelo* Court expressly refused to address this question, stating in a footnote that the fairness of the measure of just compensation "while important, … [is] not before us in this litigation."[34] The challenge, then, is to determine to what extent, if any, a property owner should be compensated beyond the monetary value of the condemned property.

Proposed Compensation Plans

Scholars have sought to advance a range of values in proposing alternative compensation schemes. Roughly, these include compensatory justice, distributive justice, and efficiency maximization. Those most concerned with compensatory justice contend that to the degree fair market value fails to reflect the total loss to the property owner, the owner has not been fully compensated for her loss. As Judge Posner stated: "the taking in effect confiscates the additional (call it 'personal') value that they obtain from the property."[35] However, the Fifth Amendment does not require "full" compensation; rather, it requires "just" compensation.

Proponents of compensatory justice schemes attempt to explain why idiosyncratic value should be compensated – particularly since government regulation such as zoning limits land value regularly with no compensation at all. If the government compensation schemes fail to internalize all the costs of a given project, the government may go forward with externality-ridden inefficient projects. Thus, they argue that efficiency can be viewed as contributing to compensatory justice. Alternatively, some of the schemes discussed below also address concerns of distributive justice and suggest that government should use eminent domain power and the just compensation provision to address current maldistributions of wealth.

Our concern, status preservation, reflects all three considerations. As recognized by the compensatory justice proponents, failing to compensate homeowners for the lost value of homeowner status is an enormous shortfall, and is avoided through status preservation. In addition, in light of the benefits of homeowner status to the homeowner and society, the failure to internalize the costs of lost homeowner status will cause avoidable inefficiencies, and again, is circumvented through status preserving compensation. Lastly, our approach reflects the concern that the most vulnerable class of homeowners will be most at risk from the potential loss

---

32 United States v. Sioux Nation of Indians, 448 U.S. 371, 417 (1980); *Monongahela Navigation Co.*, 148 U.S. at 327.

33 United States v. Commodities Trading Corp., 339 U.S. 121, 123 (1950).

34 Kelo v. City of New London, 545 U.S. 469, 489 n.21 (2005).

35 Coniston Corp. v. Vill. of Hoffman Estates, 844 F.2d 461, 464 (7th Cir. 1988) (quoted in Barros, *supra* note 1, at 298).

of homeowner status. Consequently, as will be explained below, status preserving compensation is the best suited to provide critical protection of homeowner status in any takings context.

Percentage Premium Plans

One of the most frequently suggested alternatives to traditional fair market valuation compensation are variants of a percentage multiplier, aimed at providing homeowners with compensation above and beyond fair market value. Some scholars propose flat percentage bonuses.[36] These percentage premium plans ("PPPs") are supposed to "act as a balm for the infringement upon autonomy brought about by any forced exchange and ... to correct the systematic underestimation of value" that occurs in fair market value compensation.[37] PPPs traditionally call for, say, ten percent premiums to be added to all home valuations.[38] Alternatively, some theorists attempt to introduce some semblance of individuation into PPPs by adjusting premiums based on length of residency,[39] relative wealth of the condemnee,[40] or relative value of the community in which the condemnee resides.[41]

The flat percentage plan, along with those plans that emphasize the length of residency or the relative value of the community, seem to be motivated primarily by the goal of more fully compensating condemnees for their loss. Proponents of this scheme argue that flat percentage schemes are preferable to attempts to truly measure an individual's subjective loss because such attempts are complex and also because they invite owners to either consciously or subconsciously exaggerate their felt loss.

However, analyzing these suggestions from a status preserving approach demonstrates fundamental theoretical and practical weaknesses. PPPs offer no assurances that a homeowner will be able to preserve his or her status as such. For example, if a homeowner in community A has a home judged by the market to be worth $300,000 and homeowner in community B has a home judged by the market to be worth $60,000, a flat percentage premium will compensate homeowner A's subjective loss at $30,000 and homeowner B's loss at $6,000. Prior to the institution of the PPP, homeowner A was in a better position to purchase a new home than homeowner B – in other words, the application of the PPP exacerbates the wealth disparity at taxpayer expense.

---

36 See, e.g., RICHARD EPSTEIN, TAKINGS: PRIVATE PROPERTY AND THE POWER OF EMINENT DOMAIN 184 (1985); Barros, *supra* note 1, at 300; Robert C. Ellickson, *Alternatives to Zoning: Covenants, Nuisance Rules, and Fines as Land Use Controls*, 40 U. CHI. L. REV. 681, 736–7 (1973) (although Ellickson was offering his compensatory plan to resolve issues of regulatory takings, the plan is equally applicable to instances of eminent domain takings).

37 EPSTEIN, *supra* note 36, at 184.

38 *Id.*

39 Barros, *supra* note 1, at 300; Ellickson, *supra* note 36, at 736–7.

40 Hanoch Dagan, *Takings and Distributive Justice*, 85 VA. L. REV. 741, 753–6 (1999).

41 Gideon Parchomovsky & Peter Siegelman, *Selling Mayberry: Communities and Individuals in Law and Economics*, 92 CAL. L. REV. 75, 141 (2004).

Additionally, there is a high degree of inefficiency and arbitrariness inherent in such proposals. PPPs are just as likely to over-compensate a homeowner as they are to under-compensate.[42] In any group of condemnees, there may be a significant number of owners who will readily accept fair market value,[43] and forcing taxpayers to pay an artificially inflated bill is not only inefficient, but also unjust.[44] Moreover, there are just as likely to be an equal number of condemnees whose subjective valuation far exceeds any premium offered by a condemner.[45] The argument that no amount of monetary compensation can ultimately be "just" does little to add to the eminent domain debate.

Troubling for similar reasons are plans that would adjust compensation based on community valuation. While we are sympathetic to the aims of community premiums, advocated most notably by Gideon Parchomovsky and Peter Siegelman,[46] as a means to recognize the unrecognized value a strong community brings homeowners and to create disincentives to destroy such communities, we are concerned that as designed, community premiums will also exacerbate existing disparities. Parchomovsky and Siegelman advance both compensatory and efficiency aims in their proposal. The value residents receive from a tightly knit community may not be reflected in the market because they accrue particularly to those in the web of relationships and history of the particular community. Therefore, a community premium (or the relocation costs of the entire community) more accurately reflects the actual loss. In addition, they argue, if the government fails to take into account the community value lost, the externalities may result in inefficient projects going forward.

Our predominant concern with the plan is that its valuation of community may result in excluding more vulnerable communities from receiving the benefit. The community premium takes into account "turnover rates" and "amenities" to craft an appropriate multiplier.[47] However, it is precisely the communities without many traditionally recognized amenities and with high turnover rates that often have been,[48] and will continue to be, targeted for economic development and blight removal takings.[49] The community premium, while laudable in some respects, fails to recognize the unique harms experienced by target communities composed of politically disempowered groups. Another concern is that in such a mass relocation, the government would be forced to pay artificially inflated premiums, creating both

---

42 Lee Anne Fennell, *The Death of Poletown: The Future of Eminent Domain and Economic Development After* County of Wayne v. Hathcock: *Taking Eminent Domain Apart*, 2004 MICH. ST. L. REV. 957, 993–4 (2004).

43 For example, the *Kelo* case dealt with a legal challenge brought by 7 homeowners even though 114 homeowners were impacted by the eminent domain proceedings.

44 United States v. Commodities Trading Corp., 339 U.S. 121, 123 (1950).

45 SANDEFUR, *supra* note 4, at 5–10 (describing the Bugryns, Kelo, other *Kelo* families).

46 Parchomovsky & Siegelman, *supra* note 41, at 139–40.

47 *Id.* at 141–2.

48 Brief for NAACP, et al. as Amici Curiae Supporting Petitioners at 7–8, Kelo v. City of New London, 545 U.S. 469 (2005).

49 Indeed, Parchomovsky and Siegelman acknowledge that communities lacking amenities and that are characterized by high turnover rates would not necessarily merit a community premium. Parchomovsky & Siegelman, *supra* 41, at 141–2.

a windfall to the property owner who sells the land used for the relocation, as well as a grossly inflated condemnation bill to the general public.

In a slightly different context – a proposed noxious land use – one of us has proposed an alternative premium that would specifically address the harms to politically disempowered groups. Rachel Godsil has argued that if a landowner seeks to impose a polluting use upon an under-protected, racially segregated community, homeowners subject to the nuisance should have the power to reject the use (impose a property rule) or alternatively receive the fair market value of their home augmented by a "segregation multiplier" (a pre-determined liability rule).[50] This would result in the amount the home would be worth in a comparable – but nonsegregated – neighborhood. Recognizing that the government would have power of eminent domain to overrule the use of the property rule, Godsil contended that in light of the government's role in creating racially segregated communities and in withholding from these same communities the land use and environmental protections provided to white communities, the government should also be required to award the segregation multiplier.

The strength of this proposal is its express protection of homeowner status and its redistributive effect. The benefits the government concludes it will gain from the proposed new project will be shared by those burdened by the loss of their homes. However, the proposal was designed to respond to communities suffering a gross overburden of noxious land uses such that the community could establish that government had failed to provide the sort of regulatory protections applied to similarly situated white communities. In light of current Supreme Court jurisprudence, such dramatic racially identifiable disparities are likely to be the only facts supporting an explicitly race based remedy.[51] This remedy will thus rarely be available – and would not apply to those in poor white homeowners who would also likely lose their status as such.

Government Structure Alternatives

Recognizing the inherent weaknesses of other compensatory schemes, such as the percentage premium plans, some legal scholars propose altering the role that government plays in providing just compensation by seeking to introduce market realities into compensation schemes through insurance- or tax-based models,[52] or elements of direct democracy referenda and community-driven bargaining processes.[53] We will evaluate these proposals in turn.

---

50 Rachel D. Godsil, *Viewing the Cathedral from Behind the Color Line: Property Rules, Liability Rules, and Environmental Justice*, 53 Emory L. J. 1808, 1875 (2003).

51 Michelle Adams, Toward a Unified Standard for Evaluating the Constitutionality of Racial Preferences (draft on file with author).

52 See generally Steve P. Calandrillo, *Eminent Domain Economics: Should "Just Compensation" Be Abolished, and Would "Takings Insurance" Work Instead?*, 64 Oh. St. L.J. 451, 500–504 (2003); Fennell, *supra* note 42, at 995–1002.

53 See generally James J. Kelly, *"We Shall Not be Moved": Urban Communities, Eminent Domain and the Socioeconomics of Just Compensation*, 80 St. John's L. Rev. 980–81 (2006); Michael A. Heller & Roderick M. Hills, Jr., *The Art of Land Assembly* 2 (Oct.

We are deeply concerned that the insurance-based schemes will exacerbate distributive justice concerns. A proposed insurance-based scheme would be offered in lieu of government-paid just compensation. Scholars contend that the introduction of a private sector actor into the just compensation element of eminent domain proceedings would reduce administrative and transactional costs[54] and mitigate the risk of moral hazard by enabling insurance companies to adjust premiums based on the condemnation risk.[55] Insurance-based models provide that property owners receive tax refunds in the amount that a government might otherwise require for condemnation proceedings, and then require the owner to purchase eminent domain insurance.[56] These plans are supposed to provide structural protection to politically disempowered groups as politicians would be inclined to make the "right placement decision" for takings, rather than reflexively targeting poor and minority neighborhoods.[57]

Other insurance based schemes call for homeowner self-valuation.[58] Specifically, homeowners would report the value of their home to the government on tax returns and would be compensated at that amount if their property were taken in an eminent domain proceeding.[59] In this way, homeowners value their homes prior to a taking and incorporate their own subjective valuation.[60] To control rampant over-valuation, homeowners would receive tax refunds based on the reported property value – the lower the reported value, the greater the refund that a homeowner would receive.[61] Thus, in a tax-based model, the premiums a homeowner would otherwise pay in an insurance-based scheme would be in the form of foregone tax returns.

Despite their commendable intentions, insurance and tax models eviscerate the very protections that the just compensation guarantee was meant to extend to stigmatized groups. For example, Calandrillo argues that an insurance-based model would protect poor and minority neighborhoods because government officials would be inclined to choose the "right" places for takings.[62] However, this assumes insurance companies have absolutely no political influence. In fact, it is more likely that economically depressed neighborhoods will be disproportionately targeted because takings in these areas will result in lower payouts by the insurer to homeowners as compared to higher priced neighborhoods.

Most disturbing is the reality that insurance companies adjust premiums based on the likelihood that the insured will eventually require a payout. For example, drivers that own sports cars, have been in accidents in the past, or live in areas

---

2005) (unpublished partial draft, on file with author) (earlier draft *available at* http://www.law.uchicago.edu/Lawecon/workshop-papers/Heller.pdf).

54 Calandrillo, *supra* note 52, at 495–9.

55 *Id.*; Bell, *supra* note 19, at 32–3.

56 Calandrillo, *supra* note 52, at 500–503; see also Bell, *supra* note 19, at 36–7 (discussing homeowner self-valuation in the context of a negligence-based compensation scheme).

57 Calandrillo, *supra* note 52, at 518–19.

58 Fennell, *supra* note 42, at 995–6.

59 *Id.*

60 *Id.* at 995.

61 *Id.* at 996.

62 Calandrillo, *supra* note 52, at 518–20.

with high vehicle theft rates pay higher insurance premiums. Similarly, residents living in neighborhoods that are prime candidates for economic redevelopment or blight removal would pay higher premiums because they present a higher risk of payout to the insurance company. Thus, the very residents who are least able to afford additional financial burdens would be most at risk of paying unfairly high premiums. Furthermore, despite the fact that auto insurance is mandatory for all car owners, many drivers do not carry insurance because it is unaffordable.[63] There is no reason to suspect homeowners would not take that risk as well. Consequently, not only would residents in economically depressed areas pay higher premiums, there is also a substantial risk that at least some homeowners would carry no insurance, leaving them completely vulnerable to a taking without any compensation.

Tax-based schemes are equally discriminatory in that they create the obvious incentive for poor homeowners to undervalue their home for the purposes of some potential taking, at some unknown time in the future, in exchange for greater tax returns that are definite, immediate, and sorely needed.

We are more sympathetic to the aims of proposed public referenda plans which seek to vest greater control in the individuals who will be most directly affected by the eminent domain process. Majority approval, or even approval by super-majorities, would obviously ensure that certain takings receive at least some degree of express public approval.[64] James Kelly suggests granting those whose homes are condemned with an alienable right of return to the post-taking community,[65] while Michael Heller and Roderick Hills argue for the introduction of the Land Assembly District ("LAD") which would allow property owners to approve or disapprove by majority vote whether to sell their neighborhood to a developer or municipal government.[66]

These alternatives seek to incorporate distributive justice concerns into hypothetical compensatory schemes, and present perhaps the most desirable alternatives to an expressly status-preserving compensation plan. Nevertheless, they fail to provide comprehensive protection to all property owners confronting the threat of eminent domain proceedings. Most significantly, the various schemes only apply when the use of eminent domain is intended to promote economic development rather than the myriad of other uses of land by government. Therefore, those property owners who lose their land to a highway, for example, remain unprotected.

A right of return that can be sold to others has significant merit. It allows that homeowner to return to their community after the redevelopment takes place or to recoup their losses by selling their right on the open market. However, we have several concerns.

First, granting the right of return will prevent the taker from having maximum flexibility in developing the land, likely leading to avoidable inefficiencies. Most

---

63 For example, as of 2004, the percentage of uninsured motorists on the road was 14.7 percent. Insurance Journal, *Uninsured Drivers Increasing; Vary by State; Miss. Highest, Maine Lowest*, Ins. J., June 28, 2006, http://www.insurancejournal.com/news/national/2006/06/28/69919.htm.

64 Kelly, *supra* note 53, at 928–9.

65 *Id.*

66 Heller & Hills, *supra* note 53, at 3.

notably, it necessarily requires the taker to include housing as part of the redevelopment scheme which may not be the optimal use for a given parcel of land. Second, the right of return as applied may be both prohibitively expensive and procedurally cumbersome. Displaced homeowners will necessarily be required to move out of the targeted community during its redevelopment (which may take years), find affordable, temporary replacement housing, and then move back to whatever is left of their former community when the redevelopment is complete. If the developer is required to shoulder these costs along with the limitations on redevelopment to allow for all current property owners to return, the incentives to develop may be inadequate. Those significant concerns aside, the right of return concept does address many distributive justice concerns. It grants owners of the property the right either to benefit directly from the redevelopment of their neighborhood and its increased amenities and job opportunities, while also granting them the choice to recoup the profits and use the proceeds to relocate.

The LAD proposed by Heller and Hills resembles in some respects Godsil's proposal described earlier by placing decision-making power in the hands of affected property owners.[67] The LAD concept is more far reaching, however, since it applies whenever eminent domain is proposed for economic development purposes to respond to the impossibility of assembling blocks of land that are owned by multiple owners.[68] LADs would not replace eminent domain, however, if a particular parcel of land is uniquely suited for a particular purpose.[69]

By allowing property owners to vote on a proposed sale, the power of the market is harnessed to increase the return property owners' receive on their property, and to allow an out should the majority conclude that they will be worse off than if they retained their homes in the community as presently constituted. The greatest risk (though one largely mitigated by Heller and Hills' proposal) is that property owners within the targeted community will be differently situated (commercial owners, residential owners and the like) and a majority vote may leave some worse off. Heller and Hills' proposal takes this concern into account by requiring a majority vote by each class of property owners rather than a majority of all property owners lumped together. The primary question this raises is whether such approval – both the process and the amount of any particular offer – would be so prohibitively expensive as to result in under-use of eminent domain for economically distressed areas. By contrast, even though the referendum process is meant to protect those who might not otherwise have a voice in the eminent domain process – outside of traditional republican processes – research suggests that a public referendum would provide little, if any, protection to traditionally stigmatized groups.[70] We are not suggesting

---

67 Heller and Hills propose that anyone with a property interest be included within the voting, including residential and commercial leaseholds. They suggest that majority approval by each class should be required. Heller & Hills, *supra* note 53, at 30–31.

68 *Id.* at 25.

69 *Id.*

70 DAVID BRODER, DEMOCRACY DERAILED: INITIATIVE CAMPAIGNS AND THE POWER OF MONEY 163 (2000) ("To a large extent, it is only those individuals and interest groups with access to big dollars who can play in the arena the Populists and Progressives created in order to balance the scales against the big-bucks operators.").

that this research is definitive, and indeed, the experience of communities organizing to oppose unwanted land uses in the environmental justice context provides strong contrary anecdotal evidence.[71] Of the many proposals intended to mitigate the unfairness associated with the use of eminent domain to promote economic development, the LAD proposal as devised by Heller and Hills seems most likely to optimize the interests of current residents. As noted above, however, it does not address the interests of those whose land the government seeks for other purposes. In addition, it seems likely that municipal governments and developers will seek to avoid the LAD proposal by arguing that the land they seek is "unique" in some way and therefore exempt from the LAD proposal. In either instance, we submit, a more specifically status preserving compensation scheme is critical to ensure that the compensation awarded is in fact "just."

Status Preserving Compensation

Traditional fair market value compensation fails to ensure the homeowner is "made whole" after a taking. To date, most alternative compensation plans are likely to leave some homeowners unable to preserve their status as a homeowner. The most effective, efficient, and just alternative is a compensatory scheme that preserves the homeowner's status as such. Additionally, this status preserving scheme also permits fiscally constrained governments to invoke the eminent domain power to expand the market of affordable housing,[72] encourage economic development,[73] and foster a tax base to support the provision of critical infrastructure and support services.[74]

Currently, the federal government, through the Uniform Relocation Assistance and Real Property Acquisition Policies for Federal and Federally Assisted Programs ("URA"), implements a status preserving scheme that should serve as a model statute for state adoption. The URA mandates that homeowners be compensated for moving expenses, mortgage costs that arise from early payment, closing costs, as well as a replacement payment to help ensure homeowners are provided with comparable post-taking housing.[75] The URA defines comparable housing as (1) decent, safe, and sanitary; (2) adequate in size to accommodate the occupants; (3) functionally equivalent to the acquired property; and (4) located in an area not subject to unreasonable adverse environmental conditions.[76]

Losing a home because of eminent domain undoubtedly carries with it lasting trauma for an unwilling seller. However, the URA's flexible definition serves to preserve homeowner status, and can move displaced residents living in substandard

---

71   See generally SHEILA FOSTER & LUKE COLE, FROM THE GROUND UP (2000).

72   Brief for Brooklyn United for Innovative Local Development et al. as Amici Curiae Supporting Respondents at 2, Kelo v. City of New London, 545 U.S. 469 (2005) [hereinafter BUILD Brief] (describing plans for redevelopment of the Atlantic Yards in Brooklyn, New York to expand the supply of affordable housing).

73   Brief of Respondent at 2–3, Kelo v. City of New London, 545 U.S. 469 (2005).

74   BUILD Brief, *supra* note 72, at 8.

75   42 U.S.C. § 4622(a)(1)–(3) (2000).

76   49 C.F.R. § 24.2(a)(6) (2006).

housing into improved living conditions. While this provision certainly does not eliminate the psychic and emotive harms caused by takings, it reinforces the condemner's obligation to displaced residents, and ensures, if nothing else, that an evicted homeowner can at least maintain his or her homeowner status. Furthermore, if the condemning authority cannot secure comparable replacement housing within the statutory relocation assistance amount, the URA contains a housing of last resort provision, which permits the condemning authority to provide compensation beyond the statutory limits.[77]

The URA status-preserving scheme eliminates inefficiencies created by the percentage premium plans discussed above. It permits the condemner to reduce the acquisition costs – thereby lowering the bill passed onto taxpayers – by paying traditional fair market value compensation to willing sellers. The URA plan extends the greatest protection to displaced homeowners and the broadest leverage to takers to adjust compensation to actual market conditions. This responsiveness is absent in flat percentage premium plans, community premiums, complete relocation plans, and premiums adjusted according to condemnees' length of residence in a community or socioeconomic status.

Status preserving compensation is also highly responsive to distributive justice concerns. It eliminates the problem of condemnation blight[78] because compensation is not based on the value of the acquired home, but on its replacement value. Furthermore, it reinforces homeownership as a core American value, it does not create perverse pressures that arise in insurance and tax-based compensation schemes, and extends the same level of protection to homeowners that condone the proceedings as to those who holdout.

Conclusion

It is rare indeed that an existing federal legislative scheme appears better suited to protect the most vulnerable among us from government abuse than a spate of scholarly proposals. When, however, Congress has enacted such a scheme, it behooves courts and state legislatures to follow suit. The Supreme Court has long held that the mandate of just compensation is met with the provision of fair market value unless manifest injustice will result. If the government's exercise of its power of eminent domain will result in the loss of homeowner status, this surely constitutes manifest injustice. The replacement provisions contained in the URA respond to this injustice.

---

77 § 4626(a); see also Garnett, *supra* note 19, at 122–3.

78 Condemnation blight describes the reduction in value of a property that occurs after it is announced that it will be condemned. Bell, *supra* note 19, at 67. Condemnation blight artificially lowers acquisition costs because fair market value is measured by "'what a willing buyer would pay in cash to a willing seller' at the time of the taking." United States v. 564.64 Acres of Land, 441 U.S. 506, 511 (1979) (quoting United States v. Miller, 317 U.S. 369, 374 (1943)).

Chapter 8

Kelo v. City of New London and the Prospects for Development after a Natural Disaster

Carol Necole Brown

Government's growing role as a participant in public-private economic development partnerships has prompted the judiciary to revisit the nature of the public use requirement under the Takings Clause of the Fifth Amendment[1] as evidenced by the United States Supreme Court's 2005 decision in *Kelo v. City of New London*.[2] Private property owners have been and are continuing to oppose joint urban development projects between government and private developers, commonly referred to as economic development takings.[3] These projects require the use of eminent domain and the transfer of private property to private developers in the pursuit of plans that serve public uses.[4] As the frequency and magnitude of these joint ventures increase, so too does the blurring of the public use versus private use distinction.

---

1 Charles M. Haar, *Reflections on* Euclid*: Social Contract and Private Purpose, in* ZONING AND THE AMERICAN DREAM 348 (Charles M. Haar & Jerold S. Kayden eds., 1989).

2 *Kelo*, 545 U.S. 469, 125 S. Ct. 2655 (2005).

3 See, e.g., Poletown v. City of Detroit, 410 Mich. 616 (1981), *overruled by* County of Wayne v. Hathcock, 471 Mich. 445 (2004) (as an example of the long history of struggle between government and private citizens regarding the propriety of economic development takings); *Kelo*, 125 S. Ct. at 2675.

4 *See, e.g.*, Ryan Chittum, *Eminent Domain: Is It Only Hope for Inner Cities?*, WALL ST. J., Oct. 5, 2005, at B1 (statement of private property owner in East St. Louis, Illinois: "'[E]minent domain is a horrible law … I feel that it's a little bit worse than communism.'"). *Id.* at B6. The court in *Poletown* held that the condemnation of private property and its transfer to General Motors Corp. for construction of an assembly plant was not a taking of private property for private use but rather for a public purpose. *Poletown*, 410 Mich. at 616, *overruled by Hathcock*, 471 Mich. at 445. More than twenty years later, the court overruled itself.

> Because *Poletown's* conception of a public use – that of "alleviating unemployment and revitalizing the economic base of the community" – has no support in the Court's eminent domain jurisprudence before the Constitution's ratification, its interpretation of "public use" … cannot reflect the common understanding of that phrase …

> *Hathcock*, 471 Mich. at 482–3.

In 1981, the Supreme Court of Michigan made history in the area of eminent domain jurisprudence in *Poletown Neighborhood Council v. City of Detroit*.[5] *Poletown* defined an era characterized by the broad interpretation of the scope of the public use doctrine to justify local and state governments' exercise of their takings power in furtherance of economic development initiatives.[6] In 2004, Michigan's highest court once again left an indelible mark on the eminent domain landscape when it overturned *Poletown* in a widely publicized decision, *County of Wayne v. Hathcock*.[7] While *Hathcock* was being decided by the Supreme Court of Michigan, *Kelo* was proceeding through the Connecticut state judicial process. Eventually, the United States Supreme Court granted certiorari in *Kelo*. The nation's highest court would consider the same question that the Michigan courts had been grappling with for years, whether the public use requirement for takings was broad enough to include the exercise of eminent domain powers solely for economic development purposes.

The devastation visited upon the Gulf Coast region in the same year that *Kelo* was decided intensified the attention directed toward *Kelo* and the exercise of eminent domain for economic development. New Orleans suffered extensive damage when Hurricane Katrina ravaged the Gulf Coast region in 2005. More than two-thirds of the City's rental housing, both affordable and market-rate, was destroyed and thousands of its citizens were displaced across the country.[8] The hardest hit populations tended to be the poor and minorities. In Hurricane Katrina's aftermath, some observers questioned whether the poor would be allowed back into New Orleans and whether *Kelo*'s affirmation of the constitutionality of economic development takings would be used by state and local government to separate the poor from their property and transfer it to wealthy developers for purposes of economic development.

This chapter considers the *Kelo* case and inquires whether an inevitable consequence of the Supreme Court's decision is increased gentrification and class segregation of our already heavily divided urban landscape, especially following a natural disaster such as the one visited upon the Gulf Coast region, specifically

---

5   *Poletown*, 410 Mich. at 616, *overruled by Hathcock*, 471 Mich. at 445.

6   Amanda S. Eckhoff & Dwight H. Merriam, *Public Use Goes Peripatetic: First, Michigan Reverses* Poletown *and Now the Supreme Court Grants Review in an Eminent Domain Case*, EMINENT DOMAIN USE AND ABUSE: KELO IN CONTEXT 33 (Dwight H. Merriam & Mary Nassaron Ross eds., 2006).

7   *Hathcock*, 471 Mich. at 445.

8   *The Road Home Rental Housing Program: Consequences for New Orleans* 1 (Bureau of Govt'l Research Sept. 2006), http://www.bgr.org/Consequences_for_N.O._091506. pdf (last visited Jan. 17, 2007); Sheila Crowley, *Presentation to Gulf Coast Recovery and Rebuilding Caucus, U.S. House of Reps.* (Mar. 7, 2006), http://www.nlihc.org/detail/article. cfm?article_id'3415&id'72 (last visited Jan. 17, 2007) (discussing, on behalf of the National Low Income Housing Coalition, the shortage of affordable housing in the broader context of the Gulf Coast region and estimating, conservatively, a loss of more than 214,400 affordable housing units in the region in 2005 from hurricanes and flooding). Dr. Crowley also noted that, as of the time of her briefing before the House of Representatives, there were in excess of 20,000 vacant rental units needing repair in New Orleans that were privately owned and that this housing could be used to provide housing to distressed people by making money for rehabilitation available to owners.

New Orleans, following Hurricane Katrina.[9] The Court in *Kelo* articulated a broad interpretation of public use and upheld the constitutionality of economic development takings. The decision has been described as a setback for private property rights and as authorizing an unprecedented and overreaching use of eminent domain to the detriment of individual property rights.[10] Moreover, many were and still are concerned that the Supreme Court's ruling in *Kelo* will make it too easy for government to use eminent domain to take private property, transfer it to private developers in pursuit of the public good, and permanently keep some homeowners out of New Orleans, all in the name of progress.

The Urban Land Institute assembled experts and an economic development advisory panel to create a redevelopment plan for New Orleans, "based on sound planning principles ... and a practical implementation strategy for rebuilding ... "[11] The Urban Land Institute's proposal anticipated using "eminent domain to acquire property located in blighted areas and to obtain land for public ownership."[12] In response, some City leaders stated that the Institute's approach for addressing the needs of "the most severely impacted areas [sent] 'the wrong message' to residents seeking to return to the [C]ity."[13]

So, what does the *Kelo* decision foretell in the context of natural disasters and redevelopment? Will *Kelo* open the door for communities such as New Orleans to disenfranchise their poor and minority citizens in the aftermath of natural disasters?[14] Will the poor disproportionately bear the burdens of urban renewal and development while reaping very few of the benefits and, if so, does *Kelo* bless this result?[15] After

---

9   Haar, *supra* note 1, at 348 (discussing "consumer gentrified central cities"); Douglas S. Massey & Nancy A. Denton, American Apartheid: Segregation and the Making of the Underclass (1993).

10   James W. Ely Jr., *Kelo: A Setback for Property Owners*, GP Solo Mag., Sept. 2006; see, e.g., Robert G. Dreher & John D. Echeverria, *Kelo's Unanswered Questions: The Policy Debate Over the Use of Eminent Domain for Economic Development* (Georgetown Envt'l Law & Policy Institute), *available at* http://www.law.georgetown.edu/gelpi/current_research/documents/GELPIReport_Kelo.pdf, at 11–12 (discussing the backlash following the *Kelo* decision and stating that "Public opinion polls showed strong popular opposition to the Supreme Court's decision, or at least the popular caricature of the decision. One Congressman denounced *Kelo* as the "*Dred Scott* decision of the 21st century.").

11   Urban Land Institute, *Executive Summary of Recommendations, A Strategy for Rebuilding New Orleans, Louisiana* 1 (Nov. 12–18, 2005), http://www.uli.org/Content/NavigationMenu/ProgramsServices/ AdvisoryServices/KatrinaPanel/exec_summary.pdf (last visited Apr. 24, 2007).

12   *Id.* at 6; Joe Gyan Jr., *Rebuilding Plan Divides N.O.: Think Tank Separates City Into Investment Zones; Hard-Hit Areas Last*, The Advocate, Nov. 29, 2005, at A01.

13   Gyan Jr., *supra* note 12, at A01.

14   *E.g.*, Dreher & Echeverria, *supra* note 10, at 14 ("Governments unfairly target minority and poor populations, and vulnerable entities such as churches, in exercising eminent domain.").

15   *E.g.*, *Kelo*, 125 S. Ct. 2655, 2687 (2005) (Thomas, J., dissenting).

Public works projects in the 1950's and 1960's destroyed predominantly minority communities in St. Paul, Minnesota, and Baltimore, Maryland. ... In 1981, urban

Kelo, should those who are most vulnerable to forced appropriation of their property be concerned that the decision defines a new era in which private developers, with the assistance of state and local governments, are increasingly able to disenfranchise vulnerable groups for the public good?[16]

I proceed first by analyzing the *Kelo*, *Hathcock*, and *Poletown* cases to discern what they individually and collectively contribute to an understanding of the Fifth Amendment's public use requirement. These three cases are united by common facts – economically depressed local economies, low property tax bases, and private companies promising additional jobs and increased revenues in exchange for local government's exercise of eminent domain to acquire the necessary property for their

---

planners in Detroit, Michigan, uprooted the largely "lower-income and elderly" Poletown neighborhood for the benefit of the General Motors Corporation. ... Urban renewal projects have long been associated with the displacement of blacks; [i]n cities across the country, urban renewal came to be known as "Negro removal."

Id. (citations omitted); Richard O. Brooks, Kelo *and the "Whaling City": The Failure of the Supreme Court's Opportunity to Articulate a Public Purpose of Sustainability, in* THE SUPREME COURT AND TAKINGS: FOUR ESSAYS 6 (2005) (discussing New London as plagued by decreasing population overall and increasing numbers of minority, low income, and elderly residents); Juliana Maantay, *Zoning Law, Health, and Environmental Justice: What's the Connection?*, 30 J. LAW MEDICINE & ETHICS 572, 578 (2002) (stating that "the inherently exclusionary 'market forces' framework of our economic system ... have a profound impact on the equity of land use practices and protections"); DIVIDED HIGHWAYS (PBS 1997) (film discussing the disproportionate impact of eminent domain on minority communities as part of the construction of the American Highway system); Andrea Bernstein, *New York Hopes to Nurture Artist Neighborhoods*, NPR Morning Edition (radio broadcast May 16, 2006), *available at* http://www.npr.org/templates/story/story.php?storyId'5407563 (discussing gentrification of areas of New York City, the East Village, Brooklyn, and Soho as resident artists are forced to move in search of affordable housing, some under pressure from eager real estate developers anxious to create real estate value by developing gourmet food shops and million dollar apartments).

16 Paul Nowell, *Banker Takes Stance Against Eminent Domain*, TUSCALOOSA NEWS, MAR. 5, 2006, at 1D, 4D.

BB&T Corp.'s John Allison ... declared in January that the nation's ninth-largest bank would no longer make loans to developers who planned to build commercial projects on land seized from private citizens through the power of eminent domain.

They really want to use it [eminent domain] as lever[age] to drive down the price," he said, adding that there have already been abuses of eminent domain rules, with the victims mostly among the poor, minorities and the elderly.

Normally, eminent domain does not even come into play until after a huge public process said Maureen McAvey, a senior fellow at the Urban Land Institute. The truth of the matter is that it is used as a last resort. No one wants to go through all the damage.

Id.

development projects.[17] Given their temporal alignment, one might inquire whether the United States Supreme Court granted certiorari in *Kelo* in order to settle the debates occurring in the media and across America about whether governments and the courts were going too far in exercising eminent domain.[18] The obvious relatedness of these cases warrants their combined analysis. Next, I consider *Kelo* and its implications for redevelopment in New Orleans and, more broadly, following natural disasters.

Kelo v. City of New London

The ambiguity attending the proper limitations that should be placed on the public use requirement under federal and state law reaches as far back as the men credited with identifying the power of eminent domain.[19] Was eminent domain only to be exercised for "public advantage" or could it be that "public utility" better defined its scope?[20] Could eminent domain be exercised when "adequate grounds" existed or "in case of necessity, and for the public safety."[21] The United States Supreme Court reexamined the scope of the public use doctrine in *Kelo v. City of New London.*

In 2000, the City of New London, Connecticut approved a development plan that focused on ninety acres of property located proximate to a new three hundred million dollar research facility that Pfizer, Inc. announced it would build. State and local officials targeted New London for economic revitalization with the assistance of the New London Development Corporation (hereinafter NLDC), a private non-profit corporation established to assist the City of New London with economic development. While the NLDC successfully negotiated the purchase of the majority of the ninety acres, nine property owners refused to sell. The NLDC initiated condemnation proceedings to acquire the remaining properties in the City's name. Later, the NLDC announced that some of the parcels would be leased to private developers.[22] Property owners alleged that the proposed condemnations violated the public use restriction of the Fifth Amendment Takings Clause. The Connecticut Superior Court held that the condemnations were valid as to some properties and invalid as to others. Both parties appealed to the Supreme Court of Connecticut. A majority of that court upheld all of the proposed condemnations; three dissenting justices urged a "heightened" standard of review because this was an economic

---

17 Eckhoff & Merriam, *supra* note 6.

18 *Id.* at 44. "The Michigan court handed down *Hathcock* 149 days after the Connecticut Supreme Court ruled in *Kelo*, and the U.S. Supreme Court granted certiorari in *Kelo* two months after *Hathcock.*" *Id.*

19 For a compelling exploration of the history of eminent domain and the public use clause, see Alberto Lopez, *Weighing and Reweighing Eminent Domain's Political Philosophies Post-Kelo*, 41 WAKE FOREST L. REV. 237, Part III.A (2006).

20 *Id.* at 256.

21 *Id.*

22 Long-term ground leases of 99 years at the nominal rent of $1 per year were contemplated though, at the time of the state court litigation, none had been signed. *Kelo*, 125 S. Ct. at 2660 n.4.

development taking.[23] The United States Supreme Court granted certiorari to determine whether economic development takings satisfied the Fifth Amendment's public use requirement.

The Court adopted a broad definition of public use.[24] It acknowledged that during the middle of the nineteenth century, many state courts defined the public use clause as literally requiring "use by the public."[25] [T]he Court stressed "the inadequacy of use by the general public as a universal test" and described it as not only impractical to administer but also as ill-suited to meeting evolving societal needs.[26] Relying on its decisions in *Berman*,[27] *Midkiff*,[28] and *Ruckelshaus*,[29] the Court articulated its support of a broad understanding of public use. Its interpretation of public use: (1) was broad enough to include the spiritual, aesthetic, and monetary components of the public welfare, (2) reflected its deference to state legislative judgments, and (3) embraced a policy that was sufficiently permissive to account for ever-changing and evolving demands by the public for government to ensure its access to a broad range of public benefits.[30]

The Court was not deterred by the fact that economic development takings and government pursuit of public benefits would also benefit private parties. As long as the government's purpose was legitimate and its means rational, the better course was judicial deference to legislative decision-making and rejection of heightened scrutiny and review. Consistent with this notion of judicial deference to legislative bodies in the area of land use policy, the Court emphasized that individual states retained the authority to adopt more rigorous public use requirements than the federal baseline mandated. Justice Kennedy, concurring, clarified that even under rational basis review, if the public benefits of a particular economic development taking were

---

23 *Id.* at 2661.

24 *Id.* at 2662.

25 *Id.*

26 *Id.*

27 Berman v. Parker, 348 U.S. 26 (1954) (concerning redevelopment of blighted areas of Washington, D.C.). "Berman dealt with the question of whether Congress had the power to condemn a particular area of Washington, D.C. in favor of an urban renewal project for the sole purpose of improving the aesthetics of the neighborhood." Daniel T. Cavarello, *From* Penn Central *to* United Artists' I & II: *The Rise to Immunity of Historic Preservation Designation From Successful Takings Challenges*, 22 B.C. ENVTL. AFF. L. REV. 593, 600 (1995).

28 Hawaii Housing Auth. et al. v. Midkiff et al., 467 U.S. 229 (1984) (permitting the forcible transfer of title from landlords to tenants upon payment of just compensation). The United States Supreme Court upheld the use of eminent domain to terminate a land oligopoly in Hawaii that was "skewing the State's residential fee simple market, inflating land prices, and injuring the public tranquility and welfare, and therefore enacted a condemnation scheme for redistributing title." *Kelo*, 125 S. Ct. at 2674.

29 Ruckelshaus v. Monsanto Co., 467 U.S. 986 (1984) (permitting the EPA access to certain trade secrets of prior applicants in evaluating subsequent applications as long as the subsequent applicants paid compensation to the prior applicants).

30 *Kelo*, 125 S. Ct. at 2662–3.

"only incidental or pretextual" the government's action would fail to meet the Fifth Amendment's public use mandate.[31]

Justices O'Connor, Thomas, and Scalia dissented and would have adopted a bright line rule; economic development takings are always unconstitutional.[32] The dissent held that economic development takings violated the public use requirement because their *incidental* public benefits merge with their *direct* private benefits, making it difficult to isolate the true motives underlying the takings and to measure the extent of the promised gains to the public. Justice Thomas was particularly disturbed by what he characterized as the majority's continuing misconstruction of the public use clause of the Fifth Amendment. He wrote that government may only take private property through eminent domain "if the government owns, or the public has a legal right to use, the property, as opposed to taking it for any public purpose or necessity whatsoever."[33] Continuing public accountability is critical; the public must have a right to use and employ property taken pursuant to the Takings Clause if the taking is to pass constitutional muster. According to Justice Thomas, mere incidental public benefit is not sufficient.

Poletown Neighborhood Council v. City of Detroit Reversed[34]

More than two decades before the United States Supreme Court decided *Kelo*, the Michigan Supreme Court was presented with a similar question, whether the concept of eminent domain was broad enough to permit the condemnation of private property and its transfer to a private entity for economic development. The question before the *Poletown* court then and most recently before the United States Supreme Court in *Kelo* required the judiciary to reflect on the historical intentions of constitutional drafters when providing for the power of eminent domain. The Michigan Supreme Court understood that its decision would impact the tenuous balance between citizens' private property rights and governments' need for broadly construed eminent domain powers. The court articulated an expanded historic understanding of the police power, sufficient to allow the exercise of eminent domain for economic development in pursuit of the public welfare.

Homeowners and members of a neighborhood association challenged the Detroit Economic Development Corporation's authority to condemn their private property for transfer to a private corporation, General Motors, to construct an assembly plant. These plaintiffs contended that the exercise of eminent domain to take private property and transfer it to a private corporation to bolster economic development violated the takings clause of the 1963 Michigan State Constitution set forth in

31 *Id.* at 2669 (Kennedy, J., concurring) ("A court applying rational-basis review under the Public Use Clause should strike down a taking that, by a clear showing, is intended to favor a particular private party, with only incidental or pretextual public benefits ... .").

32 *Id.* at 2673 (O'Connor, J., dissenting; Thomas and Scalia, JJ., concurring in dissent).

33 *Id.* at 2679 (Thomas, J., dissenting).

34 For one of the most comprehensive discussions of the Poletown dilemma and history, see Bryan D. Jones & Lynn W. Bachelor, The Sustaining Hand: Community Leadership and Corporate Power (2d ed. 1993).

article 10, section 2.[35] Article 10, section 2 prohibited the government's forcible acquisition of private property for public use without paying just compensation and had "been interpreted as requiring that the power of eminent domain not be invoked except to further a public use or purpose."[36]

Plaintiffs argued in favor of a restricted understanding of public use. Through the Economic Development Corporations Act, the Michigan Legislature authorized municipalities to acquire property by eminent domain, when necessary, as a means of partnering with private industry to expand commercial activities for the purpose of increasing municipal facilities, improving services, and revitalizing the state and local economies.[37] Plaintiffs did not challenge the Michigan Legislature's assertion that fulfillment of the above objectives constituted valid public purposes; however, they did disagree with the defendants' and with the court's contention that this project was an appropriate use for eminent domain. According to the plaintiffs, the public benefits derived from the proposed project were merely incidental; General Motors was the primary beneficiary. Therefore, condemning land and transferring it to General Motors for uncontrolled profit-making was a taking of private property for *private use* and constituted a substantive due process violation of article 10, section 2 of the Michigan Constitution.

Defendants disputed the plaintiffs' characterization of the public purpose as merely incidental. They framed the public purpose – ameliorating fiscal distress and reducing unemployment through creation of an industrial facility – as central and argued that the fact that this objective would be achieved through a public-private partnership did not defeat the fundamentally public purpose focus of the enterprise. The trial court ruled in favor of the defendants. The plaintiffs appealed the trial court decision and filed an application to bypass the appellate court and have the matter considered by the Michigan Supreme Court. Their application was granted.

In a five-to-two decision, the Michigan Supreme Court affirmed the holding of the trial court and found that the proposed condemnations were constitutionally valid. The court crafted its opinion circumspectly, leaving itself opportunity to reject future efforts to use eminent domain in furtherance of economic development. It used the terms public use and public purpose interchangeably to justify the use of eminent domain in instances that would primarily benefit the public. The court stated that a heightened level of review was appropriate in cases where identifiable private parties would receive direct benefits.[38]

Poletown did not usher in a rash of economic development takings, as was feared by some, and in this regard it enjoyed limited precedential value. In the years following

---

35 *Poletown*, 410 Mich. at 629 (citing MICH. CONST. art. X, 2).

36 *Id.*

37 Economic Development Corporations Act, MICH. COMP. LAWS §§ 125.1601–36 (2007).

38 *Poletown*, 410 Mich. at 634–5. In *County of Wayne v. Hathcock*, the Michigan Supreme Court considered *Poletown*'s "heightened scrutiny" test as discussed in an earlier Michigan Supreme Court case on which the defendants unsuccessfully relied, *City of Lansing v. Edward Rose Realty, Inc.*, 442 Mich. 626 (1993). The *Hathcock* court spent considerable judicial time parsing the constitutional meaning of public use and public purpose. *Hathcock*, 471 Mich. at 468–73 (discussing public use as a legal term of art).

the decision, state and local governments largely used their traditional police power authority to justify the acquisition of private property by eminent domain.[39]

Twenty-three years later, the Michigan Supreme Court reversed *Poletown* in *County of Wayne v. Hathcock.*[40] Wayne County sought to revive southeast Michigan's struggling economy by exercising its power of eminent domain to condemn private property and construct a business and technology park. The defendant property owners in *Hathcock* challenged plaintiff Wayne County's attempt to condemn nineteen parcels of private property as part of a county approved plan to construct a one thousand three hundred acre business and technology park. According to the plan, the condemned property would be transferred to a private entity for development.

The trial and appellate courts held that the condemnations were authorized by the Economic Development Corporations Act and were constitutionally permitted pursuant to article 10, section 2 of the 1963 Michigan Constitution. The *Poletown* decision carried heavy precedential value as the lower courts considered the case.

The Michigan Supreme Court granted the defendants' appeal application primarily for the purpose of reconsidering the public use test articulated in *Poletown.*[41] Thus the stage was set once again to address the difficult constitutional dilemma of framing the meaning of public use as ratified in article 10, section 2. Would the court pursue a more moderate path, escheating clearly defined rules and articulating yet another poorly defined principle of limited guidance in the area of eminent domain and land use law?[42] Or, would the court articulate an extreme view of public use? According to one extreme, the existence of a public use for eminent domain purposes only exists when the public is vested with a right or entitlement to physically use or enjoy the subject property. Pursuant to the other extreme, public use exists in "anything which [will] enlarge the resources, increase the industrial energies, and promote the

---

39 William A. Fischel, *The Political Economy of Public Use in* Poletown: *How Federal Grants Encourage Excessive Use of Eminent Domain*, 2004 MICH. ST. L. REV. 929. "Local governments are generally responsive to the concerns of their communities, especially when the issues involve spending their own tax money. When using their own resources, they do not usually displace their own citizens without strong reasons." *Id.* at 954.

40 *Hathcock*, 471 Mich. at 445.

41 *Id.*

Our grant order directed the parties to the following issues:
... (2) whether the proposed taking[s], which are at least partly intended to result in later transfers to private entities, are for a "public purpose," pursuant to *Poletown* ... ; and (3) whether the "public purpose" test set forth in *Poletown*, ... is consistent with Const 1963, art 10, 2 and, if not, whether this test should be overruled.

Id. at 454–5.

42 Carol Necole Brown, *Taking the Takings Claim; A Policy and Economic Analysis of the Survival of Takings Claims After Property Transfers,* 36 CONN. L. REV. 7, 21–3 (2003) (discussing the persisting murkiness of the doctrine of investment-backed expectations to regulatory takings claims); *Poletown*, 410 Mich. at 643–64 (Fitzgerald, J., dissenting) (stating that "while it is difficult and perhaps futile to categorize individual states as utilizing a 'broad' or 'narrow' interpretation of 'public use' for condemnation purposes, Michigan law seems most consistent with that of states that give a more limited construction to the term.").

productive power of any considerable number of the inhabitants of a section of the state, or which leads to the growth of towns and the creation of new resources for the employment of capital and labor."[43]

The court chose the more moderate path and declined to articulate one comprehensive definition of the public use requirement.[44] Instead, it relied upon the dissenting opinion in *Poletown* and held that the proposed condemnations were unconstitutional. According to the court, the project lacked the three elements necessary to justify the exercise of eminent domain and the transfer of private property to a private corporation in cases not involving instrumentalities of commerce: "(1) public necessity of the extreme sort, (2) continuing accountability to the public, and (3) selection of land according to facts of independent public significance."[45]

The majority characterized the *Poletown* decision as an unauthorized, even radical, departure from the Michigan Supreme Court's eminent domain jurisprudence, one which "rendered nugatory the constitutional public use requirement."[46] *Poletown* was thus overruled and, according to the court, the law of eminent domain and its public use requirement were returned to their pre-*Poletown* condition.

Though *Poletown* has been reversed, assume that instead of transferring condemned land to General Motors, the City of Detroit had retained title to the land and entered into long-term ground leases with General Motors, similar to those contemplated in *Kelo*.[47] Under these altered facts, is it more likely that the *Hathcock* court would have affirmed rather than reversed *Poletown*? Does the alteration of the facts to leave title vested in the local government but with a long-term present possessory interest in a private party somehow make it clearer that the exercise of eminent domain is truly in direct furtherance of a public use? The displacement is the same under both plans and the promise of economic revitalization is the catalyst.[48]

> The enduring fact is that almost all projects that employ eminent domain are for economic development. This is true even for those undertaken and run by the government itself. New roads, municipal buildings, and parks are as much a part of economic development and redevelopment as are shopping centers and manufacturing facilities.[49]

Fairness and justice should be at the forefront of the eminent domain debate especially when vulnerable cities and their citizens are struggling to recover from catastrophes. The world is a changing and evolving place. Governments need the authority to adjust economic burdens within the boundaries of fairness for all of its citizens. No longer do citizens merely seek abundant roads, an ample supply of fire stations, and safe schools. Citizens are increasingly demanding more from government and as government strains to meet these needs, it must do so in light of important justice concerns that attend the redistribution of property.

---

43 1 PHILIP NICHOLS, THE LAW OF EMINENT DOMAIN 130–31(2d ed. 1917).

44 *Poletown*, 410 Mich. at 674–5 (Ryan, J., dissenting); *Hathcock*, 471 Mich. at 473.

45 410 Mich. at 674 (Ryan, J., dissenting) (cited by *Hathcock*, 471 Mich. at 493).

46 *Hathcock*, 471 Mich. at 483.

47 *Kelo*, 125 S. Ct. at 2660 n.4.

48 *Id.*

49 Fischel, *supra* note 39, at 946.

Gentrification by Disaster and *Kelo*, Do the Two Mix?

The business of eminent domain is not a science; rather, there is an element of preference and prejudice that sometimes injures the legitimate but socially disfavored property rights of select citizens. Whether the *Kelo* Court's deference to the States on matters of eminent domain and constitutional interpretation is appropriate is a subject rich for debate. The *Kelo* case does not address the public use versus private property rights dilemma in the context of natural disasters. *Kelo*'s future impact can be discerned only by understanding the legislative and judicial constraints historically placed on the use of eminent domain in the context of disastrous situations. Because *Kelo* did not involve a case of natural disaster, it is especially important to discuss the intersection of public and private interests in the context of New Orleans' more recent history with natural disasters.

A Select History of New Orleans' Experience with Disaster

Most of New Orleans lies between five and ten feet below sea level. Flooding is a permanent part of New Orleans' history and likely its future. Situated only fifty miles from the Gulf of Mexico and surrounded by a chain of levees, reservoirs, pumping and drainage stations, channels and floodways, New Orleans has been described as "a study in the very defiance of water."[50]

Hurricane Katrina is not the first storm to challenge New Orleans and other Gulf Coast cities with the mammoth task of remaking themselves, though it is the worst disaster to strike the United States in terms of cost.[51] The Mississippi River Flood of 1927 hit the Gulf South with tremendous force, killing as many as five hundred people, dislocating another six hundred thirty-seven thousand and flooding more than sixteen million acres of land in seven states.[52] By 1927, levees extended for a thousand miles, from Memphis, Tennessee to New Orleans, Louisiana.[53] Several days of rain preceded the April 1927 flood which is recalled as one of the greatest floods in American history.[54]

The 1927 flood is particularly relevant because just as Hurricane Katrina is a defining event in twenty-first century American life, so too was the 1927 flood for

---

50 Oliver A. Houck, *Rising Water: The National Flood Insurance Program and Louisiana*, 60 Tul. L. Rev. 61, 64 (1985).

51 Richard M. Rosan, *Rebuilding New Orleans and the Gulf Coast – A Long Look Ahead*, http://europe.uli.org/AM/Template.cfm?Section'ULI_Europe_Home&Template'/CM/HTMLDisplay.cfm&ContentID'34304 (last visited Mar. 28, 2007).

52 Rick Shenkman, *Interview with Pete Daniel: The Great Flood of 1927*, http://hnn.us/ articles/15370.html (last visited June 9, 2006); John M. Barry, Rising Tide: The Great Mississippi Flood of 1927 and How It Changed America 285–6, 289, 330–31 (1998) (discussing deaths and economic loss estimates by the American Red Cross).

53 Barry, *supra* note 52, at 40; William Alexander Percy, Lanterns on the Levee: Recollections of a Planter's Son 245–55 (Knopf 1941) (1973).

54 See Percy, *supra* note 53 (discussing the legacy of the flood in general); see Barry, *supra* note 52 (discussing the impact of the flood in general).

the twentieth century.[55] Though New Orleans was saved from the ravages of the 1927 flood by cutting the levee fourteen miles south of New Orleans and diverting the waters to less fortunate lands, the similarities in the two events and in the national response prove useful backdrops for understanding *Kelo* and the likelihood of it serving as a tool for achieving gentrification in disaster contexts.[56] As with Hurricane Katrina, the repercussions of the 1927 flood crossed color and class lines and required coordinated efforts from federal, state, and local government.

There are important similarities and distinctions between the 1927 flood and Hurricane Katrina. The federal government was intricately involved with both relief efforts. Herbert Hoover, Secretary of Commerce, was appointed by President Calvin Coolidge to coordinate the 1927 relief effort which apparently proceeded with greater facility and efficiency than the Hurricane Katrina relief efforts of 2005. Hoover oversaw the Red Cross in 1927 which established more than one hundred fifty refugee camps and worked efficiently to aid rescue efforts and provide food and healthcare in the camps. In the aftermath of Hurricane Katrina, the Red Cross also facilitated relief efforts. During both disasters, citizens on the Gulf Coast and across the nation rallied to provide their support. People of all stations cooperated to feed, clothe, shelter, and evacuate as many as possible.

On a less noble note, poverty and racial strife contributed to the devastation of the 1927 flood and of Hurricane Katrina.[57] The Red Cross camps during the 1927 flood were forcibly segregated and the evidence suggests that some blacks were detained in flood areas and forced to work on the levees in an effort to fight back the Mississippi River.[58] Similarly, during and in the aftermath of Hurricane Katrina, poor and minority citizens were disproportionately impacted and had greater difficulty evacuating than other segments of the population. Some parish authorities erected barriers between the Ninth Ward of New Orleans and neighboring white suburban parishes and even issued shoot-to-kill orders to police officials.[59] The nation responded to both disasters resolute to: (1) develop better disaster plans and cooperation between the various levels of government, (2) rebuild the levees, and (3) improve infrastructure.[60]

---

55 See BARRY, *supra* note 52 (providing a comprehensive account of the impacts of the 1927 flood).

56 David Dillon, *How Should City Rebuild Neighborhoods and Infrastructure, Reinvent Economy? Problems Plentiful, Certainties Few As Big Easy Plans Recovery*, DALLAS MORNING NEWS, Nov. 20, 2005, at 1A. New Orleans and its Lower Ninth Ward were not so fortunate in 1965 with Hurricane Betsy. Many in the Ninth Ward believe that city officials permitted the intentional flooding of that area in order to save affluent, predominately white neighborhoods.

57 PERCY *supra* note 53, at 252.

58 *Id.* at 256–58; Lee Hancock, *Is It Black and White? In A City Split and Sinking Before Storm, Racial Issues Boil*, DALLAS MORNING NEWS, Dec. 4, 2005, at 1A.

59 *Id.* at 1A.

60 Shenkman, *supra* note 52; Urban Land Institute, *Executive Summary of Recommendations, A Strategy for Rebuilding New Orleans, Louisiana* 1 (Nov. 12–18, 2005), http://www.uli.org/Content/ NavigationMenu/ProgramsServices/AdvisoryServices/ KatrinaPanel/exec_summary.pdf (last visited Apr. 24, 2007).

With New Orleans' history of natural disaster and the likelihood of recurrence, smart planning and land use are especially necessary. Katrina laid bare the disparities that have affected many poor residents for decades.[61] This history is partly responsible for the fear of some that residents of the estimated one hundred fifty thousand flooded homes, many located in predominantly poor, minority, low-lying areas will be forced out and their neighborhoods gentrified. This fear was legitimized when investors and prospectors quickly began contacting local real estate agents attempting to purchase both habitable and flooded homes while residents and evacuees were still reeling from the devastation of Hurricane Katrina.

Private Economy and the Public Interest

In natural disaster situations, under what circumstances does safeguarding the public welfare and safety justify government's exercise of its police power and of the power of eminent domain?[62] Zoning and regulating to prevent development in flood plains is an example of one of the oldest and most established uses of the police power to

---

61 E.g., Liza Featherstone, *The Other Side of the Big Easy*, Grist Mag., http://www. alternet. org/story/25278 (last visited June 24, 2006) (stating that many of the toxins that now pollute New Orleans' streets are the product of environmental injustice and may make many parts of the city uninhabitable for years); Steven M. Presley et al., *Assessment of Pathogens and Toxicants in New Orleans, LA Following Hurricane Katrina*, 40(2) Envtl. Sci. & Tech. 468–74 (2006); Martha Carr, *National Experts Focus on N.O.; Los Angeles Gathering Takes Holistic Approach*, Times Picayune (New Orleans), Nov. 4, 2005, at 1 ("While most city residents remain focused on when they can return to their homes and rebuild on their property, [Urban Land Institute] members said residents need to begin thinking about where that property might fit into the city's long-term redevelopment. Many warned it will take at least 10 years for the city to build enough housing to restore the city's original population."); Shaheen Pasha, *Property Grabs and the Gulf: Local Governments Will Likely Use Eminent Domain to Rebuild: Who Will That Help?*, http://money.cnn.com/2005/10/05/news/economy/eminent_domain_katrina/ (last visited Mar. 29, 2007); David Streitfeld, *Speculators Rushing In as the Water Recedes*, Sept. 15, 2006, http://www.pipeline.com/~rougeforum/spectatorsrushing.html.

62 Dillon, *supra* note 56, at 1A.

The footprint of New Orleans in 1878 and the unflooded areas after Katrina are virtually identical. In 19th-century New Orleans, development was confined to the higher ground on the east bank of the Mississippi … while the areas that flooded in 2005 (the Lower Ninth Ward, New Orleans East and Lakeview) were uninhabited cypress swamp. Earlier residents knew what the river and the tides could do and built defensively.

All of which suggests an orderly retreat to higher ground. If New Orleans were merely an abstract planning problem – detached from people, politics and history – that is probably what would happen. The city would redline, or write off, New Orleans East, the Lower Ninth Ward and parts of Lakeview, compensate and relocate the property owners, and turn the abandoned land into parks, wetlands and playing fields. The goal would be to reinforce the historic core of the city, with its dense, mixed-use development laid out along transit lines.

Id.; Martha Carr, *Rebuilding Should Begin on High Ground, Group Says; Planners Warn Against Haphazard Development*, Times–Picayune (New Orleans), Nov. 19, 2005, at 1.

prevent public harm, essentially protecting the public from itself. "[P]ioneering work on flood control gradually convinced cities and the federal government that it would be more efficient to recognize that floods are positive natural processes and that humans should adapt to them by not putting costly permanent structures in flood plains."[63]

Governments have long recognized that they are safely within their police power discretion to use zoning and even eminent domain to prevent loss of life and property to those who would be inclined to ignore the perils of developing and residing in flood plains and federal policy even requires flood plain zoning.[64] The above is a clear example of police power exercise to accomplish general welfare zoning. Regardless of one's personal or political views regarding how and to what extent New Orleans should be rebuilt, comprehensive planning will be necessary.[65] Eminent domain and zoning are crucial aspects of comprehensive planning.

Broadly understood, the police power allows state and federal governments to regulate private citizens' property and liberty.[66] *Commonwealth v. Alger*[67] is frequently cited as the beginning point for a discussion of the history of the police power and the state of regulation in America. Chief Justice Lemuel Shaw's decision in *Alger*,

---

Tackling what is certain to be the most controversial aspect of any rebuilding plan, the contingent from the Urban Land Institute said Friday that the city should use its *original footprint*, as well as lessons learned from Hurricane Katrina, as a guide in determining what areas are most logical for redevelopment.

"Your housing is now a public resource," said Tony Salazar, a developer with McCormack, Baron and Salazar in Los Angeles. "You can't think of it as private property any more."

Id. (emphasis added).

63 A. Dan Tarlock, *Local Government Protection of Biodiversity: What is Its Niche?*, 60 U. Chi. L. Rev. 555, 576 (1993) (citations omitted).

64 *Id.* at 576–77; *see also* David G. Tucker & Alfred O. Bragg, III, *Florida's Law of Storms: Emergency Management, Local Government, and the Police Power*, 30 Stetson L. Rev. 837 (2001) (discussing the police power in the context of states of emergency). Specifically as it pertains to New Orleans, when it became clear that houses sustaining substantial damage (defined as houses requiring repairs that cost more than fifty percent of the cost to completely rebuild) would have to be built to one hundred year elevation standards in order to remain eligible for the federal government's flood insurance program, New Orleans authorities allowed many homeowners to appeal their assessed damage percentage and seek a downward revision to avoid having to elevate the homes they were rebuilding. When FEMA stated that all new and rebuilt houses should be raised an additional three feet above grade, New Orleans officials resisted strongly and have delayed passing a local ordinance implementing the FEMA requirement. FEMA and the Louisiana Recovery Authority, though, may mandate adherence to the above stated requirement as a condition for qualifying to receive Community Bloc Grants. See Brian Thevenot, *Finally, Rules for Rebuilding*, Times Picayune (New Orleans), Apr. 13, 2006, at 1.

65 Nicholas Lemann, *In the Ruins*, New Yorker, Sept. 12, 2005, http://www.newyorker.com/printables/ talk/050912ta_talk_lemann.

66 Lochner v. New York, 198 U.S. 45, 53 (1905).

67 Commonwealth v. Alger, 61 Mass. (7 Cush.) 53 (1851).

specifically his justification of the public restriction of private property rights, is considered to be one of the most compelling explanations of the police power:

> All property in this commonwealth ... is derived directly or indirectly from the government, and held subject to those general regulations, which are necessary to the common good and general welfare. Rights of property, like all other social and conventional rights, are subject to such reasonable limitations in their enjoyment, as shall prevent them from being injurious, and to such reasonable restraints and regulations established by law, as the legislature, under the governing and controlling power vested in them by the constitution, may think necessary and expedient. ... The power we allude to is ... the police power; the power vested in the legislature by the constitution to make, ordain, and establish all manner of wholesome and reasonable laws, statutes, and ordinances, either with penalties or without, not repugnant to the constitution, as they shall judge to be for the good and welfare of the Commonwealth. ... It is much easier to perceive and realize the existence and sources of this power than to mark its boundaries, or prescribe limits to its exercise.[68]

When natural disasters are constantly threatening, one does not need to rely upon cases such as *Kelo*, *Poletown*, or *Hathcock* that are struggling to fit economic development into the takings framework. Zoning and condemnation in pursuit of the public welfare and safety have always been embraced within the understanding of public use. Eminent domain is sometimes employed to address needs arising from catastrophes and in these instances, a broad and permissive understanding of public use helps government. Particularly, when strategizing to rebuild urban areas that have been repeatedly devastated by disasters, such as New Orleans, traditional police power jurisprudence permits taking decisions to be made based upon long-established police power principles and obviates the need to rely on nuanced or vague cases of constitutional interpretation.

Citizens rely upon government to secure the public welfare when an area is altered by natural disaster. Local and state governments should employ responsible land use planning and development policies following disaster situations. The goal is to redevelop and reconstitute communities so as to best provide for the public welfare and to avoid spot redevelopment, the epitome of poor planning. Instances of catastrophe and disaster reflect the most traditional uses of eminent domain – that of slum clearance and urban renewal – and are different from pure economic development takings unaccompanied by natural disaster.

"An intelligent city plan thinks impartially for all parts of the city at the same time, and does not forget the greater needs of tomorrow in the press of today."[69] Exercise of the police power and of the related power of eminent domain as tools for rebuilding in the aftermath of natural disasters may be necessary if government is to function properly and serve the public's best interest. Those concerned about the *Kelo* decision are afraid that government will increasingly use eminent domain for private development.[70] But even *Kelo*'s opponents concede that it is well established that

---

68 WILLIAM J. NOVAK, THE PEOPLES WELFARE LAW & REGULATION IN NINETEENTH-CENTURY AMERICA 19–20 (1996) (citing *Alger*, 61 Mass. (7 Cush.) at 84–85).

69 Rosan, *supra* note 51.

70 Brown, *supra* note 42, at 17.

government may regulate by exercise of its police power for purposes of maintaining public health, safety, morals and general welfare.

There are short term and long term costs of rebuilding New Orleans. These costs may justify the condemnation of significant amounts of private property that are especially prone to flood hazards, either because of their location or their population density. The police power in American constitutional law has been a source of ambiguity and of some confusion which, in a quizzical way, makes it the perfect reprieve from the social tensions and debate surrounding the *Kelo* decision. When disaster situations arise, governments will not need to rely upon *Kelo* as a basis for their authority to exercise eminent domain; rather, the police power, even with its shadowy history, provides virtually unequivocal authority for governments to exercise their takings power in these situations.[71]

Conclusion

The Fifth Amendment Takings Clause has always mediated between government and its citizens in the enjoyment of their private property.[72] One purpose of the Fifth Amendment's compensation requirement is to restrain government from infringing too heavily on private property interests. In framing the Fifth Amendment's Taking Clause, James Madison intended to protect propertied citizens from government's overly aggressive intrusion upon their land.[73] "Madison's and other's high regard for physical rights to private property reflected prevailing notions that land, as the most treasured form of private property, was the gateway to individual autonomy and a necessary prerequisite for full societal participation."[74]

The business of eminent domain is not a science; rather, there is an element of preference and prejudice which sometimes injures the legitimate but socially disfavored property rights of select citizens. At some level, the definition of public use is a political question and has been for a long time. *Kelo* does not condone all public–private partnerships nor does it condemn them.

Private entities can play an important role in closing the chasm between citizens' demands and governments' abilities to meet them. *Kelo* leaves in place meaningful mechanisms for citizens to challenge regulatory decisions by government. These mechanisms are essential to ensuring equity and fairness in allocating the burdens and benefits of citizenship. While it is likely that some good people will lose their homes following Hurricane Katrina and other good people will lament their loss, this tension is inherent in the Takings Clause and is not unduly exacerbated by *Kelo*.

---

71 RICHARD A. EPSTEIN, TAKINGS: PRIVATE PROPERTY AND THE POWER OF EMINENT DOMAIN 107 (1985).

72 Brown, *supra* note 42, at 7–9.

73 *Id.* at 17. William Michael Treanor, *The Original Understanding of the Takings Clause and the Political Process*, 95 COLUM. L. REV. 782 (1995).

74 Carol Necole Brown & Serena M. Williams, *The Houses that Eminent Domain and Housing Tax Credits Built: Imagining a Better New Orleans*, 34 FORDHAM URBAN L.J. 101, 110–11 (2007).

Appendix

SUSETTE KELO, et al., Petitioners v. CITY OF NEW LONDON,
CONNECTICUT, et al.

SUPREME COURT OF THE UNITED STATES

545 U.S. 469; 125 S. Ct. 2655; 162 L. Ed. 2d 439

February 22, 2005, Argued
June 23, 2005, Decided

OPINION: Justice **Stevens** delivered the opinion of the Court.

In 2000, the city of New London approved a development plan that, in the words of the Supreme Court of Connecticut, was "projected to create in excess of 1,000 jobs, to increase tax and other revenues, and to revitalize an economically distressed city, including its downtown and waterfront areas." *268 Conn. 1, 5, 843 A.2d 500, 507 (2004)*. In assembling the land needed for this project, the city's development agent has purchased property from willing sellers and proposes to use the power of eminent domain to acquire the remainder of the property from unwilling owners in exchange for just compensation. The question presented is whether the city's proposed disposition of this property qualifies as a "public use" within the meaning of the *Takings Clause of the Fifth Amendment to the Constitution.*[1]

I

The city of New London (hereinafter City) sits at the junction of the Thames River and the Long Island Sound in southeastern Connecticut. Decades of economic decline led a state agency in 1990 to designate the City a "distressed municipality." In 1996, the Federal Government closed the Naval Undersea Warfare Center, which had been located in the Fort Trumbull area of the City and had employed over 1,500 people. In 1998, the City's unemployment rate was nearly double that of the State, and its population of just under 24,000 residents was at its lowest since 1920.

These conditions prompted state and local officials to target New London, and particularly its Fort Trumbull area, for economic revitalization. To this end, respondent New London Development Corporation (NLDC), a private nonprofit

---

1   "[N]or shall private property be taken for public use, without just compensation." *U.S. Const., Amdt. 5*. That Clause is made applicable to the States by the *Fourteenth Amendment*. See *Chicago, B. & Q. R. Co. v. Chicago, 166 U.S. 226, 41 L. Ed. 979, 17 S. Ct. 581 (1897)*.

entity established some years earlier to assist the City in planning economic development, was reactivated. In January 1998, the State authorized a $5.35 million bond issue to support the NLDC's planning activities and a $10 million bond issue toward the creation of a Fort Trumbull State Park. In February, the pharmaceutical company Pfizer Inc. announced that it would build a $300 million research facility on a site immediately adjacent to Fort Trumbull; local planners hoped that Pfizer would draw new business to the area, thereby serving as a catalyst to the area's rejuvenation. After receiving initial approval from the city council, the NLDC continued its planning activities and held a series of neighborhood meetings to educate the public about the process. In May, the city council authorized the NLDC to formally submit its plans to the relevant state agencies for review.[2] Upon obtaining state-level approval, the NLDC finalized an integrated development plan focused on 90 acres of the Fort Trumbull area.

The Fort Trumbull area is situated on a peninsula that juts into the Thames River. The area comprises approximately 115 privately owned properties, as well as the 32 acres of land formerly occupied by the naval facility (Trumbull State Park now occupies 18 of those 32 acres). The development plan encompasses seven parcels. Parcel 1 is designated for a waterfront conference hotel at the center of a "small urban village" that will include restaurants and shopping. This parcel will also have marinas for both recreational and commercial uses. A pedestrian "riverwalk" will originate here and continue down the coast, connecting the waterfront areas of the development. Parcel 2 will be the site of approximately 80 new residences organized into an urban neighborhood and linked by public walkway to the remainder of the development, including the state park. This parcel also includes space reserved for a new U.S. Coast Guard Museum. Parcel 3, which is located immediately north of the Pfizer facility, will contain at least 90,000 square feet of research and development office space. Parcel 4A is a 2.4-acre site that will be used either to support the adjacent state park, by providing parking or retail services for visitors, or to support the nearby marina. Parcel 4B will include a renovated marina, as well as the final stretch of the riverwalk. Parcels 5, 6, and 7 will provide land for office and retail space, parking, and water-dependent commercial uses. App. 109–13.

The NLDC intended the development plan to capitalize on the arrival of the Pfizer facility and the new commerce it was expected to attract. In addition to creating jobs, generating tax revenue, and helping to "build momentum for the revitalization of downtown New London," *id.,* at 92, the plan was also designed to make the City more attractive and to create leisure and recreational opportunities on the waterfront and in the park.

The city council approved the plan in January 2000, and designated the NLDC as its development agent in charge of implementation. See *Conn. Gen. Stat. § 8–188*

---

2   Various state agencies studied the project's economic, environmental, and social ramifications. As part of this process, a team of consultants evaluated six alternative development proposals for the area, which varied in extensiveness and emphasis. The Office of Policy and Management, one of the primary state agencies undertaking the review, made findings that the project was consistent with relevant state and municipal development policies. See App. 89–95.

(2005). The city council also authorized the NLDC to purchase property or to acquire property by exercising eminent domain in the City's name. *§ 8–193*. The NLDC successfully negotiated the purchase of most of the real estate in the 90-acre area, but its negotiations with petitioners failed. As a consequence, in November 2000, the NLDC initiated the condemnation proceedings that gave rise to this case.[3]

II

Petitioner Susette Kelo has lived in the Fort Trumbull area since 1997. She has made extensive improvements to her house, which she prizes for its water view. Petitioner Wilhelmina Dery was born in her Fort Trumbull house in 1918 and has lived there her entire life. Her husband Charles (also a petitioner) has lived in the house since they married some 60 years ago. In all, the nine petitioners own 15 properties in Fort Trumbull – 4 in parcel 3 of the development plan and 11 in parcel 4A. Ten of the parcels are occupied by the owner or a family member; the other five are held as investment properties. There is no allegation that any of these properties is blighted or otherwise in poor condition; rather, they were condemned only because they happen to be located in the development area.

In December 2000, petitioners brought this action in the New London Superior Court. They claimed, among other things, that the taking of their properties would violate the "public use" restriction in the *Fifth Amendment*. After a 7-day bench trial, the Superior Court granted a permanent restraining order prohibiting the taking of the properties located in parcel 4A (park or marina support). It, however, denied petitioners relief as to the properties located in parcel 3 (office space). App. to Pet. for Cert. 343–50.[4]

After the Superior Court ruled, both sides took appeals to the Supreme Court of Connecticut. That court held, over a dissent, that all of the City's proposed takings were valid. It began by upholding the lower court's determination that the takings were authorized by chapter 132, the State's municipal development statute. See Conn. *Gen. Stat. § 8–186 et seq* (2005). That statute expresses a legislative determination that the taking of land, even developed land, as part of an economic development project is a "public use" and in the "public interest." *268 Conn., at 18–28, 843 A. 2d, at 515–21*. Next, relying on cases such as *Hawaii Housing Authority v. Midkiff, 467 U.S. 229, 81 L. Ed. 2d 186, 104 S. Ct. 2321 (1984)*, and *Berman v. Parker, 348 U.S. 26, 99 L. Ed. 27, 75 S. Ct. 98 (1954)*, the court held that such economic development qualified as a valid public use under both the Federal and State Constitutions. *268 Conn., at 40, 843 A. 2d, at 527*.

---

3 In the remainder of the opinion we will differentiate between the City and the NLDC only where necessary.

4 While this litigation was pending before the Superior Court, the NLDC announced that it would lease some of the parcels to private developers in exchange for their agreement to develop the land according to the terms of the development plan. Specifically, the NLDC was negotiating a 99-year ground lease with Corcoran Jennison, a developer selected from a group of applicants. The negotiations contemplated a nominal rent of $1 per year, but no agreement had yet been signed. See *268 Conn. 1, 9, 61, 843 A.2d 500, 509–10, 540 (2004)*.

Finally, adhering to its precedents, the court went on to determine, first, whether the takings of the particular properties at issue were "reasonably necessary" to achieving the City's intended public use, *id., at 82–4, 843 A. 2d, at 552–3*, and, second, whether the takings were for "reasonably foreseeable needs," *id., at 93–4, 843 A. 2d, at 558–9*. The court upheld the trial court's factual findings as to parcel 3, but reversed the trial court as to parcel 4A, agreeing with the City that the intended use of this land was sufficiently definite and had been given "reasonable attention" during the planning process. *Id., at 120–21, 843 A. 2d, at 574*.

The three dissenting justices would have imposed a "heightened" standard of judicial review for takings justified by economic development. Although they agreed that the plan was intended to serve a valid public use, they would have found all the takings unconstitutional because the City had failed to adduce "clear and convincing evidence" that the economic benefits of the plan would in fact come to pass. *Id., at 144, 146, 843 A. 2d, at 587, 588* (Zarella, J., joined by Sullivan, C.J., and Katz, J., concurring in part and dissenting in part).

We granted *certiorari* to determine whether a city's decision to take property for the purpose of economic development satisfies the "public use" requirement of the *Fifth Amendment. 542 U.S. 965, 159 L. Ed. 2d 857, 125 S. Ct. 27 (2004)*.

III

Two polar propositions are perfectly clear. On the one hand, it has long been accepted that the sovereign may not take the property of *A* for the sole purpose of transferring it to another private party *B*, even though *A* is paid just compensation. On the other hand, it is equally clear that a State may transfer property from one private party to another if future "use by the public" is the purpose of the taking; the condemnation of land for a railroad with common-carrier duties is a familiar example. Neither of these propositions, however, determines the disposition of this case.

As for the first proposition, the City would no doubt be forbidden from taking petitioners' land for the purpose of conferring a private benefit on a particular private party. See *Midkiff, 467 U.S., at 245, 81 L. Ed. 2d 186, 104 S. Ct. 2321* ("A purely private taking could not withstand the scrutiny of the public use requirement; it would serve no legitimate purpose of government and would thus be void"); *Missouri Pacific R. Co. v. Nebraska, 164 U.S. 403, 41 L. Ed. 489, 17 S. Ct. 130 (1896)*.[5] Nor would the City be allowed to take property under the mere pretext of a public purpose, when its actual purpose was to bestow a private benefit. The takings before us, however, would be executed pursuant to a "carefully considered" development

---

5   See also *Calder v. Bull, 3 U.S. 386, 3 Dall. 386, 1 L. Ed. 648 (1798)* ("An act of the Legislature (for I cannot call it a law) contrary to the great first principles of the social compact, compact, cannot be considered a rightful exercise of legislative authority. ... A few instances will suffice to explain what I mean ... [A] law that takes property from A and gives it to B: It is against all reason and justice, for a people to entrust a Legislature with such powers; and, therefore, it cannot be presumed that they have done it. The genius, the nature, and the spirit, of our State Governments, amount to a prohibition of such acts of legislation; and the general principles of law and reason forbid them" (emphasis deleted)).

plan. *268 Conn., at 54, 843 A. 2d, at 536.* The trial judge and all the members of the Supreme Court of Connecticut agreed that there was no evidence of an illegitimate purpose in this case.[6] Therefore, as was true of the statute challenged in *Midkiff, 467 U.S., at 245, 81 L. Ed. 2d 186, 104 S. Ct. 2321*, the City's development plan was not adopted "to benefit a particular class of identifiable individuals."

On the other hand, this is not a case in which the City is planning to open the condemned land – at least not in its entirety – to use by the general public. Nor will the private lessees of the land in any sense be required to operate like common carriers, making their services available to all comers. But although such a projected use would be sufficient to satisfy the public use requirement, this "Court long ago rejected any literal requirement that condemned property be put into use for the general public." *Id., at 244, 81 L. Ed. 2d 186, 104 S. Ct. 2321.* Indeed, while many state courts in the mid-19th century endorsed "use by the public" as the proper definition of public use, that narrow view steadily eroded over time. Not only was the "use by the public" test difficult to administer (e.g., what proportion of the public need have access to the property? at what price?),[7] but it proved to be impractical given the diverse and always evolving needs of society.[8] Accordingly, when this

---

6   See *268 Conn., at 159, 843 A. 2d, at 595* (Zarella, J., concurring in part and dissenting in part) ("The record clearly demonstrates that the development plan was not intended to serve the interests of Pfizer, Inc., or any other private entity, but rather, to revitalize the local economy by creating temporary and permanent jobs, generating a significant increase in tax revenue, encouraging spin-off economic activities and maximizing public access to the waterfront"). And while the City intends to transfer certain of the parcels to a private developer in a long-term lease – which developer, in turn, is expected to lease the office space and so forth to other private tenants – the identities of those private parties were not known when the plan was adopted. It is, of course, difficult to accuse the government of having taken *A*'s property to benefit the private interests of *B* when the identity of *B* was unknown.

7   See, e.g., *Dayton Gold & Silver Mining Co. v. Seawell, 11 Nev. 394, 410 (1876)* ("If public occupation and enjoyment of the object for which land is to be condemned furnishes the only and true test for the right of eminent domain, then the legislature would certainly have the constitutional authority to condemn the lands of any private citizen for the purpose of building hotels and theaters. Why not? A hotel is used by the public as much as a railroad. The public have the same right, upon payment of a fixed compensation, to seek rest and refreshment at a public inn as they have to travel upon a railroad").

8   From upholding the Mill Acts (which authorized manufacturers dependent on power-producing dams to flood upstream lands in exchange for just compensation), to approving takings necessary for the economic development of the West through mining and irrigation, many state courts either circumvented the "use by the public" test when necessary or abandoned it completely. See Nichols, The Meaning of Public Use in the Law of Eminent Domain, 20 B.U.L. Rev. 615, 619–24 (1940) (tracing this development and collecting cases). For example, in rejecting the "use by the public" test as overly restrictive, the Nevada Supreme Court stressed that "[m]ining is the greatest of the industrial pursuits in this state. All other interests are subservient to it. Our mountains are almost barren of timber, and our valleys could never be made profitable for agricultural purposes except for the fact of a home market having been created by the mining developments in different sections of the state. The mining and milling interests give employment to many men, and the benefits derived from this business are distributed as much, and sometimes more, among the laboring classes than with

Court began applying the *Fifth Amendment* to the States at the close of the 19th century, it embraced the broader and more natural interpretation of public use as "public purpose." See, e.g., *Fallbrook Irrigation Dist. v. Bradley, 164 U.S. 112, 158–64, 41 L. Ed. 369, 17 S. Ct. 56 (1896)*. Thus, in a case upholding a mining company's use of an aerial bucket line to transport ore over property it did not own, Justice Holmes' opinion for the Court stressed "the inadequacy of use by the general public as a universal test." *Strickley v. Highland Boy Gold Mining Co., 200 U.S. 527, 531, 50 L. Ed. 581, 26 S. Ct. 301 (1906)*.[9] We have repeatedly and consistently rejected that narrow test ever since.[10]

The disposition of this case therefore turns on the question whether the City's development plan serves a "public purpose." Without exception, our cases have defined that concept broadly, reflecting our longstanding policy of deference to legislative judgments in this field.

In *Berman v. Parker, 348 U.S. 26, 99 L. Ed. 27, 75 S. Ct. 98 (1954)*, this Court upheld a redevelopment plan targeting a blighted area of Washington, D.C., in which most of the housing for the area's 5,000 inhabitants was beyond repair. Under the plan, the area would be condemned and part of it utilized for the construction of streets, schools, and other public facilities. The remainder of the land would be leased or sold to private parties for the purpose of redevelopment, including the construction of low-cost housing.

The owner of a department store located in the area challenged the condemnation, pointing out that his store was not itself blighted and arguing that the creation of a "better balanced, more attractive community" was not a valid public use. *Id., at 31, 99 L. Ed. 27, 75 S. Ct. 98*. Writing for a unanimous Court, Justice Douglas refused to evaluate this claim in isolation, deferring instead to the legislative and agency judgment that the area "must be planned as a whole" for the plan to be successful. *Id., at 34, 99 L. Ed. 27, 75 S. Ct. 98*. The Court explained that "community redevelopment programs need not, by force of the Constitution, be on a piecemeal basis – lot by lot, building by building." *Id., at 35, 99 L. Ed. 27, 75 S. Ct. 98*. The public use underlying the taking was unequivocally affirmed:

> We do not sit to determine whether a particular housing project is or is not desirable. The concept of the public welfare is broad and inclusive. ... The values it represents are spiritual as well as physical, aesthetic as well as monetary. It is within the power of

---

the owners of the mines and mills. ... The present prosperity of the state is entirely due to the mining developments already made, and the entire people of the state are directly interested in having the future developments unobstructed by the obstinate action of any individual or individuals." *Dayton Gold & Silver Mining Co., 11 Nev., at 409–10*.

9   See also *Clark v. Nash, 198 U.S. 361, 49 L. Ed. 1085, 25 S. Ct. 676 (1905)* (upholding a statute that authorized the owner of arid land to widen a ditch on his neighbor's property so as to permit a nearby stream to irrigate his land).

10   See, e.g., *Mt. Vernon-Woodberry Cotton Duck Co. v. Alabama Interstate Power Co., 240 U.S. 30, 32, 60 L. Ed. 507, 36 S. Ct. 234 (1916)* ("The inadequacy of use by the general public as a universal test is established"); *Ruckelshaus v. Monsanto Co., 467 U.S. 986, 1014–15, 81 L. Ed. 2d 815, 104 S. Ct. 2862 (1984)* ("This Court, however, has rejected the notion that a use is a public use only if the property taken is put to use for the general public").

the legislature to determine that the community should be beautiful as well as healthy, spacious as well as clean, well-balanced as well as carefully patrolled. In the present case, the Congress and its authorized agencies have made determinations that take into account a wide variety of values. It is not for us to reappraise them. If those who govern the District of Columbia decide that the Nation's Capital should be beautiful as well as sanitary, there is nothing in the *Fifth Amendment* that stands in the way. *Id., at 33, 99 L. Ed. 27, 75 S. Ct. 98.*

In *Hawaii Housing Authority v. Midkiff, 467 U.S. 229, 81 L. Ed. 2d 186, 104 S. Ct. 2321 (1984)*, the Court considered a Hawaii statute whereby fee title was taken from lessors and transferred to lessees (for just compensation) in order to reduce the concentration of land ownership. We unanimously upheld the statute and rejected the Ninth Circuit's view that it was "a naked attempt on the part of the state of Hawaii to take the property of A and transfer it to B solely for B's private use and benefit." *Id., at 235, 81 L. Ed. 2d 186, 104 S. Ct. 2321* (internal quotation marks omitted). Reaffirming *Berman*'s deferential approach to legislative judgments in this field, we concluded that the State's purpose of eliminating the "social and economic evils of a land oligopoly" qualified as a valid public use. *467 U.S., at 241–2, 81 L. Ed. 2d 186, 104 S. Ct. 2321.* Our opinion also rejected the contention that the mere fact that the State immediately transferred the properties to private individuals upon condemnation somehow diminished the public character of the taking. "[I]t is only the taking's purpose, and not its mechanics," we explained, that matters in determining public use. *Id., at 244, 81 L. Ed. 2d 186, 104 S. Ct. 2321.*

In that same Term we decided another public use case that arose in a purely economic context. In *Ruckelshaus v. Monsanto Co., 467 U.S. 986, 81 L. Ed. 2d 815, 104 S. Ct. 2862 (1984)*, the Court dealt with provisions of the *Federal Insecticide, Fungicide, and Rodenticide Act* under which the Environmental Protection Agency could consider the data (including trade secrets) submitted by a prior pesticide applicant in evaluating a subsequent application, so long as the second applicant paid just compensation for the data. We acknowledged that the "most direct beneficiaries" of these provisions were the subsequent applicants, *id., at 1014, 81 L. Ed. 2d 815, 104 S. Ct. 2862*, but we nevertheless upheld the statute under *Berman* and *Midkiff*. We found sufficient Congress' belief that sparing applicants the cost of time-consuming research eliminated a significant barrier to entry in the pesticide market and thereby enhanced competition. *467 U.S., at 1015, 81 L. Ed. 2d 815, 104 S. Ct. 2862.*

Viewed as a whole, our jurisprudence has recognized that the needs of society have varied between different parts of the Nation, just as they have evolved over time in response to changed circumstances. Our earliest cases in particular embodied a strong theme of federalism, emphasizing the "great respect" that we owe to state legislatures and state courts in discerning local public needs. See *Hairston v. Danville & Western R. Co., 208 U.S. 598, 606–607, 52 L. Ed. 637, 28 S. Ct. 331 (1908)* (noting that these needs were likely to vary depending on a State's "resources, the capacity of the soil, the relative importance of industries to the general public welfare, and the long-established methods and habits of the people").[11] For more than a century, our public use jurisprudence has wisely eschewed rigid formulas and intrusive scrutiny in favor of affording legislatures broad latitude in determining what public needs justify the use of the takings power.

IV

Those who govern the City were not confronted with the need to remove blight in the Fort Trumbull area, but their determination that the area was sufficiently distressed to justify a program of economic rejuvenation is entitled to our deference. The City has carefully formulated an economic development plan that it believes will provide appreciable benefits to the community, including – but by no means limited to – new jobs and increased tax revenue. As with other exercises in urban planning and development,[12] the City is endeavoring to coordinate a variety of commercial, residential, and recreational uses of land, with the hope that they will form a whole greater than the sum of its parts. To effectuate this plan, the City has invoked a state statute that specifically authorizes the use of eminent domain to promote economic development. Given the comprehensive character of the plan, the thorough deliberation that preceded its adoption, and the limited scope of our review, it is appropriate for us, as it was in *Berman*, to resolve the challenges of the individual owners, not on a piecemeal basis, but rather in light of the entire plan. Because that plan unquestionably serves a public purpose, the takings challenged here satisfy the public use requirement of the *Fifth Amendment*.

To avoid this result, petitioners urge us to adopt a new bright-line rule that economic development does not qualify as a public use. Putting aside the unpersuasive suggestion that the City's plan will provide only purely economic benefits, neither precedent nor logic supports petitioners' proposal. Promoting economic development is a traditional and long accepted function of government. There is, moreover, no principled way of distinguishing economic development from the other public purposes that we have recognized. In our cases upholding takings that facilitated

---

11 See also *Clark, 198 U.S., at 367–8, 49 L. Ed. 1085, 25 S. Ct. 676*; *Strickley v. Highland Boy Gold Mining Co., 200 U.S. 527, 531, 50 L. Ed. 581, 26 S. Ct. 301 (1906)* ("In the opinion of the legislature and the Supreme Court of Utah the public welfare of that State demands that aerial lines between the mines upon its mountain sides and railways in the valleys below should not be made impossible by the refusal of a private owner to sell the right to cross his land. The Constitution of the United States does not require us to say that they are wrong"); *O'Neill v. Leamer, 239 U.S. 244, 253, 60 L. Ed. 249, 36 S. Ct. 54 (1915)* ("States may take account of their special exigencies, and when the extent of their arid or wet lands is such that a plan for irrigation or reclamation according to districts may fairly be regarded as one which promotes the public interest, there is nothing in the Federal Constitution which denies to them the right to formulate this policy or to exercise the power of eminent domain in carrying it into effect. With the local situation the state court is peculiarly familiar and its judgment is entitled to the highest respect").

12 Cf. *Village of Euclid v. Ambler Realty Co., 272 U.S. 365, 71 L. Ed. 303, 47 S. Ct. 114, 4 Ohio Law Abs. 816 (1926)*.

agriculture and mining, for example, we emphasized the importance of those industries to the welfare of the States in question, see, e.g., *Strickley, 200 U.S. 527, 50 L. Ed. 581, 26 S. Ct. 301*; in *Berman,* we endorsed the purpose of transforming a blighted area into a "well-balanced" community through redevelopment, *348 U.S., at 33, 99 L. Ed. 27, 75 S. Ct. 98*;[13] in *Midkiff,* we upheld the interest in breaking up a land oligopoly that "created artificial deterrents to the normal functioning of the State's residential land market," *467 U.S., at 242, 81 L. Ed. 2d 186, 104 S. Ct. 2321*; and in *Monsanto,* we accepted Congress' purpose of eliminating a "significant barrier to entry in the pesticide market," *467 U.S., at 1014–15, 81 L. Ed. 2d 815, 104 S. Ct. 2862.* It would be incongruous to hold that the City's interest in the economic benefits to be derived from the development of the Fort Trumbull area has less of a public character than any of those other interests. Clearly, there is no basis for exempting economic development from our traditionally broad understanding of public purpose.

Petitioners contend that using eminent domain for economic development impermissibly blurs the boundary between public and private takings. Again, our cases foreclose this objection. Quite simply, the government's pursuit of a public purpose will often benefit individual private parties. For example, in *Midkiff,* the forced transfer of property conferred a direct and significant benefit on those lessees who were previously unable to purchase their homes. In *Monsanto,* we recognized that the "most direct beneficiaries" of the data-sharing provisions were the subsequent pesticide applicants, but benefiting them in this way was necessary to promoting competition in the pesticide market. *467 U.S., at 1014, 81 L. Ed. 2d 815, 104 S. Ct. 2862.*[14] The owner of the department store in *Berman* objected to "taking from one businessman for the benefit of another businessman," *348 U.S., at 33, 99*

---

13 It is a misreading of *Berman* to suggest that the only public use upheld in that case was the initial removal of blight. See Reply Brief for Petitioners 8. The public use described in *Berman* extended beyond that to encompass the purpose of *developing* that area to create conditions that would prevent a reversion to blight in the future. See *348 U.S., at 34–5, 99 L. Ed. 27, 75 S. Ct. 98* ("It was not enough, [the experts] believed, to remove existing buildings that were insanitary or unsightly. It was important to redesign the whole area so as to eliminate the conditions that cause slums. ... The entire area needed redesigning so that a balanced, integrated plan could be developed for the region, including not only new homes, but also schools, churches, parks, streets, and shopping centers. In this way it was hoped that the cycle of decay of the area could be controlled and the birth of future slums prevented"). Had the public use in *Berman* been defined more narrowly, it would have been difficult to justify the taking of the plaintiff's nonblighted department store.

14 Any number of cases illustrate that the achievement of a public good often coincides with the immediate benefiting of private parties. See, e.g., *National Railroad Passenger Corporation v. Boston & Maine Corp., 503 U.S. 407, 422, 118 L. Ed. 2d 52, 112 S. Ct. 1394 (1992)* (public purpose of *(1992)* (public purpose of "facilitating Amtrak's rail service" served by taking rail track from one private company and transferring it to another private company); *Brown v. Legal Foundation of Wash., 538 U.S. 216, 155 L. Ed. 2d 376, 123 S. Ct. 1406 (2003)* (provision of legal services to the poor is a valid public purpose). It is worth noting that in *Hawaii Housing Authority v. Midkiff, 467 U.S. 229, 81 L. Ed. 2d 186, 104 S. Ct. 2321 (1984),* *Monsanto,* and *Boston & Maine Corp.,* the property in question retained the same use even after the change of ownership.

L. Ed. 27, 75 S. Ct. 98, referring to the fact that under the redevelopment plan land would be leased or sold to private developers for redevelopment.[15] Our rejection of that contention has particular relevance to the instant case: "The public end may be as well or better served through an agency of private enterprise than through a department of government – or so the Congress might conclude. We cannot say that public ownership is the sole method of promoting the public purposes of community redevelopment projects." *Id., at 34, 99 L. Ed. 27, 75 S. Ct. 98.*[16]

It is further argued that without a bright-line rule nothing would stop a city from transferring citizen *A*'s property to citizen *B* for the sole reason that citizen *B* will put the property to a more productive use and thus pay more taxes. Such a one-to-one transfer of property, executed outside the confines of an integrated development plan, is not presented in this case. While such an unusual exercise of government power would certainly raise a suspicion that a private purpose was afoot,[17] the hypothetical cases posited by petitioners can be confronted if and when they arise.[18] They do not warrant the crafting of an artificial restriction on the concept of public use.[19]

---

15 Notably, as in the instant case, the private developers in *Berman* were required by contract to use the property to carry out the redevelopment plan. See *348 U.S., at 30, 99 L. Ed. 27, 75 S. Ct. 98.*

16 Nor do our cases support Justice O'Connor's novel theory that the government may only take property and transfer it to private parties when the initial taking eliminates some "harmful property use." *Post, at 501, 162 L. Ed. 2d, at 465* (dissenting opinion). There was nothing "harmful" about the nonblighted department store at issue in *Berman, 348 U.S. 26, 99 L. Ed. 27, 75 S. Ct. 98*; see also n. 13, *supra;* nothing "harmful" about the lands at issue in the mining and agriculture cases, see, e.g., *Strickley, 200 U.S. 527, 50 L. Ed. 581, 26 S. Ct. 301*; see also nn 9, 11, *supra;* and certainly nothing "harmful" about the trade secrets owned by the pesticide manufacturers in *Monsanto, 467 U.S. 986, 81 L. Ed. 2d 815, 104 S. Ct. 2862.* In each case, the public purpose we upheld depended on a private party's *future* use of the concededly nonharmful property that was taken. By focusing on a property's future use, as opposed to its past use, our cases are faithful to the text of the *Takings Clause.* See *U.S. Const., Amdt. 5.* ("[N]or shall private property be taken for public use, without just compensation"). Justice O'Connor's intimation that a "public purpose" may not be achieved by the action of private parties, see *post, at 500–501, 162 L. Ed. 2d, at 465*, confuses the *purpose* of a taking with its *mechanics*, a mistake we warned of in *Midkiff, 467 U.S., at 244, 81 L. Ed. 2d 186, 104 S. Ct. 2321.* See also *Berman, 348 U.S., at 33–4, 99 L. Ed. 27, 75 S. Ct. 98* ("The public end may be as well or better served through an agency of private enterprise than through a department of government").

17 Courts have viewed such aberrations with a skeptical eye. See, e.g., *99 Cents Only Stores v. Lancaster Redevelopment Agency, 237 F. Supp. 2d 1123 (CD Cal. 2001)*; cf. *Cincinnati v. Vester, 281 U.S. 439, 448, 74 L. Ed. 950, 50 S. Ct. 360 (1930)* (taking invalid under state eminent domain statute for lack of a reasoned explanation). These types of takings may also implicate other constitutional guarantees. See *Village of Willowbrook v. Olech, 528 U.S. 562, 145 L. Ed. 2d 1060, 120 S. Ct. 1073 (2000) (per curiam).*

18 Cf. *Panhandle Oil Co. v. Mississippi ex rel. Knox, 277 U.S. 218, 223, 72 L. Ed. 857, 48 S. Ct. 451 (1928)* (Holmes, J., dissenting) ("The power to tax is not the power to destroy while this Court sits").

19 A parade of horribles is especially unpersuasive in this context, since the *Takings Clause* largely "operates as a conditional limitation, permitting the government to do what it wants so long as it pays the charge." *Eastern Enterprises v. Apfel, 524 U.S. 498, 545, 141*

Alternatively, petitioners maintain that for takings of this kind we should require a "reasonable certainty" that the expected public benefits will actually accrue. Such a rule, however, would represent an even greater departure from our precedent. "When the legislature's purpose is legitimate and its means are not irrational, our cases make clear that empirical debates over the wisdom of takings – no less than debates over the wisdom of other kinds of socioeconomic legislation – are not to be carried out in the federal courts." *Midkiff, 467 U.S., at 242, 81 L. Ed. 2d 186, 104 S. Ct. 2321.*[20] Indeed, earlier this Term we explained why similar practical concerns (among others) undermined the use of the "substantially advances" formula in our regulatory takings doctrine. See *Lingle v. Chevron U.S.A. Inc., 544 U.S. 528, 544, 161 L. Ed. 2d 876, 125 S. Ct. 2074 (2005)* (noting that this formula "would empower – and might often require – courts to substitute their predictive judgments for those of elected legislatures and expert agencies"). The disadvantages of a heightened form of review are especially pronounced in this type of case. Orderly implementation of a comprehensive redevelopment plan obviously requires that the legal rights of all interested parties be established before new construction can be commenced. A constitutional rule that required postponement of the judicial approval of every condemnation until the likelihood of success of the plan had been assured would unquestionably impose a significant impediment to the successful consummation of many such plans.

Just as we decline to second-guess the City's considered judgments about the efficacy of its development plan, we also decline to second-guess the City's determinations as to what lands it needs to acquire in order to effectuate the project. "It is not for the courts to oversee the choice of the boundary line nor to sit in review on the size of a particular project area. Once the question of the public purpose has been decided, the amount and character of land to be taken for the project and the

---

L. Ed. 2d 451, 118 S. Ct. 2131 (1998) (Kennedy, J., concurring in judgment and dissenting in part). Speaking of the takings power, Justice Iredell observed that "[i]t is not sufficient to urge, that the power may be abused, for, such is the nature of all power, – such is the tendency of every human institution: and, it might as fairly be said, that the power of taxation, which is only circumscribed by the discretion of the Body, in which it is vested, ought not to be granted, because the Legislature, disregarding its true objects, might, for visionary and useless projects, impose a tax to the amount of nineteen shillings in the pound. We must be content to limit power where we can, and where we cannot, consistently with its use, we must be content to repose a salutory confidence." *Calder, 3 Dall., at 400, 1 L. Ed. 648* (opinion concurring in result).

20 See also *Boston & Maine Corp., 503 U.S., at 422–3, 118 L. Ed. 2d 52, 112 S. Ct. 1394* ("[W]e need not make a specific factual determination whether the condemnation will accomplish its objectives"); *Monsanto, 467 U.S., at 1015, n. 18, 81 L. Ed. 2d 815, 104 S. Ct. 2862* ("Monsanto argues that EPA and, by implication, Congress, misapprehended the true 'barriers to entry' in the pesticide industry and that the challenged provisions of the law create, rather than reduce, barriers to entry. ... Such economic arguments are better directed to Congress. The proper inquiry before this Court is not whether the provisions in fact will accomplish their stated objectives. Our review is limited to determining that the purpose is legitimate and that Congress rationally could have believed that the provisions would promote that objective").

need for a particular tract to complete the integrated plan rests in the discretion of the legislative branch." *Berman, 348 U.S., at 35–6, 99 L. Ed. 27, 75 S. Ct. 98.*

In affirming the City's authority to take petitioners' properties, we do not minimize the hardship that condemnations may entail, notwithstanding the payment of just compensation.[21] We emphasize that nothing in our opinion precludes any State from placing further restrictions on its exercise of the takings power. Indeed, many States already impose "public use" requirements that are stricter than the federal baseline. Some of these requirements have been established as a matter of state constitutional law,[22] while others are expressed in state eminent domain statutes that carefully limit the grounds upon which takings may be exercised.[23] As the submissions of the parties and their *amici* make clear, the necessity and wisdom of using eminent domain to promote economic development are certainly matters of legitimate public debate.[24] This Court's authority, however, extends only to determining whether the City's proposed condemnations are for a "public use" within the meaning of the *Fifth Amendment to the Federal Constitution.* Because over a century of our case law interpreting that provision dictates an affirmative answer to that question, we may not grant petitioners the relief that they seek.

The judgment of the Supreme Court of Connecticut is affirmed. It is so ordered.

---

21 The *amici* raise questions about the fairness of the measure of just compensation. See, e.g., Brief for American Planning Association et al. as *Amici Curiae* 26–30. While important, these questions are not before us in this litigation.

22 See, e.g., *County of Wayne v. Hathcock, 471 Mich. 445, 684 N.W.2d 765 (2004).*

23 Under California law, for instance, a city may only take land for economic development purposes in blighted areas. *Cal. Health & Safety Code Ann. §§ 33030–37* (West 1999). See, e.g., *Redevelopment Agency of Chula Vista v. Rados Bros., 95 Cal. App. 4th 309, 115 Cal. Rptr. 2d 234 (2002).*

24 For example, some argue that the need for eminent domain has been greatly exaggerated because private developers can use numerous techniques, including secret negotiations or precommitment strategies, to overcome holdout problems and assemble lands for genuinely profitable projects. See Brief for Jane Jacobs as *Amicus Curiae* 13–15; see also Brief for John Norquist as *Amicus Curiae.* Others argue to the contrary, urging that the need for eminent domain is especially great with regard to older, small cities like New London, where centuries of development have created an extreme overdivision of land and thus a real market impediment to land assembly. See Brief for Connecticut Conference of Municipalities et al. as *Amici Curiae* 13, 21; see also Brief for National League of Cities et al. as *Amici Curiae.*

CONCUR: Justice **Kennedy**, concurring.

I join the opinion for the Court and add these further observations:

This Court has declared that a taking should be upheld as consistent with the Public Use Clause, *U.S. Const., Amdt. 5*, as long as it is "rationally related to a conceivable public purpose." *Hawaii Housing Authority v. Midkiff, 467 U.S. 229, 241, 81 L. Ed. 2d 186, 104 S. Ct. 2321 (1984)*; see also *Berman v. Parker, 348 U.S. 26, 99 L. Ed. 27, 75 S. Ct. 98 (1954)*. This deferential standard of review echoes the rational-basis test used to review economic regulation under the *Due Process* and *Equal Protection Clauses*, see, e.g., *FCC v. Beach Communications, Inc., 508 U.S. 307, 313–14, 124 L. Ed. 2d 211, 113 S. Ct. 2096 (1993)*; *Williamson v. Lee Optical of Okla., Inc., 348 U.S. 483, 99 L. Ed. 563, 75 S. Ct. 461 (1955)*. The determination that a rational-basis standard of review is appropriate does not, however, alter the fact that transfers intended to confer benefits on particular, favored private entities, and with only incidental or pretextual public benefits, are forbidden by the *Public Use Clause*.

A court applying rational-basis review under the *Public Use Clause* should strike down a taking that, by a clear showing, is intended to favor a particular private party, with only incidental or pretextual public benefits, just as a court applying rational-basis review under the *Equal Protection Clause* must strike down a government classification that is clearly intended to injure a particular class of private parties, with only incidental or pretextual public justifications. See *Cleburne v. Cleburne Living Center, Inc., 473 U.S. 432, 446–7, 450, 87 L. Ed. 2d 313, 105 S. Ct. 3249 (1985)*; *Department of Agriculture v. Moreno, 413 U.S. 528, 533–6, 37 L. Ed. 2d 782, 93 S. Ct. 2821 (1973)*. As the trial court in this case was correct to observe: "Where the purpose [of a taking] is economic development and that development is to be carried out by private parties or private parties will be benefited, the court must decide if the stated public purpose – economic advantage to a city sorely in need of it – is only incidental to the benefits that will be confined on private parties of a development plan." App. to Pet. for Cert. 263. See also *ante, at 477–8, 162 L. Ed. 2d, at 450.*

A court confronted with a plausible accusation of impermissible favoritism to private parties should treat the objection as a serious one and review the record to see if it has merit, though with the presumption that the government's actions were reasonable and intended to serve a public purpose. Here, the trial court conducted a careful and extensive inquiry into "whether, in fact, the development plan is of primary benefit to ... the developer [i.e., Corcoran Jennison], and private businesses which may eventually locate in the plan area [e.g., Pfizer], and in that regard, only of incidental benefit to the city." App. to Pet. for Cert. 261. The trial court considered testimony from government officials and corporate officers; *id.*, at 266–71; documentary evidence of communications between these parties, *ibid.*; respondents' awareness of New London's depressed economic condition and evidence corroborating the validity of this concern, *id.*, at 272–3, 278–9; the substantial commitment of public funds by the State to the development project before most of the private beneficiaries were known, *id.*, at 276; evidence that respondents reviewed a variety of development plans and chose a private developer from a group of applicants rather than picking out a particular transferee beforehand, *id.*, at 273, 278; and the fact that the other private beneficiaries of the project are still unknown because the office space proposed to be built has not yet been rented, *id.*, at 278.

The trial court concluded, based on these findings, that benefiting Pfizer was not "the primary motivation or effect of this development plan"; instead, "the primary motivation for [respondents] was to take advantage of Pfizer's presence." *Id.*, at 276. Likewise, the trial court concluded that "[t]here is nothing in the record to indicate that ... [respondents] were motivated by a desire to aid [other] particular private entities." *Id.*, at 278. See also *ante, at 478, 162 L. Ed. 2d, at 450–51.* Even the dissenting justices on the Connecticut Supreme Court agreed that respondents' development plan was intended to revitalize the local economy, not to serve the interests of Pfizer, Corcoran Jennison, or any other private party. *268 Conn. 1, 159, 843 A.2d 500, 595 (2004)* (Zarella, J., concurring in part and dissenting in part). This case, then, survives the meaningful rational basis review that in my view is required under the *Public Use Clause.*

Petitioners and their *amici* argue that any taking justified by the promotion of economic development must be treated by the courts as *per se* invalid, or at least presumptively invalid. Petitioners overstate the need for such a rule, however, by making the incorrect assumption that review under *Berman* and *Midkiff* imposes no meaningful judicial limits on the government's power to condemn any property it likes. A broad *per se* rule or a strong presumption of invalidity, furthermore, would prohibit a large number of government takings that have the purpose and expected effect of conferring substantial benefits on the public at large and so do not offend the *Public Use Clause.*

My agreement with the Court that a presumption of invalidity is not warranted for economic development takings in general, or for the particular takings at issue in this case, does not foreclose the possibility that a more stringent standard of review than that announced in *Berman* and *Midkiff* might be appropriate for a more narrowly drawn category of takings. There may be private transfers in which the risk of undetected impermissible favoritism of private parties is so acute that a presumption (rebuttable or otherwise) of invalidity is warranted under the *Public Use Clause.* Cf. *Eastern Enterprises v. Apfel, 524 U.S. 498, 549–50, 141 L. Ed. 2d 451, 118 S. Ct. 2131 (1998)* (Kennedy, J., concurring in judgment and dissenting in part) (heightened scrutiny for retroactive legislation under the *Due Process Clause*). This demanding level of scrutiny, however, is not required simply because the purpose of the taking is economic development.

This is not the occasion for conjecture as to what sort of cases might justify a more demanding standard, but it is appropriate to underscore aspects of the instant case that convince me no departure from *Berman* and *Midkiff* is appropriate here. This taking occurred in the context of a comprehensive development plan meant to address a serious city-wide depression, and the projected economic benefits of the project cannot be characterized as *de minimis.* The identities of most of the private beneficiaries were unknown at the time the city formulated its plans. The city complied with elaborate procedural requirements that facilitate review of the record and inquiry into the city's purposes. In sum, while there may be categories of cases in which the transfers are so suspicious, or the procedures employed so prone to abuse, or the purported benefits are so trivial or implausible, that courts should presume an impermissible private purpose, no such circumstances are present in this case.

For the foregoing reasons, I join in the Court's opinion.

DISSENT: Justice **O'Connor,** with whom the **Chief Justice,** Justice **Scalia,** and Justice **Thomas** join, dissenting.

Over two centuries ago, just after the *Bill of Rights* was ratified, Justice Chase wrote:

> An Act of the Legislature (for I cannot call it a law) contrary to the great first principles of the social compact, cannot be considered a rightful exercise of legislative authority ... A few instances will suffice to explain what I mean. ... [A] law that takes property from A and gives it to B: It is against all reason and justice, for a people to entrust a Legislature with such powers; and, therefore, it cannot be presumed that they have done it. *Calder v. Bull, 3 U.S. 386, 3 Dallas 386, 1 L. Ed. 648 (1798)* (emphasis deleted).

Today the Court abandons this long-held, basic limitation on government power. Under the banner of economic development, all private property is now vulnerable to being taken and transferred to another private owner, so long as it might be upgraded – i.e., given to an owner who will use it in a way that the legislature deems more beneficial to the public – in the process. To reason, as the Court does, that the incidental public benefits resulting from the subsequent ordinary use of private property render economic development takings "for public use" is to wash out any distinction between private and public use of property – and thereby effectively to delete the words "for public use" from the *Takings Clause of the Fifth Amendment*. Accordingly I respectfully dissent.

I

Petitioners are nine resident or investment owners of 15 homes in the Fort Trumbull neighborhood of New London, Connecticut. Petitioner Wilhelmina Dery, for example, lives in a house on Walbach Street that has been in her family for over 100 years. She was born in the house in 1918; her husband, petitioner Charles Dery, moved into the house when they married in 1946. Their son lives next door with his family in the house he received as a wedding gift, and joins his parents in this suit. Two petitioners keep rental properties in the neighborhood.

In February 1998, Pfizer Inc., the pharmaceuticals manufacturer, announced that it would build a global research facility near the Fort Trumbull neighborhood. Two months later, New London's city council gave initial approval for the New London Development Corporation (NLDC) to prepare the development plan at issue here. The NLDC is a private, nonprofit corporation whose mission is to assist the city council in economic development planning. It is not elected by popular vote, and its directors and employees are privately appointed. Consistent with its mandate, the NLDC generated an ambitious plan for redeveloping 90 acres of Fort Trumbull in order to "complement the facility that Pfizer was planning to build, create jobs, increase tax and other revenues, encourage public access to and use of the city's waterfront, and eventually 'build momentum' for the revitalization of the rest of the city." App. to Pet. for Cert. 5.

Petitioners own properties in two of the plan's seven parcels – Parcel 3 and Parcel 4A. Under the plan, Parcel 3 is slated for the construction of research and office space as a market develops for such space. It will also retain the existing Italian Dramatic Club (a private cultural organization) though the homes of three plaintiffs in that parcel are to be demolished. Parcel 4A is slated, mysteriously, for "'park support.'" *Id.,* at 345–6. At oral argument, counsel for respondents conceded the vagueness of this proposed use, and offered that the parcel might eventually be used for parking. Tr. of Oral Arg. 36.

To save their homes, petitioners sued New London and the NLDC, to whom New London has delegated eminent domain power. Petitioners maintain that the *Fifth Amendment* prohibits the NLDC from condemning their properties for the sake of an economic development plan. Petitioners are not holdouts; they do not seek increased compensation, and none is opposed to new development in the area. Theirs is an objection in principle: They claim that the NLDC's proposed use for their confiscated property is not a "public" one for purposes of the *Fifth Amendment*. While the government may take their homes to build a road or a railroad or to eliminate a property use that harms the public, say petitioners, it cannot take their property for the private use of other owners simply because the new owners may make more productive use of the property.

II

The *Fifth Amendment to the Constitution*, made applicable to the States by the *Fourteenth Amendment*, provides that "private property [shall not] be taken for public use, without just compensation." When interpreting the Constitution, we begin with the unremarkable presumption that every word in the document has independent meaning, "that no word was unnecessarily used, or needlessly added." *Wright v. United States, 302 U.S. 583, 588, 82 L. Ed. 439, 58 S. Ct. 395, 86 Ct. Cl. 764 (1938).* In keeping with that presumption, we have read the *Fifth Amendment*'s language to impose two distinct conditions on the exercise of eminent domain: "the Taking must be for a 'public use' and 'just compensation' must be paid to the owner." *Brown v. Legal Foundation of Wash., 538 U.S. 216, 231–2, 155 L. Ed. 2d 376, 123 S. Ct. 1406 (2003).*

These two limitations serve to protect "the security of Property," which Alexander Hamilton described to the Philadelphia Convention as one of the "great obj[ects] of Gov[ernment]." 1 Records of the Federal Convention of 1787, p. 302 (M. Farrand ed. 1911). Together they ensure stable property ownership by providing safeguards against excessive, unpredictable, or unfair use of the government's eminent domain power – particularly against those owners who, for whatever reasons, may be unable to protect themselves in the political process against the majority's will.

While the *Takings Clause* presupposes that government can take private property without the owner's consent, the just compensation requirement spreads the cost of condemnations and thus "prevents the public from loading upon one individual more than his just share of the burdens of government." *Monongahela Nav. Co. v. United States, 148 U.S. 312, 325, 37 L. Ed. 463, 13 S. Ct. 622 (1893)*; see also *Armstrong v. United States, 364 U.S. 40, 49, 4 L. Ed. 2d 1554, 80 S. Ct. 1563 (1960)*. The public use requirement, in turn, imposes a more basic limitation, circumscribing the very scope of the eminent domain power: Government may compel an individual to forfeit her property for the *public*'s use, but not for the benefit of another private person. This requirement promotes fairness as well as security. Cf. *Tahoe-Sierra Preservation Council, Inc. v. Tahoe Regional Planning Agency, 535 U.S. 302, 336, 152 L. Ed. 2d 517, 122 S. Ct. 1465 (2002)* ("The concepts of 'fairness and justice' ... underlie the *Takings Clause*").

Where is the line between "public" and "private" property use? We give considerable deference to legislatures' determinations about what governmental activities will advantage the public. But were the political branches the sole arbiters of the public-private distinction, the *Public Use Clause* would amount to little more than hortatory fluff. An external, judicial check on how the public use requirement is interpreted, however limited, is necessary if this constraint on government power is to retain any meaning. See *Cincinnati v. Vester, 281 U.S. 439, 446, 74 L. Ed. 950, 50 S. Ct. 360 (1930)* ("It is well established that ... the question [of] what is a public use is a judicial one").

Our cases have generally identified three categories of takings that comply with the public use requirement, though it is in the nature of things that the boundaries between these categories are not always firm. Two are relatively straightforward and uncontroversial. First, the sovereign may transfer private property to public ownership – such as for a road, a hospital, or a military base. See, e.g., *Old Dominion Land Co. v. United States, 269 U.S. 55, 70 L. Ed. 162, 46 S. Ct. 39 (1925)*; *Rindge Co. v. County of Los Angeles, 262 U.S. 700, 67 L. Ed. 1186, 43 S. Ct. 689 (1923)*. Second, the sovereign may transfer private property to private parties, often common carriers, who make the property available for the public's use – such as with a railroad, a public utility, or a stadium. See, e.g., *National Railroad Passenger Corporation v. Boston & Maine Corp., 503 U.S. 407, 118 L. Ed. 2d 52, 112 S. Ct. 1394 (1992)*; *Mt. Vernon-Woodberry Cotton Duck Co. v. Alabama Interstate Power Co., 240 U.S. 30, 60 L. Ed. 507, 36 S. Ct. 234 (1916)*. But "public ownership" and "use-by-the-public" are sometimes too constricting and impractical ways to define the scope of the *Public Use Clause*. Thus we have allowed that, in certain circumstances and to meet certain exigencies, takings that serve a public purpose also satisfy the Constitution even if the property is destined for subsequent private use. See, e.g., *Berman v. Parker, 348 U.S. 26, 99 L. Ed. 27, 75 S. Ct. 98 (1954)*; *Hawaii Housing Authority v. Midkiff, 467 U.S. 229, 81 L. Ed. 2d 186, 104 S. Ct. 2321 (1984)*.

This case returns us for the first time in over 20 years to the hard question of when a purportedly "public purpose" taking meets the public use requirement. It presents an issue of first impression: Are economic development takings constitutional? I would hold that they are not. We are guided by two precedents about the taking of real property by eminent domain. In *Berman*, we upheld takings within a blighted neighborhood of Washington, D.C. The neighborhood had so deteriorated that, for example, 64.3 percent of its dwellings were beyond repair. *348 U.S., at 30, 99 L. Ed. 27, 75 S. Ct. 98*. It had become burdened with "overcrowding of dwellings," "lack of adequate streets and alleys," and "lack of light and air." *Id., at 34, 99 L. Ed. 27, 75 S. Ct. 98.* Congress had determined that the neighborhood had become "injurious to the public health, safety, morals, and welfare" and that it was necessary to "eliminat[e] all such injurious conditions by employing all means necessary and appropriate for the purpose," including eminent domain. *Id., at 28, 99 L. Ed. 27, 75 S. Ct. 98.* (internal quotation omitted). Mr. Berman's department store was not itself blighted. Having approved of Congress' decision to eliminate the harm to the public emanating from the blighted neighborhood, however, we did not second-guess its decision to treat the neighborhood as a whole rather than lot-by-lot. *Id., at 34–5, 99 L. Ed. 27, 75 S. Ct. 98*; see also *Midkiff, 467 U.S., at 244, 81 L. Ed. 2d 186, 104 S. Ct. 2321* ("[I]t is only the taking's purpose, and not its mechanics, that must pass scrutiny").

In *Midkiff*, we upheld a land condemnation scheme in Hawaii whereby title in real property was taken from lessors and transferred to lessees. At that time, the State and Federal Governments owned nearly 49 percent of the State's land, and another 47 percent was in the hands of only 72 private landowners. Concentration of land ownership was so dramatic that on the State's most urbanized island, Oahu, 22 landowners owned 72.5 percent of the fee simple titles. *Id., at 232, 81 L. Ed. 2d 186, 104 S. Ct. 2321.* The Hawaii Legislature had concluded that the oligopoly in land ownership was "skewing the State's residential fee simple market, inflating land prices, and injuring the public tranquility and welfare," and therefore enacted a condemnation scheme for redistributing title. *Ibid.*

In those decisions, we emphasized the importance of deferring to legislative judgments about public purpose. Because courts are ill equipped to evaluate the efficacy of proposed legislative initiatives, we rejected as unworkable the idea of courts' "'deciding on what is and is not a governmental function and … invalidating legislation on the basis of their view on that question at the moment of decision, a practice which has proved impracticable in other fields.'" *Id., at 240–41, 81 L. Ed. 2d 186, 104 S. Ct. 2321* (quoting *United States ex rel. TVA v. Welch, 327 U.S. 546, 552, 90 L. Ed. 843, 66 S. Ct. 715 (1946))*; see *Berman, supra, at 32, 99 L. Ed. 27, 75 S. Ct. 98* ("[T]he legislature, not the judiciary, is the main guardian of the public needs to be served by social legislation"); see also *Lingle v. Chevron U.S.A., Inc., 544 U.S. 528, 161 L. Ed. 2d 876, 125 S. Ct. 2074 (2005)*. Likewise, we recognized our inability to evaluate whether, in a given case, eminent domain is a necessary means by which to pursue the legislature's ends. *Midkiff, supra, at 242, 81 L. Ed. 2d 186, 104 S. Ct. 2321; Berman, supra, at 33, 99 L. Ed. 27, 75 S. Ct. 98.*

Yet for all the emphasis on deference, *Berman* and *Midkiff* hewed to a bedrock principle without which our public use jurisprudence would collapse: "A purely private taking could not withstand the scrutiny of the public use requirement; it would serve no legitimate purpose of government and would thus be void." *Midkiff, 467 U.S., at 245, 81 L. Ed. 2d 186, 104 S. Ct. 2321; id., at 241, 81 L. Ed. 2d 186, 104 S. Ct. 2321* ("[T]he Court's cases have repeatedly stated that 'one person's property may not be taken for the benefit of another private person without a justifying public purpose, even though compensation be paid'" (quoting *Thompson v. Consolidated Gas Util. Corp., 300 U.S. 55, 80, 81 L. Ed. 510, 57 S. Ct. 364 (1937)))*; see also *Missouri Pacific R. Co. v. Nebraska, 164 U.S. 403, 417, 41 L. Ed. 489, 17 S. Ct. 130 (1896)*. To protect that principle, those decisions reserved "a role for courts to play in reviewing a legislature's judgment of what constitutes a public use ... [though] the Court in *Berman* made clear that it is 'an extremely narrow' one." *Midkiff, supra, at 240, 81 L. Ed. 2d 186, 104 S. Ct. 2321* (quoting *Berman, supra, at 32, 99 L. Ed. 27, 75 S. Ct. 98*).

The Court's holdings in *Berman* and *Midkiff* were true to the principle underlying the *Public Use Clause*. In both those cases, the extraordinary, precondemnation use of the targeted property inflicted affirmative harm on society – in *Berman* through blight resulting from extreme poverty and in *Midkiff* through oligopoly resulting from extreme wealth. And in both cases, the relevant legislative body had found that eliminating the existing property use was necessary to remedy the harm. *Berman, supra, at 28–9, 99 L. Ed. 27, 75 S. Ct. 98; Midkiff, supra, at 232, 81 L. Ed. 2d 186, 104 S. Ct. 2321.* Thus a public purpose was realized when the harmful use was eliminated. Because each taking *directly* achieved a public benefit, it did not matter that the property was turned over to private use. Here, in contrast, New London does not claim that Susette Kelo's and Wilhelmina Dery's well-maintained homes are the source of any social harm. Indeed, it could not so claim without adopting the absurd argument that any single-family home that might be razed to make way for an apartment building, or any church that might be replaced with a retail store, or any small business that might be more lucrative if it were instead part of a national franchise, is inherently harmful to society and thus within the government's power to condemn.

In moving away from our decisions sanctioning the condemnation of harmful property use, the Court today significantly expands the meaning of public use. It holds that the sovereign may take private property currently put to ordinary private use, and give it over for new, ordinary private use, so long as the new use is predicted to generate some secondary benefit for the public – such as increased tax revenue, more jobs, maybe even esthetic pleasure. But nearly any lawful use of real private property can be said to generate some incidental benefit to the public. Thus, if predicted (or even guaranteed) positive side effects are enough to render transfer from one private party to another constitutional, then the words "for public use" do not realistically exclude *any* takings, and thus do not exert any constraint on the eminent domain power.

There is a sense in which this troubling result follows from errant language in *Berman* and *Midkiff*. In discussing whether takings within a blighted neighborhood were for a public use, *Berman* began by observing: "We deal, in other words, with what traditionally has been known as the police power." *348 U.S., at 32, 99 L. Ed. 27, 75 S. Ct. 98.* From there it declared that "[o]nce the object is within the authority of Congress, the right to realize it through the exercise of eminent domain is clear." *Id., at 33, 99 L. Ed. 27, 75 S. Ct. 98.* Following up, we said in *Midkiff* that "[t]he 'public use' requirement is coterminous with the scope of a sovereign's police powers." *467 U.S., at 240, 81 L. Ed. 2d 186, 104 S. Ct. 2321.* This language was unnecessary to the specific holdings of those decisions. *Berman* and *Midkiff* simply did not put such language to the constitutional test, because the takings in those cases were within the police power but also for "public use" for the reasons I have described. The case before us now demonstrates why, when deciding if a taking's purpose is constitutional, the police power and "public use" cannot always be equated.

The Court protests that it does not sanction the bare transfer from A to B for B's benefit. It suggests two limitations on what can be taken after today's decision. First, it maintains a role for courts in ferreting out takings whose sole purpose is to bestow a benefit on the private transferee – without detailing how courts are to conduct that complicated inquiry. *Ante, at 477–8, 162 L. Ed. 2d, at 450.* For his part, Justice Kennedy suggests that courts may divine illicit purpose by a careful review of the record and the process by which a legislature arrived at the decision to take – without specifying what courts should look for in a case with different facts, how they will know if they have found it, and what to do if they do not. *Ante, at 491–2, 162 L. Ed. 2d, at 459–60* (concurring opinion). Whatever the details of Justice Kennedy's as-yet-undisclosed test, it is difficult to envision anyone but the "stupid staff[er]" failing it. See *Lucas v. South Carolina Coastal Council, 505 U.S. 1003, 1025–6, n. 12, 120 L. Ed. 2d 798, 112 S. Ct. 2886 (1992).* The trouble with economic development takings is that private benefit and incidental public benefit are, by definition, merged and mutually reinforcing. In this case, for example, any boon for Pfizer or the plan's developer is difficult to disaggregate from the promised public gains in taxes and jobs. See App. to Pet. for Cert. 275–7.

Even if there were a practical way to isolate the motives behind a given taking, the gesture toward a purpose test is theoretically flawed. If it is true that incidental public benefits from new private use are enough to ensure the "public purpose" in a taking, why should it matter, as far as the *Fifth Amendment* is concerned, what inspired the taking in the first place? How much the government does or does not desire to benefit a favored private party has no bearing on whether an economic development taking will or will not generate secondary benefit for the public. And whatever the reason for a given condemnation, the effect is the same from the constitutional perspective – private property is forcibly relinquished to new private ownership.

A second proposed limitation is implicit in the Court's opinion. The logic of today's decision is that eminent domain may only be used to upgrade – not downgrade – property. At best this makes the *Public Use Clause* redundant with the *Due Process Clause*, which already prohibits irrational government action. See *Lingle, 544 U.S. 528, 161 L. Ed. 2d 876, 125 S. Ct. 2074.* The Court rightfully admits, however, that the judiciary cannot get bogged down in predictive judgments about whether the public will actually be better off after a property transfer. In any event, this constraint has no realistic import. For who among us can say she already makes the most productive or attractive possible use of her property? The specter of condemnation hangs over all property. Nothing is to prevent the State from replacing any Motel 6 with a Ritz-Carlton, any home with a shopping mall, or any farm with a factory. Cf. *Bugryn v. Bristol, 63 Conn. App. 98, 774 A.2d 1042 (2001)* (taking the homes and farm of four owners in their 70's and 80's and giving it to an "industrial park"); *99 Cents Only Stores v. Lancaster Redevelopment Agency, 237 F. Supp. 2d 1123 (CD Cal. 2001)* (attempted taking of 99 Cents store to replace with a Costco); *Poletown Neighborhood Council v. Detroit, 410 Mich. 616, 304 N.W.2d 455 (1981)* (taking a working-class, immigrant community in Detroit and giving it to a General Motors assembly plant), overruled by *County of Wayne v. Hathcock, 471 Mich. 445, 684 N.W.2d 765 (2004)*; Brief for Becket Fund for Religious Liberty as *Amicus Curiae* 4–11 (describing takings of religious institutions' properties); Institute for Justice, D. Berliner, Public Power, Private Gain:

A Five-Year, State-by-State Report Examining the Abuse of Eminent Domain (2003) (collecting accounts of economic development takings).

The Court also puts special emphasis on facts peculiar to this case: The NLDC's plan is the product of a relatively careful deliberative process; it proposes to use eminent domain for a multipart, integrated plan rather than for isolated property transfer; it promises an array of incidental benefits (even esthetic ones), not just increased tax revenue; it comes on the heels of a legislative determination that New London is a depressed municipality. See, e.g., *ante, at 487, 162 L. Ed. 2d, at 456* ("[A] one-to-one transfer of property, executed outside the confines of an integrated development plan, is not presented in this case"). Justice Kennedy, too, takes great comfort in these facts. *Ante, at 493, 162 L. Ed. 2d, at 460* (concurring opinion). But none has legal significance to blunt the force of today's holding. If legislative prognostications about the secondary public benefits of a new use can legitimate a taking, there is nothing in the Court's rule or in Justice Kennedy's gloss on that rule to prohibit property transfers generated with less care, that are less comprehensive, that happen to result from less elaborate process, whose only projected advantage is the incidence of higher taxes, or that hope to transform an already prosperous city into an even more prosperous one.

Finally, in a coda, the Court suggests that property owners should turn to the States, who may or may not choose to impose appropriate limits on economic development takings. *Ante, at 489, 162 L. Ed. 2d, at 457–8.* This is an abdication of our responsibility. States play many important functions in our system of dual sovereignty, but compensating for our refusal to enforce properly the Federal Constitution (and a provision meant to curtail state action, no less) is not among them.

It was possible after *Berman* and *Midkiff* to imagine unconstitutional transfers from A to B. Those decisions endorsed government intervention when private property use had veered to such an extreme that the public was suffering as a consequence. Today nearly all real property is susceptible to condemnation on the Court's theory. In the prescient words of a dissenter from the infamous decision in *Poletown*, "[n]ow that we have authorized local legislative bodies to decide that a different commercial or industrial use of property will produce greater public benefits than its present use, no homeowner's, merchant's or manufacturer's property, however productive or valuable to its owner, is immune from condemnation for the benefit of other private interests that will put it to a 'higher' use." *410 Mich., at 644–5, 304 N. W. 2d, at 464* (opinion of Fitzgerald, J.). This is why economic development takings "seriously jeopardiz[e] the security of all private property ownership." *Id., at 645, 304 N. W. 2d, at 465* (Ryan, J., dissenting).

Any property may now be taken for the benefit of another private party, but the fallout from this decision will not be random. The beneficiaries are likely to be those citizens with disproportionate influence and power in the political process, including large corporations and development firms. As for the victims, the government now has license to transfer property from those with fewer resources to those with more. The Founders cannot have intended this perverse result. "[T]hat alone is a *just* government," wrote James Madison, "which *impartially* secures to every man, whatever is his *own*." For the National Gazette, Property (Mar. 27, 1792), reprinted in 14 Papers of James Madison 266 (R. Rutland et al. eds. 1983).

I would hold that the takings in both Parcel 3 and Parcel 4A are unconstitutional, reverse the judgment of the Supreme Court of Connecticut, and remand for further proceedings.

Justice **Thomas,** dissenting.

Long ago, William Blackstone wrote that "the law of the land … postpone[s] even public necessity to the sacred and inviolable rights of private property." 1 Commentaries on the Laws of England 134–5 (1765) (hereinafter Blackstone). The Framers embodied that principle in the Constitution, allowing the government to take property not for "public necessity," but instead for "public use." *Amdt. 5.* Defying this understanding, the Court replaces the *Public Use Clause* with a "'[P]ublic [P]urpose'" Clause, *ante, at 479–80, 162 L. Ed. 2d, at 451–2* (or perhaps the "Diverse and Always Evolving Needs of Society" Clause, *ante, at 479, 162 L. Ed. 2d, at 451* (capitalization added)), a restriction that is satisfied, the Court instructs, so long as the purpose is "legitimate" and the means "not irrational," *ante, at 488, 162 L. Ed. 2d, at 456* (internal quotation marks omitted). This deferential shift in phraseology enables the Court to hold, against all common sense, that a costly urban-renewal project whose stated purpose is a vague promise of new jobs and increased tax revenue, but which is also suspiciously agreeable to the Pfizer Corporation, is for a "public use."

I cannot agree. If such "economic development" takings are for a "public use," any taking is, and the Court has erased the *Public Use Clause* from our Constitution, as Justice O'Connor powerfully argues in dissent. *Ante, at 494, 501–5, 162 L. Ed. 2d, at 460–61, 464–8.* I do not believe that this Court can eliminate liberties expressly enumerated in the Constitution and therefore join her dissenting opinion. Regrettably, however, the Court's error runs deeper than this. Today's decision is simply the latest in a string of our cases construing the *Public Use Clause* to be a virtual nullity, without the slightest nod to its original meaning. In my view, the *Public Use Clause*, originally understood, is a meaningful limit on the government's eminent domain power. Our cases have strayed from the Clause's original meaning, and I would reconsider them.

I

The *Fifth Amendment* provides:

> No person shall be held to answer for a capital, or otherwise infamous crime, unless on a presentment or indictment of a Grand Jury, except in cases arising in the land or naval forces, or in the Militia, when in actual service in time of War or public danger; nor shall any person be subject for the same offence to be twice put in jeopardy of life or limb, nor shall be compelled in any criminal case to be a witness against himself, nor be deprived of life, liberty, or property, without due process of law; *nor shall private property be taken for public use, without just compensation* (emphasis added.)

It is the last of these liberties, the *Takings Clause*, that is at issue in this case. In my view, it is "imperative that the Court maintain absolute fidelity to" the Clause's express limit on the power of the government over the individual, no less than with every other liberty expressly enumerated in the *Fifth Amendment* or the *Bill of Rights* more generally. *Shepard v. United States, 544 U.S. 13, 28, 161 L. Ed. 2d 205, 125 S. Ct. 1254 (2005)* (Thomas, J., concurring in part and concurring in judgment) (internal quotation marks omitted).

Though one component of the protection provided by the *Takings Clause* is that the government can take private property only if it provides "just compensation" for the taking, the *Takings Clause* also prohibits the government from taking property except "for public use." Were it otherwise, the *Takings Clause* would either be meaningless or empty. If the *Public Use Clause* served no function other than to state that the government may take property through its eminent domain power – for public or private uses – then it would be surplusage. See *ante, at 496, 162 L. Ed. 2d, at 462* (O'Connor, J., dissenting); see also *Marbury v. Madison, 5 U.S. 137, 1 Cranch 137, 174, 2 L. Ed. 60 (1803)* ("It cannot be presumed that any clause in the constitution is intended to be without effect"); *Myers v. United States, 272 U.S. 52, 151, 71 L. Ed. 160, 47 S. Ct. 21 (1926)*. Alternatively, the Clause could distinguish those takings that require compensation from those that do not. That interpretation, however, "would permit private property to be taken or appropriated for private use without any compensation whatever." *Cole v. La Grange, 113 U.S. 1, 8, 28 L. Ed. 896, 5 S. Ct. 416 (1885)* (interpreting same language in the *Missouri Public Use Clause*). In other words, the Clause would require the government to compensate for takings done "for public use," leaving it free to take property for purely private uses without the payment of compensation. This would contradict a bedrock principle well established by the time of the founding: that all takings required the payment of compensation. 1 Blackstone 135; 2 J. Kent, Commentaries on American Law 275 (1827) (hereinafter Kent); For the National Property Gazette (Mar. 27, 1792), in 14 Papers of James Madison 266, 267 (R. Rutland et al. eds. 1983) (arguing that no property "shall be taken *directly* even for public use without indemnification to the owner").[1] The *Public Use Clause*, like the *Just Compensation Clause*, is therefore an express limit on the government's power of eminent domain.

The most natural reading of the Clause is that it allows the government to take property only if the government owns, or the public has a legal right to use, the property, as opposed to taking it for any public purpose or necessity whatsoever. At the time of the founding, dictionaries primarily defined the noun "use" as "[t]he act of employing any thing to any purpose." 2 S. Johnson, A Dictionary of the English Language 2194 (4th ed. 1773) (hereinafter Johnson). The term "use," moreover, "is from the Latin *utor*, which means 'to use, make use of, avail one's self of, employ,

---

1   Some state constitutions at the time of the founding lacked *just compensation clauses* and took property even without providing compensation. See *Lucas v. South Carolina Coastal Council, 505 U.S. 1003, 1056–7, 120 L. Ed. 2d 798, 112 S. Ct. 2886 (1992)* (Blackmun, J., dissenting). The Framers of the *Fifth Amendment* apparently disagreed, for they expressly prohibited uncompensated takings, and the *Fifth Amendment* was not incorporated against the States until much later. See *id., at 1028, n. 15, 120 L. Ed. 2d 798, 112 S. Ct. 2886*.

apply, enjoy, etc.'" J. Lewis, Law of Eminent Domain § 165, p 224, n. 4 (1888) (hereinafter Lewis). When the government takes property and gives it to a private individual, and the public has no right to use the property, it strains language to say that the public is "employing" the property, regardless of the incidental benefits that might accrue to the public from the private use. The term "public use," then, means that either the government or its citizens as a whole must actually "employ" the taken property. See *id.*, at 223 (reviewing founding-era dictionaries).

Granted, another sense of the word "use" was broader in meaning, extending to "[c]onvenience" or "help," or "[q]ualities that make a thing proper for any purpose." 2 Johnson 2194. Nevertheless, read in context, the term "public use" possesses the narrower meaning. Elsewhere, the Constitution twice employs the word "use," both times in its narrower sense. Claeys, Public-Use Limitations and Natural Property Rights, *2004 Mich. St. L. Rev. 877, 897* (hereinafter Public Use Limitations). Article I, § 10 provides that "the net Produce of all Duties and Imposts, laid by any State on Imports or Exports, shall be for the Use of the Treasury of the United States," meaning the Treasury itself will control the taxes, not use it to any beneficial end. And Article I, § 8 grants Congress power "[t]o raise and support Armies, but no Appropriation of Money to that Use shall be for a longer Term than two Years." Here again, "use" means "employed to raise and support Armies," not anything directed to achieving any military end. The same word in the *Public Use Clause* should be interpreted to have the same meaning.

Tellingly, the phrase "public use" contrasts with the very different phrase "general Welfare" used elsewhere in the Constitution. See *ibid.* ("Congress shall have Power To ... provide for the common Defence and general Welfare of the United States"); preamble (Constitution established "to promote the general Welfare"). The Framers would have used some such broader term if they had meant the *Public Use Clause* to have a similarly sweeping scope. Other founding-era documents made the contrast between these two usages still more explicit. See Sales, Classical Republicanism and the *Fifth Amendment*'s "Public Use" Requirement, *49 Duke L. J. 339, 367–8 (1999)* (hereinafter Sales) (noting contrast between, on the one hand, the term "public use" used by 6 of the first 13 States and, on the other, the terms "public exigencies" employed in the Massachusetts *Bill of Rights* and the Northwest Ordinance, and the term "public necessity" used in the Vermont Constitution of 1786). The Constitution's text, in short, suggests that the *Takings Clause* authorizes the taking of property only if the public has a right to employ it, not if the public realizes any conceivable benefit from the taking.

The Constitution's common-law background reinforces this understanding. The common law provided an express method of eliminating uses of land that adversely impacted the public welfare: nuisance law. Blackstone and Kent, for instance, both carefully distinguished the law of nuisance from the power of eminent domain. Compare 1 Blackstone 135 (noting government's power to take private property with compensation) with 3 *id.*, at 216 (noting action to remedy "*public* ... nuisances, which affect the public, and are an annoyance to *all* the king's subjects"); see also 2 Kent 274–6 (distinguishing the two). Blackstone rejected the idea that private property could be taken solely for purposes of any public benefit. "So great ... is the regard of the law for private property," he explained, "that it will not authorize the least violation of it; no, not even for the general good of the whole community." 1 Blackstone 135. He continued: "If a new road ... were to be made through the grounds of a private person, it might perhaps be extensively beneficial to the public; but the law permits no man, or set of men, to do this without the consent of the owner of the land." *Ibid.* Only "by giving [the landowner] full indemnification" could the government take property, and even then "[t]he public [was] now considered as an individual, treating with an individual for an exchange." *Ibid.* When the public took property, in other words, it took it as an individual buying property from another typically would: for one's own use. The *Public Use Clause*, in short, embodied the Framers' understanding that property is a natural, fundamental right, prohibiting the government from "tak[ing] *property* from A and giv[ing] it to B." *Calder v. Bull, 3 Dall. 386, 388, 1 L. Ed. 648 (1798)*; see also *Wilkinson v. Leland, 27 U.S. 627, 2 Pet. 627, 658, 7 L. Ed. 542 (1829)*; *Vanhorne's Lessee v. Dorrance, 2 U.S. 304, 2 Dallas 304, 1 L. Ed. 391 (CC Pa. 1795)*.

The public purpose interpretation of the *Public Use Clause* also unnecessarily duplicates a similar inquiry required by the Necessary and Proper Clause. The *Takings Clause* is a prohibition, not a grant of power: The Constitution does not expressly grant the Federal Government the power to take property for any public purpose whatsoever. Instead, the Government may take property only when necessary and proper to the exercise of an expressly enumerated power. See *Kohl v. United States, 91 U.S. 367, 371–2, 23 L. Ed. 449 (1876)* (noting Federal Government's power under the Necessary and Proper Clause to take property "needed for forts, armories, and arsenals, for navy-yards and light-houses, for custom-houses, post-offices, and court-houses, and for other public uses"). For a law to be within the Necessary and Proper Clause, as I have elsewhere explained, it must bear an "obvious, simple, and direct relation" to an exercise of Congress' enumerated powers, *Sabri v. United States, 541 U.S. 600, 613, 158 L. Ed. 2d 891, 124 S. Ct. 1941 (2004)* (Thomas, J., concurring in judgment), and it must not "subvert basic principles of" constitutional design, *Gonzales v. Raich, ante, at 65, 162 L. Ed. 2d 1, 125 S. Ct. 2195* (Thomas, J., dissenting). In other words, a taking is permissible under the Necessary and Proper Clause only if it serves a valid public purpose. Interpreting the *Public Use Clause* likewise to limit the government to take property only for sufficiently public purposes replicates this inquiry. If this is all the Clause means, it is, once again, surplusage. See *supra, at 507, 162 L. Ed. 2d, at 469*. The Clause is thus most naturally read to concern whether the property is used by the public or the government, not whether the purpose of the taking is legitimately public.

II

Early American eminent domain practice largely bears out this understanding of the *Public Use Clause*. This practice concerns state limits on eminent domain power, not the *Fifth Amendment*, since it was not until the late 19th century that the Federal Government began to use the power of eminent domain, and since the *Takings Clause* did not even arguably limit state power until after the passage of the *Fourteenth Amendment*. See Note, The Public Use Limitation on Eminent Domain:

An Advance Requiem, 58 Yale L. J. 567, 599–600, and nn. 3–4 (1949); *Barron ex rel. Tiernan v. Mayor of Baltimore, 32 U.S. 243, 7 Pet. 243, 250–51, 8 L. Ed. 672 (1833)* (holding the *Takings Clause* inapplicable to the States of its own force). Nevertheless, several early state constitutions at the time of the founding likewise limited the power of eminent domain to "public uses." See Sales 367–9, and n. 137 (emphasis deleted). Their practices therefore shed light on the original meaning of the same words contained in the *Public Use Clause*.

States employed the eminent domain power to provide quintessentially public goods, such as public roads, toll roads, ferries, canals, railroads, and public parks. Lewis §§ 166, 168–71, 175, at 227–8, 234–41, 243. Though use of the eminent domain power was sparse at the time of the founding, many States did have so-called Mill Acts, which authorized the owners of grist mills operated by water power to flood upstream lands with the payment of compensation to the upstream landowner. See, e.g., *id.*, § 178, at 245–6; *Head v. Amoskeag Mfg. Co., 113 U.S. 9, 16–19, 28 L. Ed. 889, 5 S. Ct. 441, and n. (1885)*. Those early grist mills "were regulated by law and compelled to serve the public for a stipulated toll and in regular order," and therefore were actually used by the public. Lewis § 178, at 246, and n. 3; see also *Head, supra, at 18–19, 28 L. Ed. 889, 5 S. Ct. 441*. They were common carriers – quasi-public entities. These were "public uses" in the fullest sense of the word, because the public could legally use and benefit from them equally. See Public Use Limitations 903 (common-carrier status traditionally afforded to "private beneficiaries of a state franchise or another form of state monopoly, or to companies that operated in conditions of natural monopoly").

To be sure, some early state legislatures tested the limits of their state-law eminent domain power. Some States enacted statutes allowing the taking of property for the purpose of building private roads. See Lewis § 167, at 230. These statutes were mixed; some required the private landowner to keep the road open to the public, and others did not. See *id.*, § 167, at 230–34. Later in the 19th century, moreover, the Mill Acts were employed to grant rights to private manufacturing plants, in addition to grist mills that had common-carrier duties. See, e.g., M. Horwitz, The Transformation of American Law 1780–1860, pp 51–2 (1977).

These early uses of the eminent domain power are often cited as evidence for the broad "public purpose" interpretation of the *Public Use Clause*, see, e.g., *ante, at 479–80, n 8, 162 L. Ed. 2d, at 450–51* (majority opinion); Brief for Respondents 30; Brief for American Planning Assn. et al. as *Amici Curiae* 6–7, but in fact the constitutionality of these exercises of eminent domain power under state public use restrictions was a hotly contested question in state courts throughout the 19th and into the 20th century. Some courts construed those clauses to authorize takings for public purposes, but others adhered to the natural meaning of "public use."[2] As

---

2   Compare *ante, at 479, 162 L. Ed. 2d, at 450–51*, and n. 8 (majority opinion) (noting that some state courts upheld the validity of applying the Mill Acts to private purposes and arguing that the "'use by the public' test" "eroded over time"), with, e.g., *Ryerson v. Brown, 35 Mich. 333, 338–9 (1877)* (holding it "essential" to the constitutionality of a Mill Act "that the statute should require the use to be public in fact; in other words, that it should contain provisions entitling the public to accommodations"); *Gaylord v. Sanitary Dist. of Chicago,*

noted above, the earliest Mill Acts were applied to entities with duties to remain open to the public, and their later extension is not deeply probative of whether that subsequent practice is consistent with the original meaning of the *Public Use Clause*. See *McIntyre v. Ohio Elections Comm'n, 514 U.S. 334, 370, 131 L. Ed. 2d 426, 115 S. Ct. 1511 (1995)* (Thomas, J., concurring in judgment). At the time of the founding, "[b]usiness corporations were only beginning to upset the old corporate model, in which the *raison d'etre* of chartered associations was their service to the public," Horwitz, *supra*, at 49–50, so it was natural to those who framed the first Public Use Clauses to think of mills as inherently public entities. The disagreement among state courts, and state legislatures' attempts to circumvent public use limits on their eminent domain power, cannot obscure that the *Public Use Clause* is most naturally read to authorize takings for public use only if the government or the public actually uses the taken property.

III

Our current *Public Use Clause* jurisprudence, as the Court notes, has rejected this natural reading of the Clause. *Ante, at 479–83, 162 L. Ed. 2d, at 450–52.* The Court adopted its modern reading blindly, with little discussion of the Clause's history and original meaning, in two distinct lines of cases: first, in cases adopting the "public purpose" interpretation of the Clause, and second, in cases deferring to legislatures' judgments regarding what constitutes a valid public purpose. Those questionable cases converged in the boundlessly broad and deferential conception of "public use" adopted by this Court in *Berman v. Parker, 348 U.S. 26, 99 L. Ed. 27, 75 S. Ct. 98 (1954),* and *Hawaii Housing Authority v. Midkiff, 467 U.S. 229, 81 L. Ed. 2d 186, 104 S. Ct. 2321 (1984),* cases that take center stage in the Court's opinion. See *ante, 480–82, 162 L. Ed. 2d, at 452–3.* The weakness of those two lines of cases, and consequently *Berman* and *Midkiff*, fatally undermines the doctrinal foundations of the Court's decision. Today's questionable application of these cases is further proof that the "public purpose" standard is not susceptible of principled application. This Court's reliance by rote on this standard is ill advised and should be reconsidered.

---

204 Ill. 576, 581–4, 68 N. E. 522, 524 (1903) (same); *Tyler v. Beacher, 44 Vt. 648, 652–6 (1871)* (same); *Sadler v. Langham, 34 Ala. 311, 332–4 (1859)* (striking down taking for purely private road and grist mill); *Varner v. Martin, 21 W. Va. 534, 546–8, 556–7, 566–7 (1883)* (grist mill and private road had to be open to public for them to constitute public use); *Harding v. Goodlett, 3 Yer. 41, 53 (Tenn. 1832)*; *Jacobs v. Clearview Water Supply Co., 220 Pa. 388, 393–5, 69 A. 870, 872 (1908)* (endorsing actual public use standard); *Minnesota Canal & Power Co. v. Koochiching Co., 97 Minn. 429, 449–51, 107 N. W. 405, 413 (1906)* (same); *Chesapeake Stone Co. v. Moreland, 126 Ky. 656, 663–7, 104 S. W. 762, 765, 31 Ky. L. Rptr. 1075 (Ct. App. 1907)* (same); Note, Public Use in Eminent Domain, 21 N.Y.U.L.Q. Rev. 285, 286, and n. 11 (1946) (calling the actual public use standard the "majority view" and citing other cases).

A

As the Court notes, the "public purpose" interpretation of the *Public Use Clause* stems from *Fallbrook Irrigation Dist. v. Bradley, 164 U.S. 112, 161–2, 41 L. Ed. 369, 17 S. Ct. 56 (1896). Ante, at 479–80, 162 L. Ed. 2d, at 452–3*. The issue in *Bradley* was whether a condemnation for purposes of constructing an irrigation ditch was for a public use. *164 U.S., at 161, 41 L. Ed. 369, 17 S. Ct. 56*. This was a public use, Justice Peckham declared for the Court, because "[t]o irrigate and thus to bring into possible cultivation these large masses of otherwise worthless lands would seem to be a public purpose and a matter of public interest, not confined to landowners, or even to any one section of the State." *Ibid.* That broad statement was dictum, for the law under review also provided that "[a]ll landowners in the district have the right to a proportionate share of the water." *Id., at 162, 41 L. Ed. 369, 17 S. Ct. 56*. Thus, the "public" did have the right to use the irrigation ditch because all similarly situated members of the public – those who owned lands irrigated by the ditch – had a right to use it. The Court cited no authority for its dictum, and did not discuss either the *Public Use Clause*'s original meaning or the numerous authorities that had adopted the "actual use" test (though it at least acknowledged the conflict of authority in state courts, see *id., at 158, 41 L. Ed. 369, 17 S. Ct. 56*; *supra, at 513–14, 162 L. Ed. 2d, at 473*, and n. 2). Instead, the Court reasoned that "[t]he use must be regarded as a public use, or else it would seem to follow that no general scheme of irrigation can be formed or carried into effect." *Bradley, supra, at 160–61, 41 L. Ed. 369, 17 S. Ct. 56*. This is no statement of constitutional principle: Whatever the utility of irrigation districts or the merits of the Court's view that another rule would be "impractical given the diverse and always evolving needs of society," *ante, at 479, 162 L. Ed. 2d, at 451*, the Constitution does not embody those policy preferences any more than it "enact[s] Mr. Herbert Spencer's Social Statics," *Lochner v. New York, 198 U.S. 45, 75, 49 L. Ed. 937, 25 S. Ct. 539 (1905)* (Holmes, J., dissenting); but see *id., at 58–62, 49 L. Ed. 937, 25 S. Ct. 539* (Peckham, J., for the Court).

This Court's cases followed *Bradley*'s test with little analysis. In *Clark v. Nash, 198 U.S. 361, 49 L. Ed. 1085, 25 S. Ct. 676 (1905)* (Peckham, J., for the Court), this Court relied on little more than a citation to *Bradley* in upholding another condemnation for the purpose of laying an irrigation ditch. *198 U.S., at 369–70, 49 L. Ed. 1085, 25 S. Ct. 676*. As in *Bradley*, use of the "public purpose" test was unnecessary to the result the Court reached. The government condemned the irrigation ditch for the purpose of ensuring access to water in which "[o]ther land owners adjoining the defendant in error ... might share," *198 U.S., at 370, 49 L. Ed. 1085, 25 S. Ct. 676*, and therefore *Clark* also involved a condemnation for the purpose of ensuring access to a resource to which similarly situated members of the public had a legal right of access. Likewise, in *Strickley v. Highland Boy Gold Mining Co., 200 U.S. 527, 50 L. Ed. 581, 26 S. Ct. 301 (1906)*, the Court upheld a condemnation establishing an aerial right-of-way for a bucket line operated by a mining company, relying on little more than *Clark*, see *Strickley, supra, at 531, 50 L. Ed. 581, 26 S. Ct. 301*. This case, too, could have been disposed of on the narrower ground that "the plaintiff [was] a carrier for itself and others," *200 U.S., at 531–32, 50 L. Ed. 581, 26 S. Ct. 301*, and therefore that the bucket line was legally open to the public. Instead, the Court unnecessarily rested its decision on the "inadequacy of use by the general public as a universal test." *Id., at 531, 50 L. Ed. 581, 26 S. Ct. 301.* This Court's cases quickly incorporated the public purpose standard set forth in *Clark* and *Strickley* by barren citation. See, e.g., *Rindge Co. v. County of Los Angeles, 262 U.S. 700, 707, 67 L. Ed. 1186, 43 S. Ct. 689 (1923)*; *Block v. Hirsh, 256 U.S. 135, 155, 65 L. Ed. 865, 41 S. Ct. 458 (1921)*; *Mt. Vernon-Woodberry Cotton Duck Co. v. Alabama Interstate Power Co., 240 U.S. 30, 32, 60 L. Ed. 507, 36 S. Ct. 234 (1916)*; *O'Neill v. Leamer, 239 U.S. 244, 253, 60 L. Ed. 249, 36 S. Ct. 54 (1915).*

B

A second line of this Court's cases also deviated from the *Public Use Clause*'s original meaning by allowing legislatures to define the scope of valid "public uses." *United States v. Gettysburg Electric R. Co., 160 U.S. 668, 40 L. Ed. 576, 16 S. Ct. 427 (1896)*, involved the question whether Congress' decision to condemn certain private land for the purpose of building battlefield memorials at Gettysburg, Pennsylvania, was for a public use. *Id., at 679–80, 40 L. Ed. 576, 16 S. Ct. 427.* Since the Federal Government was to use the lands in question, *id., at 682, 40 L. Ed. 576, 16 S. Ct. 427,* there is no doubt that it was a public use under any reasonable standard. Nonetheless, the Court, speaking through Justice Peckham, declared that "when the legislature has declared the use or purpose to be a public one, its judgment will be respected by the courts, unless the use be palpably without reasonable foundation." *Id., at 680, 40 L. Ed. 576, 16 S. Ct. 427.* As it had with the "public purpose" dictum in *Bradley,* the Court quickly incorporated this dictum into its *Public Use Clause* cases with little discussion. See, e.g., *United States ex rel. TVA v. Welch, 327 U.S. 546, 552, 90 L. Ed. 843, 66 S. Ct. 715 (1946)*; *Old Dominion Land Co. v. United States, 269 U.S. 55, 66, 70 L. Ed. 162, 46 S. Ct. 39 (1925).*

There is no justification, however, for affording almost insurmountable deference to legislative conclusions that a use serves a "public use." To begin with, a court owes no deference to a legislature's judgment concerning the quintessentially legal question of whether the government owns, or the public has a legal right to use, the taken property. Even under the "public purpose" interpretation, moreover, it is most implausible that the Framers intended to defer to legislatures as to what satisfies the *Public Use Clause,* uniquely among all the express provisions of the *Bill of Rights.* We would not defer to a legislature's determination of the various circumstances that establish, for example, when a search of a home would be reasonable, see, e.g., *Payton v. New York, 445 U.S. 573, 589–90, 63 L. Ed. 2d 639, 100 S. Ct. 1371 (1980)*, or when a convicted double-murderer may be shackled during a sentencing proceeding without on-the-record findings, see *Deck v. Missouri, 544 U.S. 622, 161 L. Ed. 2d 953, 125 S. Ct. 2007 (2005)*, or when state law creates a property interest protected by the *Due Process Clause,* see, e.g., *Castle Rock v. Gonzales, post, at 756–8, 162 L. Ed. 2d 658, 125 S. Ct. 2796*; *Board of Regents of State Colleges v. Roth, 408 U.S. 564, 576, 33 L. Ed. 2d 548, 92 S. Ct. 2701 (1972)*; *Goldberg v. Kelly, 397 U.S. 254, 262–3, 25 L. Ed. 2d 287, 90 S. Ct. 1011 (1970).*

Still worse, it is backwards to adopt a searching standard of constitutional review for nontraditional property interests, such as welfare benefits, see, e.g., *Goldberg, supra*, while deferring to the legislature's determination as to what constitutes a public use when it exercises the power of eminent domain, and thereby invades individuals' traditional rights in real property. The Court has elsewhere recognized "the overriding respect for the sanctity of the home that has been embedded in our traditions since the origins of the Republic," *Payton, supra, at 601, 63 L. Ed. 2d 639, 100 S. Ct. 1371,* when the issue is only whether the government may search a home. Yet today the Court tells us that we are not to "second-guess the City's considered judgments," *ante, at 488, 162 L. Ed. 2d, at 457,* when the issue is, instead, whether the government may take the infinitely more intrusive step of tearing down petitioners' homes. Something has gone seriously awry with this Court's interpretation of the Constitution. Though citizens are safe from the government in their homes, the homes themselves are not. Once one accepts, as the Court at least nominally does, *ante, at 477, 162 L. Ed. 2d, at 450,* that the *Public Use Clause* is a limit on the eminent domain power of the Federal Government and the States, there is no justification for the almost complete deference it grants to legislatures as to what satisfies it.

C

These two misguided lines of precedent converged in *Berman v. Parker, 348 U.S. 26, 99 L. Ed. 27, 75 S. Ct. 98 (1954),* and *Hawaii Housing Authority v. Midkiff, 467 U.S. 229, 81 L. Ed. 2d 186, 104 S. Ct. 2321 (1984).* Relying on those lines of cases, the Court in *Berman* and *Midkiff* upheld condemnations for the purposes of slum clearance and land redistribution, respectively. "Subject to specific constitutional limitations," *Berman* proclaimed, "when the legislature has spoken, the public interest has been declared in terms well-nigh conclusive. In such cases the legislature, not the judiciary, is the main guardian of the public needs to be served by social legislation." *348 U.S., at 32, 99 L. Ed. 27, 75 S. Ct. 98.* That reasoning was question begging, since the question to be decided was whether the "specific constitutional limitation" of the *Public Use Clause* prevented the taking of the appellant's (concededly "nonblighted") department store. *Id., at 31, 34, 99 L. Ed. 27, 75 S. Ct. 98. Berman* also appeared to reason that any exercise by Congress of an enumerated power (in this case, its plenary power over the District of Columbia) was *per se* a "public use" under the *Fifth Amendment. Id., at 33, 99 L. Ed. 27, 75 S. Ct. 98.* But the very point of the *Public Use Clause* is to limit that power. See *supra, at 508, 162 L. Ed. 2d, at 469–70.*

More fundamentally, *Berman* and *Midkiff* erred by equating the eminent domain power with the police power of States. See *Midkiff, supra, at 240, 81 L. Ed. 2d 186, 104 S. Ct. 2321* ("The 'public use' requirement is … coterminous with the scope of a sovereign's police powers"); *Berman, supra 32, 99 L. Ed. 27, 75 S. Ct. 98.* Traditional uses of that regulatory power, such as the power to abate a nuisance, required no compensation whatsoever, see *Mugler v. Kansas, 123 U.S. 623, 668–9, 31 L. Ed. 205, 8 S. Ct. 273 (1887),* in sharp contrast to the takings power, which has always required compensation, see *supra, at 508, 162 L. Ed. 2d, at 469–70,* and n. 1. The question whether the State can take property using the power of eminent domain is therefore distinct from the question whether it can regulate property pursuant to the police power. See, e.g., *Lucas v. South Carolina Coastal Council, 505 U.S. 1003,*

1014, 120 L. Ed. 2d 798, 112 S. Ct. 2886 (1992); *Mugler, supra, at 668–9, 31 L. Ed. 205, 8 S. Ct. 273*. In *Berman*, for example, if the slums at issue were truly "blighted," then state nuisance law, see, e.g., *supra, at 510, 162 L. Ed. 2d, at 463–4*; *Lucas, supra, at 1029, 120 L. Ed. 2d 798, 112 S. Ct. 2886*, not the power of eminent domain, would provide the appropriate remedy. To construe the *Public Use Clause* to overlap with the States' police power conflates these two categories.[3]

The "public purpose" test applied by *Berman* and *Midkiff* also cannot be applied in principled manner. "When we depart from the natural import of the term 'public use,' and substitute for the simple idea of a public possession and occupation, that of public utility, public interest, common benefit, general advantage or convenience … we are afloat without any certain principle to guide us." *Bloodgood v. Mohawk & Hudson R. Co., 18 Wend. 9, 60–61 (NY 1837)* (opinion of Tracy, Sen.). Once one permits takings for public purposes in addition to public uses, no coherent principle limits what could constitute a valid public use-at least, none beyond Justice O'Connor's (entirely proper) appeal to the text of the Constitution itself. See *ante, at 494, 501–5, 162 L. Ed. 2d, at 460 61, 464–8* (dissenting opinion). I share the Court's skepticism about a public use standard that requires courts to second-guess the policy wisdom of public works projects. *Ante, at 486–9, 162 L. Ed. 2d, at 456–7*. The "public purpose" standard this Court has adopted, however, demands the use of such judgment, for the Court concedes that the *Public Use Clause* would forbid a purely private taking. *Ante, at 477–8, 162 L. Ed. 2d, at 450–51*. It is difficult to imagine how a court could find that a taking was purely private except by determining that the taking did not, in fact, rationally advance the public interest. Cf. *ante, at 502–3, 162 L. Ed. 2d, at 465–6* (O'Connor, J., dissenting) (noting the complicated inquiry the Court's test requires). The Court is therefore wrong to criticize the "actual use" test as "difficult to administer." *Ante, at 479, 162 L. Ed. 2d, at 451*. It is far easier to analyze whether the government owns or the public has a legal right to use the taken property than to ask whether the taking has a "purely private purpose" – unless the Court means to eliminate public use scrutiny of takings entirely. *Ante, at 477–8, 488–9, 162 L. Ed. 2d, at 450–51, 456–7*. Obliterating a provision of the Constitution, of course, guarantees that it will not be misapplied.

For all these reasons, I would revisit our *Public Use Clause* cases and consider returning to the original meaning of the *Public Use Clause*: that the government may take property only if it actually uses or gives the public a legal right to use the property.

---

3   Some States also promoted the alienability of property by abolishing the feudal "quit rent" system, i.e., long-term leases under which the proprietor reserved to himself the right to perpetual payment of rents from his tenant. See Vance, The Quest for Tenure in the United States, 33 Yale L. J. 248, 256–7, 260–63 (1923). In *Hawaii Housing Authority v. Midkiff, 467 U.S. 229, 81 L. Ed. 2d 186, 104 S. Ct. 2321 (1984)*, the Court cited those state policies favoring the alienability of land *Ct. 2321*. But they were uses of the States' regulatory power, not the takings power, and therefore were irrelevant to the issue in *Midkiff*. This mismatch underscores the error of conflating a State's regulatory power with its taking power.

IV

The consequences of today's decision are not difficult to predict, and promise to be harmful. So-called "urban renewal" programs provide some compensation for the properties they take, but no compensation is possible for the subjective value of these lands to the individuals displaced and the indignity inflicted by uprooting them from their homes. Allowing the government to take property solely for public purposes is bad enough, but extending the concept of public purpose to encompass any economically beneficial goal guarantees that these losses will fall disproportionately on poor communities. Those communities are not only systematically less likely to put their lands to the highest and best social use, but are also the least politically powerful. If ever there were justification for intrusive judicial review of constitutional provisions that protect "discrete and insular minorities," *United States v. Carolene Products Co., 304 U.S. 144, 152, n. 4, 82 L. Ed. 1234, 58 S. Ct. 778 (1938)*, surely that principle would apply with great force to the powerless groups and individuals the *Public Use Clause* protects. The deferential standard this Court has adopted for the *Public Use Clause* is therefore deeply perverse. It encourages "those citizens with disproportionate influence and power in the political process, including large corporations and development firms," to victimize the weak. *Ante, at 505, 162 L. Ed. 2d, at 468* (O'Connor, J., dissenting).

Those incentives have made the legacy of this Court's "public purpose" test an unhappy one. In the 1950's, no doubt emboldened in part by the expansive understanding of "public use" this Court adopted in *Berman*, cities "rushed to draw plans" for downtown development. B. Frieden & L. Sagalyn, Downtown, Inc. How America Rebuilds Cities 17 (1989). "Of all the families displaced by urban renewal from 1949 through 1963, 63 percent of those whose race was known were nonwhite, and of these families, 56 percent of nonwhites and 38 percent of whites had incomes low enough to qualify for public housing, which, however, was seldom available to them." *Id.*, at 28. Public works projects in the 1950's and 1960's destroyed predominantly minority communities in St. Paul, Minnesota, and Baltimore, Maryland. *Id.*, at 28–9. In 1981, urban planners in Detroit, Michigan, uprooted the largely "lower-income and elderly" Poletown neighborhood for the benefit of the General Motors Corporation. J. Wylie, Poletown: Community Betrayed 58 (1989). Urban renewal projects have long been associated with the displacement of blacks; "[i]n cities across the country, urban renewal came to be known as 'Negro removal.'" Pritchett, The "Public Menace" of Blight: Urban Renewal and the Private Uses of Eminent Domain, *21 Yale L. & Pol'y Rev. 1, 47 (2003)*. Over 97 percent of the individuals forcibly removed from their homes by the "slum-clearance" project upheld by this Court in *Berman* were black. *348 U.S., at 30, 99 L. Ed. 27, 75 S. Ct. 98*. Regrettably, the predictable consequence of the Court's decision will be to exacerbate these effects.

The Court relies almost exclusively on this Court's prior cases to derive today's far-reaching, and dangerous, result. See *ante, at 479–83, 162 L. Ed. 2d, at 451–3*. But the principles this Court should employ to dispose of this case are found in the *Public Use Clause* itself, not in Justice Peckham's high opinion of reclamation laws, see *supra, at 515–16, 162 L. Ed. 2d, at 474*. When faced with a clash of constitutional principle and a line of unreasoned cases wholly divorced from the text, history, and structure of our founding document, we should not hesitate to resolve the tension in favor of the Constitution's original meaning. For the reasons I have given, and for the reasons given in Justice O'Connor's dissent, the conflict of principle raised by this boundless use of the eminent domain power should be resolved in petitioners' favor. I would reverse the judgment of the Connecticut Supreme Court.

Table of Cases

Bibliography

Adams, Michelle, Toward a Unified Standard for Evaluating the Constitutionality of Racial Preferences (draft on file with author).

Adler, Matthew D. & Kreimer, Seth F., *The New Etiquette of Federalism*: New York, Printz, and Yeskey, 1998 SUP.CT. REV. 71.

ALLEN, TOM, PROPERTY AND THE HUMAN RIGHTS ACT, 1998 (2005).

ALLEN, TOM, THE RIGHT TO PROPERTY IN COMMONWEALTH CONSTITUTIONS (2000).

Answer given by Mr. Monti on behalf of the Commission to a Written Question by Pere Esteve and Camilo Nogueira Román, 2003 O.J. (161 E) 57 (Jul. 10, 2003).

AWAKENING FROM THE DREAM: CIVIL RIGHTS UNDER SIEGE AND THE NEW STRUGGLE FOR EQUAL JUSTICE (Denise C. Morgan, Rachil Godsil & Joy Moses, eds., 2006).

Ayres, Susan, *The Rhetorics of Takings Cases: It's Mine v. Let's Share*, 5 NEV. L.J. 615 (2005).

Barbash, Fred, *Court Sustains Hawaiian Law Dividing Large Land Holdings*, WASH. POST, May 31, 1984, at A2.

Barros, D. Benjamin, *Home as a Legal Concept*, 46 SANTA CLARA L. REV. 255 (2006).

Barros, D. Benjamin, *At Last, Some Clarity: The Potential Long-Term Impact of Lingle v. Chevron and the Separation of Takings and Substantive Due Process*, 69 ALB. L. REV. 343 (2005).

Barros, D. Benjamin, *The Police Power and the Takings Clause*, 58 U. MIAMI L. REV. 471 (2004).

BARRY, JOHN M., RISING TIDE: THE GREAT MISSISSIPPI FLOOD OF 1927 AND HOW IT CHANGED AMERICA (1998).

Bayer, Jared, *Re-Balancing State and Federal Power: Toward a Political Principle of Subsidiarity in the United States*, 53 AM. U. L. REV. 1421 (2004).

Beard, Matthew, Businesses on Olympic Site Fight to Avoid Eviction, THE INDEPENDENT (London, England), Aug. 13, 2005, at 42.

Bell, Abraham & Parchomovsky, Gideon, *Of Property and Federalism*, 115 YALE L.J. 72 (2005).

Bell, Abraham, *Not Just Compensation*, 13 J. CONTEMP. LEGAL ISSUES 29 (2003).

BERLINER, DANA, PUBLIC POWER, PRIVATE GAIN: A FIVE-YEAR, STATE-BY-STATE REPORT EXAMINING THE ABUSE OF EMINENT DOMAIN (2003).

Bermstein, Andrea, *New York Hopes to Nurture Artist Neighborhoods*, National Public Radio Morning Edition (May 16, 2006).

4 BLACKSTONE, WILLIAM, COMMENTARIES ON ENGLISH LAW 223 (1765–69).

Blumm, Michael C. & Ritchie, Lucus, Lucas's *Unlikely Legacy: The Rise of Background Principles as Categorical Takings Defenses*, 29 HARV. ENVT'L L. REV. 321 (2005).

Breemer, J. David, *You Can Check Out But You Can Never Leave: The Story of San Remo Hotel – the Supreme Court Relegates Federal Takings Claims to State Courts Under a Rule Intended to Ripen the Claims for Federal Review*, 33 B.C. Envtl. Aff. L. Rev. 247 (2006).

Breemer, J. David, *Overcoming Williamson County's Troubling State Procedures Rule: How the England Reservation, Issue Preclusion Exceptions, and the Inadequacy Exception Open the Federal Courthouse Door to Ripe Takings Claims*, 18 J. Land Use & Envtl. L. 209 (2003).

Brief Amicus Curiae of John Norquist, President, Congress for New Urbanism, in Support of Petitioners, Kelo v. City of New London, No. 04-108 (filed December 3, 2004) (available at 2004 WL 2811055).

Briffault, Richard, *Our Localism, Part I – The Structure of Local Government Law*, 90 Colum. L. Rev. 1 (1990).

Briffault, Richard, *Our Localism, Part II – Localism and Legal Theory*, 90 Colum. L. Rev. 346 (1990).

Broder, David, Democracy Derailed: Initiative Campaigns and the Power of Money (2000).

Brooks, Richard O., Kelo *and the "Whaling City": The Failure of the Supreme Court's Opportunity to Articulate a Public Purpose of Sustainability, in* The Supreme Court and Takings: Four Essays 6th ed. (2005).

Brown, Carol Necole & Williams, Serena M., *The Houses that Eminent Domain and Housing Tax Credits Built: Imagining a Better New Orleans*, 34 Fordham Urban L.J.110 (2007).

Brown, Carol Necole, *Taking the Takings Claim; A Policy and Economic Analysis of the Survival of Takings Claims After Property Transfers*, 36 Conn. L. Rev. 7 (2003).

Calandrillo, Steve P., *Eminent Domain Economics: Should "Just Compensation" Be Abolished, and Would "Takings Insurance" Work Instead?*, 64 Oh. St. L.J. 451 (2003).

Callies, David L. & Saxer, Shelley Ross, *Is Fair Market Value Just Compensation? An Underlying Issue Surfaced in Kelo*, in Eminent Domain Use and Abuse: Kelo in Context 137 (Dwight H. Merriam & Mary Massaron Ross, eds, 2006).

Cameron, Stuart, *Gentrification, Housing Redifferentiation and Urban Regeneration: "Going for Growth" in Newcastle Upon Tyne*, 40 Urban Studies 2367 (2003).

Cao, Pei, Real Estate Law in China (1998).

Carr, Martha, *Rebuilding Should Begin on High Ground, Group Says; Planners Warn Against Haphazard Development*, Times Picayune (New Orleans), Nov. 19, 2005.

Carr, Martha, *National Experts Focus on N.O.; Los Angeles Gathering Takes Holistic Approach*, Times Picayune (New Orleans), Nov. 4, 2005.

Castle Coalition: Citizens Fighting Eminent Domain Abuse, *available at* http://www.castlecoalition.com/.

Cavarello, Daniel T., from Penn Central to United Artists' I & II: The Rise to Immunity of Historic Preservation Designation From Successful Takings Challenges, 22 B.C. Envtl. Aff. L. Rev. 593 (1995).

CBS Evening News, May 30, 1984 (recording in possession of author).

CBS News Transcripts, CBS Evening News: Supreme Court Affirms the Power of Local Governments to Seize Private Property, June 23, 2005 (available on LEXIS).

Chemerinsky, Erwin, *The Values of Federalism*, 47 FLA. L. REV. 499 (1995).

Chemerinsky, Erwin, *Parity Reconsidered: Defining a Role for the Federal Judiciary*, 36 U.C.L.A.L. REV. 233 (1988).

Chittum, Ryan, *Eminent Domain: Is It Only Hope for Inner Cities?*, WALL ST. J., Oct. 5, 2005, at B1.

Claeys, Eric R., *Don't Waste a Teaching Moment:* Kelo, *Urban Renewal, and Blight*, 15 J. AFFORDABLE HOUS. 14 (2006).

Claeys, Eric R., *That '70s Show: Eminent Domain Reform and the Administrative Law Revolution*, 46 SANTA CLARA L. REV. 867 (2006).

Claeys, Eric R., *Euclid Lives? The Uneasy Legacy of Progressivism in Zoning*, 73 FORDHAM L. REV. 731 (2004).

Claeys, Eric R., *Public Use Limitations and Natural Property Rights*, 2004 MICH. ST. L. REV. 877 (2004).

Cochrane, Allan, *Devolving the Heartland: Making Up A New Social Policy for the "South East"* 26 CRITICAL SOCIAL POLICY 685 (2006).

Cohen, Charles E., *Eminent Domain After* Kelo v. City of New London*: An Argument For Banning Economic Development Takings*, 29 HARV. J.L. & PUB. POL'Y 491 (2006).

COKE, SIR EDWARD, THIRD INSTITUTE OF THE LAWS OF ENGLAND (1644).

Collin, Robert W. & Collin, Robin Morris, *The Role of Communities in Environmental Decisionmaking: Communities Speaking for Themselves*, 13 J. ENVTL. L. & LITIG. 37 (1998).

Congress Upheld in Slum Clearing: Supreme Court Says Federal and State Legislatures Have Wide Redevelopment Power, N.Y. TIMES, Nov. 23, 1954, at 49.

COOLEY, THOMAS M., A TREATISE ON THE CONSTITUTIONAL LIMITATIONS WHICH REST UPON THE LEGISLATIVE POWER OF THE STATES OF THE AMERICAN UNION 299 and n. 3 (1st ed. 1868).

Cowell, Richard & Thomas, Huw, *Managing Nature and Narratives of Dispossession: Reclaiming Territory in Cardiff Bay*, 39 URBAN STUDIES 1241 (2002).

COYLE, DENNIS J., PROPERTY RIGHTS AND THE CONSTITUTION (1993).

Cribbet, John, *Changing Concepts in the Law of Land Use*, 50 IOWA L. REV. 245 (1965).

Crowley, Sheila, *Presentation to Gulf Coast Recovery and Rebuilding Caucus, U.S. House of Reps.* (Mar. 7, 2006), http://www.nlihc.org/detail/article.cfm?article_id'3415&id'72.

Dagan, Hanoch, *Takings and Distributive Justice*, 85 VA. L. REV. 741 (1999).

DeBow, Michael, *Unjust Compensation: The Continuing Need for Reform*, 46 S.C. L. REV. 579 (1995).

DEGAETANO, ALAN AND KLEMANSKI, JOHN S., POWER AND CITY GOVERNANCE: COMPARATIVE PERSPECTIVES ON URBAN DEVELOPMENT (1999).

Desai, Anuj C., *Filters and Federalism: Public Library Internet Access, Local Control, and the Federal Spending Power*, 7 U. PA. J. CONST. L. 1 (2004).

DeSoto, Hernando, The Mystery of Capital: Why Capitalism Triumphs in the West and Fails Everywhere Else (2000).

Dickson, Del, The Supreme Court in Conference, 1940–1985: The Private Discussions Behind Nearly 300 Supreme Court Decisions (2001).

Dillon, David, *How Should City Rebuild Neighborhoods and Infrastructure, Reinvent Economy? Problems Plentiful, Certainties Few As Big Easy Plans Recovery*, Dallas Morning News, Nov. 20, 2005.

Dodd, Philip, *Supreme Court Delays Segregation Action: Arguments Await 9th Justice*, Chicago Daily Tribune, Nov. 23, 1954, at 7.

Doremus, Holly, *Takings and Transitions*, 19 J. Land Use & Envtl. L. 1 (2003).

Dowling, Timothy J., *How to Think About Kelo after the Shouting Stops, in* Eminent Domain Use and Abuse: Kelo in Context (Dwight H. Merriam & Mary Massaron Ross eds, 2006).

Dreher, Robert G. & Echeverria, John D., *Kelo's Unanswered Questions: The Policy Debate Over the Use of Eminent Domain for Economic Development* (Georgetown Environmental Law & Policy Institute, Georgetown University Law Center), available at http://www.law.georgetown.edu/gelpi/current_research/documents/GELPIReport_Kelo.pdf at 11–12.

Duncan, Myrl L., *Property as a Public Conversation, Not a Lockean Soliloquy: A Role for Intellectual and Legal History in Takings Analysis*, 26 Envtl. L. 1095 (1996).

Durchslag, Melvin R., *Forgotten Federalism: The Takings Clause and Local Land Use Decisions*, 59 Md. L. Rev. 464 (2000).

Eckhoff, Amanda S. & Merriam, Dwight H., Public Use Goes Peripatetic: First, Michigan Reverses Poletown and Now the Supreme Court Grants Review in an Eminent Domain Case, Eminent Domain Use and Abuse: Kelo in Context, 33 (eds Dwight H. Merriam & Mary Nassaron Ross, ABA 2006).

Editorial, *A Wide Decision on Blighted Areas*, L.A. Times, Nov. 26, 1954, at II–4.

Editorial, *City's Right to Beauty*, Wash. Post & Times Herald, Nov. 24, 1954, at 12.

Editorial, *Eminent Latitude*, Washington Post, June 24, 2005, at A30.

Editorial, *Eminent Sense on Eminent Domain*, N.Y. Times, June 1, 1984, at A30.

Editorial, *Lords of the Manor*, Wall St. Journal, June 1, 1984, at 1.

Editorial, *Paradise Divvied*, Christian Science Monitor, June 1, 1984, at 15.

Editorial, *Tear Down the Castle*, St. Louis Post-Dispatch, June 24, 2005, at B8.

Editorial, *The Limits of Property Rights*, N.Y. Times, June 24, 2005, at A22.

Ellickson, Robert C., *Alternatives to Zoning: Covenants, Nuisance Rules, and Fines as Land Use Controls*, 40 U. Chi. L. Rev. 681 (1973).

Ely Jr., James W., *Real Estate Law Kelo: A Setback for Property Owners*, GPSolo Magazine, Sept. 2006.

Epstein, Richard A., How Progressives Rewrote the Constitution (2006).

Epstein, Richard A. *Property, Speech, and the Politics of Distrust*, 59 U. Chi. L. Rev. 41 (1992).

Epstein, Richard A., Takings: Private Property and the Power of Eminent Domain (1985).

EU to Look Into Real Property Deal, The Times, March 4, 2004, 47.

Exec. Order No. 13, 406 (June 23, 2006).

Farber, Daniel A., *Economic Analysis and Just Compensation*, 12 Int'l Rev. L. & Econ. 125 (1992).

Farber, Daniel A., *Public Choice and Just Compensation*, 9 Const. Commentary 279 (1992).

Featherstone, Liza, *The Other Side of the Big Easy*, Grist Magazine, http://www. alternet.org/story/25278 (last visited June 24, 2006).

Fee, John, *Reforming Eminent Domain*, in Eminent Domain Use and Abuse: Kelo in Context 125 (Dwight H. Merriam & Mary Massaron Ross eds, 2006).

Feinberg, Lawrence, *30 Years After Brown Decision, Its Impact Debated*, Wash. Post, May 18, 1984, at C1.

Fennell, Lee Anne, *The Death of Poletown: The Future of Eminent Domain and Economic Development After* County of Wayne v. Hathcock*: Taking Eminent Domain Apart*, 2004 Mich. St. L. Rev. 957 (2004).

Fenster, Mark, *The Takings Clause, Version 2005: The Legal Process of Constitutional Property Rights*, 9 U. Pa. J. Const. L. 667 (2007).

Fenster, Mark, *Takings Formalism and Regulatory Formulas: Exactions and the Consequences of Clarity*, 92 Cal. L. Rev. 609 (2004).

Fischel, William A., *The Political Economy of Public Use in* Poletown*: How Federal Grants Encourage Excessive Use of Eminent Domain*, 2004 Mich. St. L. Rev. 929.

Fischel, William A., The Homevoter Hypothesis: How Home Values Influence Local Government Taxation, School Finance, and Land-Use Policies (2001).

Fischel, William A., Regulatory Takings: Law, Economics, and Politics (1995).

Foster, Sheila, and Cole, Luke, From the Ground Up (2000).

Freyfogle, Eric T., *Owning the Land: Four Contemporary Narratives*, 13 J. Land Use & Envtl. L. 279 (1998).

Garnett, Nicole Stelle, *The Neglected Political Economy of Eminent Domain*, 105 Mich. L. Rev. 101 (2006).

Garnett, Nicole Stelle, *The Public-Use Question as a Takings Problem*, 71 Geo. Wash. L. Rev. 934 (2003).

Gauna, Eileen, *The Environmental Justice Misfit: Public Participation and the Paradigm Paradox*, 17 Stan. Envtl. L.J. 3 (1998).

Geneslaw, Howard D. & Federgreen, Shepard A., *The New Rules of Redevelopment: Courts More Skeptical of "Area in Need of Redevlopment" Designations*, 190 N.J.L.J. 402 (2007).

Gest, Ted, et al., *School Desegregation Grinds to a Halt in the South*, U.S. News & World Report, May 21, 1984, at 49.

Gibson, Gail, *High Court Upholds Eminent Domain; Private Homes, Businesses Can Be Seized as Part of Economic Revitalization; Cities Are Handed Broad Powers*, Baltimore Sun, June 24, 2005, at 1A.

Gillette, Clayton P., *Kelo and the Local Political Process*, 34 Hofstra L. Rev. 13 (2005).

Girling, Richard, "Save Our Streets", Sunday Times Magazine, September 19, 2004.

Godsil, Rachel D., Viewing the Cathedral from Behind the Color Line: *Property Rules, Liability Rules, and Environmental Justice*, 53 Emory L. J. 1808 (2003).

Gonzales, Carmen G., *Beyond Eco-Imperialism: An Environmental Justice Critique of Free Trade*, 78 DENV. U. L. REV. 979 (2001).

Goodman, Walter, *Brown v. Board of Education: Uneven Results 30 Years Later*, N.Y. TIMES, May 17, 1984, at B18.

Gordon, Colin, *Blighting the Way: Urban Renewal, Economic Development, and the Elusive Definition of Blight*, 31 FORDHAM URB. L.J. 305 (2004).

GREEN, MATTHEW, AND MARSHALL, ADAM, ECONOMIC DEVELOPMENT TOOLS – INTERNATIONAL COMPARISONS (2005).

Greenhouse, Linda, *Justice Weighs Desire v. Duty (Duty Prevails)*, N.Y. TIMES, Aug. 25, 2005, at A1.

Gyan Jr., Joe, Rebuilding Plan Divides N.O.: *Think Tank Separates City Into Investment Zones; Hard-Hit Areas Last*, THE ADVOCATE A01 (Nov. 29, 2005).

HAAR, CHARLES M., REFLECTIONS ON EUCLID: SOCIAL CONTRACT AND PRIVATE PURPOSE, IN ZONING AND THE AMERICAN DREAM 348 (Charles M. Haar & Jerold S. Kayden eds, 1989).

Hager, Philip, *Hawaiian Law on Breakup of Estates Upheld; High Court Expands Government's Power of Eminent Domain*, L.A. TIMES, May 31, 1984, at 1.

Hancock, Lee, *Is It Black and White? In A City Split and Sinking Before Storm, Racial Issues Boil*, DALLAS MORNING NEWS, Dec. 4, 2005.

Harrington, Matthew P., *"Public Use" and the Original Understanding of the So-Called "Takings" Clause*, 53 HASTINGS L.J. 1245 (2002).

Harsanyi, David, *Court Gives Land Robbery a Thumbs Up*, Denver Post, June 27, 2005, at B-01 (column).

Hart, John F., *Colonial Land Use Law and Its Significance for Modern Takings Doctrine*, 109 HARV. L. REV. 1252 (1996).

HART, JR. HENRY M. & SACKS, ALBERT M., THE LEGAL PROCESS (William N. Eskridge, Jr. & Philip P. Frickey eds., 1994).

HEALEY, PATSY, ET. AL., REBUILDING THE CITY: PROPERTY-LED URBAN REGENERATION (1992).

Heller, Michael A. & Hills, Jr., Roderick M., *The Art of Land Assembly* 2 (Oct. 2005) (unpublished partial draft, on file with contributing author, Rachel D. Godsil).

Heller, Michael, *The Tragedy of the Anticommons: Property in Transition from Marx to Markets*, 111 HARV. L. REV. 621 (1998).

High Court Upholds Slum Re-Reprojecting: Ruling Okays Broad Powers of Federal, State Legislatures, ATLANTA CONSTITUTION, Nov. 23, 1954, at 2 (from New York Times News Service).

Hills, Jr., Roderick M. *Is Federalism Good for Localism? The Localist Case for Federal Regimes*, 21 J. L. & POL. 187 (2005).

Houck, Oliver A., *Rising Water: The National Flood Insurance Program and Louisiana*, 60 TUL. L. REV. 61 (1985).

Hubbard, F. Patrick, Palazzolo, *Lucas and Penn Central: The Need for Pragmatism, Symbolism, and Ad Hoc Balancing*, 80 NEB. L. REV. 465 (2001).

Hulsebosch, Daniel J., *The Tools of Law and the Rule of Law: Teaching Regulatory Takings after* Palazzolo, 46 ST. LOUIS U.L. REV. 713 (2002).

Huston, Luther A., *School Bias Case to Await Harlan: Implementation Arguments Delayed by Supreme Court Till There is a Full Bench*, N.Y. TIMES, at 49.

Immigration Debate Put Off, CHRISTIAN SCIENCE MONITOR, Nov. 22, 1954, at 7.

Imrie, Rob and Thomas, Huw, *Law, Legal Struggles and Urban Regeneration: Rethinking the Relationships*, 34 URBAN STUDIES 1401 (1997).

Integration Hearings Postponed: Supreme Court to Wait for Full Membership Before Acting, MORNING TRIBUNE (Tampa, Florida), Nov. 23, 1954, at 1.

Jacobs, Sonji, *Legislators Give Property Seizure Laws High Priority*, ATLANTA JOURNAL CONSTITUTION, Aug. 25, 2005 at 1C.

Jeffries, Shavar, *The Structural Inadequacy of Public Schools for Stigmatized Minorities: The Need for Institutional Remedies*, HASTINGS CONST. L.Q. (*forthcoming* 2007).

JONES, BRYAN D. & BACHELOR, LYNN W., THE SUSTAINING HAND: COMMUNITY LEADERSHIP AND CORPORATE POWER (2nd ed. 1993).

Jones, Walter, *Expropriation in Roman Law*, 45 L.Q. 512 (1929).

JUSTICE HAROLD BURTON PAPERS, Manuscript Division, Library of Congress, Washington, D.C., Box 251, Folder 15.

JUSTICE LEWIS F. POWELL, JR. PAPERS, Washington & Lee University, Lexington, Virginia.

JUSTICE STANLEY REED PAPERS, University of Kentucky Library, Lexington, Kentucky.

JUSTICE WILLIAM BRENNAN PAPERS, Manuscript Division, Library of Congress, Washington D.C., Box 627, Folder 5.

JUSTICE WILLIAM O. DOUGLAS PAPERS, Manuscript Division, Library of Congress, Washington, D.C.

Karkkainen, Bradley C., *The Police Power Revisited: Phantom Incorporation and the Roots of the Takings Muddle*, 90 MINN. L. REV. 826 (2006).

Kasindorf, Martin, *Voters Get a Say on Land Rights; State Laws Limit High Court Ruling*, USA TODAY, Sept. 25, 2006, at 1A.

Kelly, James J., *"We Shall Not be Moved": Urban Communities, Eminent Domain and the Socioeconomics of Just Compensation*, 80 ST. JOHN'S L. REV. 980–81 (2006).

Kendall, Douglas T. & Lord, Charles P., *The Takings Project: A Critical Analysis and Assessment of the Progress So Far*, 25 B.C. ENVTL. AFF. L. REV. 509 (1998).

Kendall, Douglas T., et al., *Choice of Forum and Finality Ripeness: The Unappreciated Hot Topics in Regulatory Takings Cases*, 33 URB. LAW. 405 (2001).

Kent, Jr., Frank R., *Development Act of D.C. Upheld: U.S. Supreme Court Opinion Removes Major Obstacle to Rebuilding Here*, WASH. POST AND TIMES HERALD, Nov. 23, 1954, at 1.

Kidalov, Max & Seamon, Richard H., *The Missing Pieces of the Debate Over Federal Property Rights Legislation*, 27 HASTINGS CONT'L L.Q. 1 (1999).

Kleinman, Mark, *Include Me Out? The New Politics of Place and Poverty*, 21 POLICY STUDIES 49 (2000).

KOSTAL, RANDE, LAW AND ENGLISH RAILWAY CAPITALISM, 1825–1875 (1994).

Kovacs, Kathryn E., *Accepting the Relegation of Takings Claims to State Courts: The Federal Courts' Misguided Attempts to Avoid Preclusion under* Williamson County, 26 ECOLOGY L.Q. 1 (1999).

Kramer, Larry, *Understanding Federalism*, 47 VAND. L. REV. 1485 (1994).

Krier, James E. & Serkin, Christopher, *Public Ruses*, 2004 MICH. ST. L. REV. 859.

Law Commission of England and Wales, Towards a Compulsory Purchase Code: (1) Compensation, Law Com. No. 286, 8–9, 159–70 (2003).

Lemann, Nicholas, *In the Ruins*, NEW YORKER, The Talk of the Town, Sept. 12, 2005, http://www.newyorker.com/printables/talk/050912ta_talk_lemann.

Levmore, Saul, *Just Compensation and Just Politics*, 22 CONN. L. REV. 285 (1990).

Li & Fung Research Centre, *The Promulgation of Property Law – A New Era for Private Property* 1–8, 38 CHINA DISTRIBUTION & TRADING (MARCH 2007).

"Lib Dems Scrap Demolition Plans", BBC News Service, June 14, 2004, available at http://news.bbc.co.uk/1/hi/england/tyne/3806827.stm.

Lopez, Alberton, *Weighing and Reweighing Eminent Domain's Political Philosophies Post-Kelo*, 41 WAKE FOREST L. REV. 237 (2006).

Loughlin, John, and Martin, Steve, with assistance from Lux, Suzannah, Options for Reforming Local Government Funding to Increase Local Streams of Funding: International Comparisons, available at http://www.lyonsinquiry.org.uk/docs/051215%20research%-20report%20cardiff.pdf.

Lunney, Jr., Glynn S., *A Critical Reexamination of the Takings Jurisprudence*, 90 MICH. L. REV. 1892 (1991).

Lyons Inquiry into Local Government, Consultation Paper & Interim Report (2005).

Maantay, Juliana, *Zoning Law, Health, and Environmental Justice: What's the Connection?*, 30 J. LAW MEDICINE & ETHICS 572 (2002).

Macy, J.E., *Constitutional Rights of Owner As Against Destruction of Building by Public Authorities*, 14 A.L.R. 2D 73 (1950).

MALLOY, ROBIN PAUL & SMITH, JAMES C., REAL ESTATE TRANSACTIONS 3RD (2007).

MALLOY, ROBIN PAUL, LAW IN A MARKET CONTEXT: AN INTRODUCTION TO MARKET CONCEPTS IN LEGAL REASONING (2004).

MALLOY, ROBIN PAUL, LAW AND MARKET ECONOMY: REINTERPRETING THE VALUES OF LAW AND ECONOMICS (2000).

MANDELKER, DANIEL R., LAND USE LAW 5TH (2005).

Mann, F.A., *Outlines of a History of Expropriation*, 75 L.Q.R. 188 (1959).

MASSEY, DOUGLAS S. & DENTON, NANCY A., AMERICAN APARTHEID: SEGREGATION AND THE MAKING OF THE UNDERCLASS (1993).

McGough, Michael, *Court Upholds Eminent Domain; Property Rights Movement Suffers Narrow Defeat*, PITTSBURGH POST-GAZETTE, June 24, 2005, at A-1.

McGreal, Stanley, Alastair Adair, Jim Berry, Bill Deddis, and Suzanne Hirst, *Accessing Private Sector Finance in Urban Regeneration: Investor and Non-Investor Perspectives*, 17 J. OF PROPERTY RESEARCH 109 (2000).

Meacham, Madeline J., *The Williamson Trap*, 32 URB. LAW. 239 (2000).

Meidinger, Errol E., *The "Public Uses" of Eminent Domain: History and Policy*, 11 ENVTL. LAW. 1 (1980).

MEMORANDUM FROM JUSTICE POWELL TO JUSTICE O'CONNOR, May 18, 1984 (Powell Papers).

Merrill, Thomas, *Incomplete Compensation for Takings*, 11 N.Y.U. ENVTL. L.J. 110 (2002).

Merrill, Thomas, *The Economics of Public Use*, 72 CORNELL L. REV. 61 (1986).

Michelman, Frank I., *Property, Federalism, and Jurisprudence: A Comment on Lucas and Judicial Conservatism*, 35 WM. & MARY L. REV. 301 (1993).

Michelman, Frank I., *Liberties, Fair Values, and Constitutional Method*, 59 U. CHI L. REV. 91 (1992).

Michelman, Frank I., *Foreword: Traces of Self-Government*, 100 HARV. L. REV. 4 (1986).

Michelman, Frank I., *Property, Utility, and Fairness: Comments on the Ethical Foundations of "Just Compensation" Law*, 80 HARV. L. REV. 1165 (1967).

MOLLENKOPF, JOHN, THE CONTESTED CITY (1983).

Montag, Brian S. & Monsen, Dawn M., *A Narrower Definition of Blight: Courts Will be Taking a Harder Look at Evidence in Support of Blight Definitions*, 190 N.J.L.J. 614 (2007).

Morgan, Denise C. & Zietlow, Rebecca E., *The New Parity Debate: Congress and Rights of Belonging*, 73 U. CINN. L. REV. 1347 (2005).

National Public Radio, Talk of the Nation: David Savage Discusses the Issue of Eminent Domain and the Constitution, June 23, 2005 (transcript available on LEXIS).

Neuborne, Burt, *The Myth of Parity*, 90 HARV. L. REV. 1105 (1977).

Neuborne, Burt, *Toward Procedural Parity in Constitutional Litigation*, 22 WM. & MARY. L. REV. 725 (1981).

New Jersey Department of the Public Advocate, *Reforming the Use of Eminent Domain for Private Redevelopment in New Jersey* (May 18, 2006).

New Heartlands, Merseyside Housing Market Renewal Pathfinder February 2004 Prospectus Executive Summary (2004), 3.

NICHOLS, PHILIP, 1 THE LAW OF EMINENT DOMAIN (2nd ed. 1917).

NOVAK, WILLIAM J., THE PEOPLES WELFARE LAW & REGULATION IN NINETEENTH-CENTURY AMERICA 19–20 (1996).

Nowell, Paul, *Banker Takes Stance Against Eminent Domain*, TUSCALOOSA NEWS, Mar. 5, 2006.

NPR: Morning Edition: Western Voters Consider Property Rights Changes, Sept. 19, 2006 (transcript available on LEXIS).

OFFICE OF THE DEPUTY PRIME MINISTER, CIRCULAR 06/04: COMPULSORY PURCHASE AND THE CRICHEL DOWN RULES (2004).

OFFICE OF THE DEPUTY PRIME MINISTER, SUSTAINABLE COMMUNITIES: BUILDING FOR THE FUTURE (2003).

OLIVER, MELVIN L. & SHAPIRO, THOMAS M., BLACK WEALTH/WHITE WEALTH: A NEW PERSPECTIVE ON RACIAL INEQUALITY 30 (1995).

Opinion, Derrick Bell, *Brown and Pocketbook Segregation*, CHRISTIAN SCIENCE MONITOR, May 17, 1984, at 18.

Parchomovsky, Gideon & Siegelman, Peter, *Selling Mayberry: Communities and Individuals in Law and Economics*, 92 CAL. L. REV. 75 (2004).

Pasha, Shaheen, *Property Grabs and the Gulf: Local Governments Will Likely Use Eminent Domain to Rebuild: Who Will That Help?*, CNN Money.com, http://money.cnn.com/2005/10/05/news/economy/eminent_domain_katrina/.

Penalver, Eduardo, *Property Metaphors and Kelo v. New London; Two Views of the Castle* (2006) 74 FORDHAM L. REV. 2971 (2006).

Penalver, Eduardo, *Property as Entrance*, 91 VA. L. REV. 1889 (2005).

PERCY, WILLIAM ALEXANDER, LANTERNS ON THE LEVEE: RECOLLECTIONS OF A PLANTER'S SON (Louisiana State University Press 2006) (1941).

Pettys, Todd E., *The Mobility Paradox*, 92 GEO. L. J. 384 (2004).

Philbrick, Francis S., Changing *Conceptions of Property in Law*, 86 U. PENN. L. REV. 691 (1938).

Poirier, Marc R., *The NAFTA Chapter 11 Expropriation Debate Through the Eyes of a Property Theorist*, 33 ENVTL. L. 851 (2003).

Poirier, Marc R., *The Virtue of Vagueness in Takings Doctrine*, 24 CARDOZO L. REV. 93 (2002).

Poirier, Marc R., *Takings and Natural Hazards Policy: Public Choice on the Beachfront*, 46 RUTGERS L. REV. 243 (1993).

POWELL ON REAL PROPERTY, § 79F.03[3][b][iv] (Michael Allan Wolf, gen. ed., 2006).

POWER, ANNE, SUSTAINABLE COMMUNITIES AND SUSTAINABLE DEVELOPMENT: A REVIEW OF THE SUSTAINABLE COMMUNITIES PLAN (2004).

POWER, SUSTAINABLE COMMUNITIES, 21; SOCIAL EXCLUSION UNIT, A NEW COMMITMENT TO NEIGHBOURHOOD RENEWAL: NATIONAL STRATEGY ACTION PLAN (2001), 5.

Presley, Steven M., et al., Assessment of Pathogens and Toxicants in New Orleans, LA Following Hurricane Katrina, Vol. 40, No. 2 *Environ. Sci. Technol.*, 468 (2006).

Pritchett, Wendell E., *The "Public Menace" of Blight: Urban Renewal and the Private Uses of Eminent Domain*, 21 YALE L. & POL'Y REV. 1 (2003).

Private Property Rights Protection Act of 2005, H.R. 4128, 109th Cong. (2005).

QUIGLEY, CONOR, AND COLLINS, ANTHONY, EC STATE AID LAW AND POLICY (2003).

Raco, Mike, *Sustainable Development, Rolled-out Neoliberalism and Sustainable Communities*, 37 ANTIPODE 324 (2005).

Radin, Margaret, *Property and Personhood*, 34 STAN. L. REV. 957 (1982).

RANDOLPH, PATRICK, CHINESE REAL ESTATE LAW (2000).

Reagan, Ronald *Inaugural Address (Jan. 20, 1981), in* Public Papers of the Presidents of the United States: Ronald Reagan, 1981: January 20 to December 31, 1981, at 1 (1981).

"Residents Win Demolition Battle," BBC News Service, September 19, 2003.

Roberts, Thomas E., *Ripeness and Forum Selection in Fifth Amendment Takings Litigation*, 11 J. LAND USE & ENVT'L L. 37 (1995).

Rogers, Jeanne, *High Court Delays School Arguments*, WASH. POST AND TIMES HERALD, Nov. 23, 1954, at 29.

Rosan, Richard M., *Rebuilding New Orleans and the Gulf Coast – A Long Look Ahead*, The Urban Land Institute, at http://europe.uli.org/AM/Temlate.cfm?Section=ULI_Home&-Template=/CM/HTMLDisplay.cfm&ContentID=34304.

Rose, Carol M., *Property and Expropriation: Themes and Variation in American Law*, 2000 UTAH L. REV. 1.

Rose, Carol M., *Takings, Federalism, Norms*, 105 YALE L.J. 1121 (1996).

ROSE, CAROL M., PROPERTY AND PERSUASION (1994).

Rose, Carol M., *The Ancient Constitution vs. The Federalist Empire: Anti-Federalism from the Attack on "Monarchism" to Modern Localism*, 84 Nw. L. Rev. 74 (1989).

Rose, Carol M., *Planning and Dealing: Piecemeal Land Controls and Problems of Local Legitimacy*, 71 Cal. L Rev. 837 (1983).

Rubin, Edward, *The Myth of Accountability and the Anti-Administrative Impulse*, 103 Mich. L. Rev. 2073 (2003).

Rubin, Edward & Feeley, Malcolm, *Federalism: Some Notes on a National Neurosis*, 41 U.C.L.A. L. Rev. 903 (1994).

Ryan, Erin, *Palazzolo, The Public Trust, and the Property Owner's Reasonable Expectations: Takings and the South Carolina Marsh Island Bridge Debate*, 15 SOUTHWESTERN ENVT'L L.J. 121 (2006).

Ruiz, Giulianna K., Student Comment, *Informing Expectations Through Visual Cues: Creating the Assurance of Justice in Regulatory Takings Jurisprudence*, 36 Seton Hall L. Rev. 1309 (2006).

Samuel, Martin, *What Paula Radcliffe Paused to do in the Streets of London, Bid Organisers are Doing to the Locals*, The Times (London), May 4, 2005, 64.

Sandefur, Timothy, Cornerstone of Liberty: Property Rights in 21st Century America (2006).

School Desegregation Thirty Years Later, MacNeil/Lehrer NewsHour, May 17, 1984 (Transcript #2254 available on LEXIS).

Searles, Sidney Z. (Chairman), *Real Estate Condemnation: Recent Developments and New Trends*, Practicing Law Institute (1976).

Segregation Arguments Postponed: U.S. High Court Acts After Senate Delays Action on Harlan Nomination, Miami Herald, Nov. 23, 1954, at 1.

Sepulveda, Peter, *The Use of The Eminent Domain Power in the Relocation of Sports Stadiums to Urban Areas: Is the Public Purpose Requirement Satisfied?* 11 Seton Hall J. Sport L.137 (2001).

Serkin, Christopher, *The Meaning of Value: Assessing Just Compensation for Regulatory Takings*, 99 Nw. U.L. Rev. 677 (2005).

Shapiro, Thomas M., *Race, Homeownership and Wealth*, 20 Wash. U. J.L. & Pol'y 53 (2006).

Shenkman, Rick, *Interview with Pete Daniel: The Great Flood of 1927*, at http://hnn.us/articles/15370.html (last visited June 9, 2006).

Sherwood, Bob, *Shadow Falls on Forgotten Face of Olympics: Many Businesses in the Designated Zone of the East End Have Not Been Offered Enough to Afford to Stay in the Area*, The Financial Times, June 5, 2006, 24.

Singer, Joseph William, *The Ownership Society and Taking Of Property: Castles, Investments, and Just Obligations*, 30 Harv. Envtl. L. Rev. 309 (2006).

Singer, Joseph William, Introduction to Property (2001).

Sixth Annual Harvard Latino Law and Policy Conference: Latino Leadership and Collective Power, 7 Harv. Latino L. Rev. 75 (2004).

Somin, Ilya, *Controlling The Grasping Hand: Economic Development Takings After Kelo*, 15 S. Ct. Econ. Rev. (forthcoming 2007).

Sterk, Stewart E., *The Federalist Dimension of Regulatory Takings Jurisprudence*, 114 Yale L.J. 203, 243–51 (2004).

Stevens, Hon. John Paul, *Judicial Predilections*, 6 NEV. L.J. 1 (2005).

Stoebuck, William B., *A General Theory of Eminent Domain*, 47 WASH. L. REV. 553 (1972).

Streitfeld, David, *Speculators Rushing in as the Water Recedes*, L.A. TIMES, Sept. 15, 2005 at http://www.pipeline.com/~rougeforum/spectatorsrushing.html.

Supreme Court Delays Segregation Action, CHICAGO DAILY TRIBUNE, at 7.

Tarlock, A. Dan, *Local Government Protection of Biodiversity: What is Its Niche?*, 60 U. CHI. L. REV. 555 (1993).

Taylor, Hali Bernstein, "Focus Provides Service to Builders, LAS VEGAS NEWSPAPERS, Jan. 17, 2004.

The Declaration of Independence (U.S. 1776).

THE FEDERALIST PAPERS, No. 10, at 45, 47 (Charles R. Kesler intro. & Clinton Rossiter ed. 1999) (Madison).

The Urban Land Institute Executive Summary of Recommendations, "A Strategy for Rebuilding New Orleans, Louisiana" 1 (November 12–18, 2005), available at http://www.uli.org/Content/NavigationMenu/ProgramsServices/AdvisoryServices/KatrinaPanel/exec_summary.pdf (last visited Feb. 7, 2007).

Thevenot, Brian, *Finally, Rules for Rebuilding*, Times Picayune (New Orleans), Apr. 13, 2006.

Tideman, T. Nicolaus, *Takings, Moral Evolution, and Justice*, 88 COLUM L. REV. 1714 (1988).

Travers, Tony, International Comparisons of Local Government Finance: Propositions and Analysis, available at http://www.lyonsinquiry.org.uk/docs/051215%20research%-20report%20travers.pdf.

Treanor, William Michael, *The Original Understanding of the Takings Clause and the Political Process*, 95 COLUM. L. REV. 782 (1995).

TREATY ESTABLISHING THE EUROPEAN COMMUNITY, Nov. 10, 1997.

Tucker, David G. & Bragg, III, Alfred O., *Florida's Law of Storms: Emergency Management, Local Government, and the Police Power*, 30 STETSON L. REV. 837 (2001).

U.S. Census Bureau, Homeownership Rates by Race and Ethnicity of Householder: 1994 to 2005.

Underkuffler, Laura S., *Tahoe's Requiem: The Death of the Scalian View of Property and Justice*, 21 CONST'L COMMENTARY 727 (2004).

UNDERKUFFLER, LAURA S., THE IDEA OF PROPERTY: ITS MEANING AND POWER (2003).

Underkuffler, Laura S., *When Should Rights "Trump"? An Examination of Speech and Property*, 52 MAINE L. REV. 311 (2000).

Underkuffler, Laura S., *Property: A Special Right*, 71 NOTRE DAME L. REV. 1033 (1996).

Valuation Office Agency, Property Market Report January 2005 (2005) (http://www.voa.gov.uk/publications/property_market_report/pmr-jan-06/index.htm.) (last visited July 28, 2005).

Ward, William J., *Reversal of Blight: New Crop of Cases Face* Gallenthin's *Substantial Credible Evidence Test*, 190 N.J.L.J. 666 (2007).

Web of Advocacy Groups Funnels Millions to Pass Property Rights Initiative, SAN FRANCISCO CHRONICLE, Oct. 5, 2006, at A1.

Weinberg, Philip, *Eminent Domain for Private Sports Stadiums: Fair Ball or Foul?* 35 ENVTL. L. 311 (2005).

Wermiel, Stephen, *Powers in Justices, in a Hawaii Land Case, Reaffirm States' Regulation of Resources*, WALL ST. JOURNAL, May 31, 1954, at 60.

Wilk, Corey J., *The Struggle Over the Public Use Clause: Survey of Holdings and Trends, 1986–2003*, 39 REAL PROP. & TR. J. 251 (2004).

Winter, Steven L., *Contingency and Community in Normative Practice*, 139 U. PA. L. REV. 963 (1991).

THE WORKS OF JAMES WILSON (Robert McCloskey ed., 1967).

Wright, Danaya C., *A New Time for Denominators: Toward a Dynamic Theory of Property in the Regulatory Takings Relevant Parcel Analysis*, 34 ENVTL. L. 175 (2004).

Yelling, J.A., Slums and Redevelopment: Policy and Practice in England, 1918–45, with particular reference to London (1992).

YELLING, J.A., SLUMS AND SLUM CLEARANCE IN VICTORIAN LONDON (1986).

Zhang, Yan & Fang, Ke, *Is History Repeating Itself? From Urban Renewal in the United States to Inner-City Redevelopment in China*, 23 JOURNAL OF PLANNING EDUCATION AND RESEARCH 286 (2004).

Legislative Acts and Statutes

Acquisition of Land Act 1981, c. 67 ss. 2, 7 (Eng.)

Ala. Code § 11-47-170(b) (2005)

District of Columbia Redevelopment Act of 1945

Economic Development Corporations Act, Mich. Comp. Laws §§ 125.1601–1636 (2007)

Ga. Code Ann. § 22-1-1 (West 2006)

Human Rights Act 1998 (Eu)

Land Compensation Act, 1973 (Eng.)

Planning and Compulsory Purchase Act, 2004, C.5 (Eng.)

Tex. Gov't Code Ann. § 2206.001

Town and Country Planning Act 1990, c.8 s.226(1) (1A) (Eng.)

US Constitutional Amend. V

Miscellaneous Websites

http://www.communities.gov.uk/embedded_object.asp?id=1162561)

http://www.dti.gov.uk/regional/regional-dev-agencies/index.html

http://www.msnbc.msn.com/id/8331097/

http://www.foxnews.com/story/0,2933,160479,00.html

http://www.cnn.com/2005/LAW/06/24/scotus.property/

http://www.rushlimbaugh.com/home/stacks/liberals_stick_it_to_the_little_guy_in_eminent_domain__06_27_05_.guest.html

http://www.stateofthenewsmedia.org/narrative_newspapers_audience.asp?cat=3&media=2

http://www.bgr.org/Consequences_for_N.O._091506.pdf
http://www.nlihc.org/detail/article.cfm?article_id=3415&id=72

Index